Debating Higher Education: Philosophical Perspectives

Volume 1

Series Editors

Paul Gibbs, Middlesex University, London, UK
Amanda Fulford, ICE, Leeds Trinity University, Leeds, UK
Ronald Barnett, University College London, Institute of Education, London, UK

Debating Higher Education: Philosophical Perspectives is a new book series launched by Springer and is motivated by two considerations.

Higher education has become a huge matter globally, both politically and socially, commanding massive resources, national and cross-national decision-making, and the hopes of many. Yet, there has been no dedicated book series that connects directly with the many debates on higher education.

In parallel, over the last four decades or so, there has been a growing interest in the academic literature in grappling with technical issues in and around higher education. In particular, work has developed drawing on philosophical perspectives and social theory. This is evident right across the world, especially in the journal literature and in research students' doctoral theses. In effect, we have witnessed the formation of a new sub-discipline, a shorthand of which is 'the philosophy of higher education', and which includes perspectives drawn not only from philosophy and social theory but also feminism, ethics, geopolitics, learning theory, and organizational studies.

Through this book series – the first of its kind in the world – the editors want to encourage the further development of this literature. We are keen to promote lively volumes which are informed about changing practices and policy frameworks in higher education and which engage seriously and deeply with matters of public interest, and are written in an accessible style.

Books will take a variety of forms, and will include both sole-authored and multi-authored formats. Importantly, each volume will have a dialogical flavour, engaging explicitly in dialogue with contemporary debates and their contending positions and, where practicable, especially in volumes with many contributors, will themselves exemplify dialogue.

The editors are keen that the series is open to many approaches. We wish to include work that focuses directly on the university as a social institution and on higher education as an educational process; on the idea of the university and on higher education as a sector with political and policy frameworks; on students and learning, and on academics and academic knowledge; and on curricula and pedagogy, and on research and knowledge processes.

Volumes will examine policy and practical issues including, for example, internationalisation, higher education as a set of 'public goods', access and fairness, and the digital era and learning as well as more conceptual and theoretical issues such as academic freedom, ethics, wellbeing, and the philosophy of social organizations.

The editors very much welcome informal inquiries at any time.

Middlesex University	Paul Gibbs
Leeds Trinity University	Amanda Fulford
UCL Institute of Education	Ronald Barnett

More information about this series at http://www.springer.com/series/15094

Søren S.E. Bengtsen • Ronald Barnett
Editors

The Thinking University

A Philosophical Examination of Thought and Higher Education

 Springer

Editors
Søren S.E. Bengtsen
Centre for Teaching Development
and Digital Media
Aarhus University
Aarhus, Denmark

Ronald Barnett
University College London
Institute of Education
London, UK

ISSN 2366-2573   ISSN 2366-2581   (electronic)
Debating Higher Education: Philosophical Perspectives
ISBN 978-3-319-77666-8   ISBN 978-3-319-77667-5   (eBook)
https://doi.org/10.1007/978-3-319-77667-5

Library of Congress Control Number: 2018938564

Printed on acid-free paper

This Springer imprint is published by the registered company Springer International Publishing AG part of Springer Nature.
The registered company address is: Gewerbestrasse 11, 6330 Cham, Switzerland

For Geoff Whitty

Acknowledgements

We express our warm thanks to the series editors Paul Gibbs (Middlesex University) and Amanda Fulford (Leeds Trinity University) for inviting us to orchestrate this volume, and for the encouragement and support they have given us.

Also, we thank all the contributors and co-authors of this volume. It has been a great experience for us to work with them and to learn about their work in this collaborative venture into the philosophy of higher education.

Finally, we express our gratitude and thanks to Annemarie Keur, the Springer editor, who has been so helpful throughout the entire publishing process. Her support for this project has been a strong source of encouragement for us.

Contents

Contributor Biographies

Sonja Arndt is a senior lecturer in Te Whiringa School of Educational Leadership and Policy in the Faculty of Education, University of Waikato, New Zealand. Her scholarly and teaching interests lie at the intersection of philosophy of/in education and early childhood education, with a particular interest in the philosophy of the subject and cultural Otherness within diverse societal and educational settings.

James Arvanitakis is professor and the Dean of the Graduate Research School at Western Sydney University. He is also a lecturer in Humanities and a member of the University's Institute for Cultural and Society. James was also the founding Head of The Academy at Western Sydney University that received an *Australian Financial Review* higher education excellence award (2016) and the *Western Sydney Leadership Dialogue* Excellence in Education Award (2017). James is internationally recognised for his innovative teaching style and was the recipient of the Prime Minister's University Teacher of the Year Award in 2012 and an Eminent Researcher Award from the Australia India Education Council in 2015. In 2017 he was appointed a Research Fellow of the Australian Indian Institute. A former economist and free market advocate, James changed his position after witnessing child and indentured labour. James is a board member of the Public Education Foundation, the Chair of Diversity Arts Australia, an Academic Fellow at the Australian India Institute and a Research Fellow at the Centre for Policy Development. A collection of his works can be found at www.jamesarvanitakis.net

Robyn Barnacle is a Senior Research Fellow in the School of Graduate Research, RMIT University, Melbourne, Australia. She is a research education specialist and coordinates professional development programs for higher degrees by research supervisors and candidates. Robyn's research field is higher education, particularly questions of the value and purpose of the PhD and being and becoming a researcher in the contemporary higher education environment. Her work draws on the phenomenological tradition and she is particularly interested in notions of care and ontology and learning.

Ronald Barnett is Emeritus Professor of Higher Education at University College London Institute of Education. For forty years, he has been advancing a social philosophy of the university, in which he has been developing creative concepts and practical principles that might enhance universities and higher education. His books have been translated into several languages and a number have won prizes. His latest book is '*The Ecological University: A Feasible Utopia*', which follows a recent trilogy of books on understanding the university (all published by Routledge). He has been described as 'one of the most eloquent defenders of the university of reason' (Michael Peters, 2014). He is the inaugural recipient of the EAIR Award for 'Outstanding Contribution to Higher Education Research, Policy and Practice' and has had a higher doctorate of the University of London and Fellowships of the Academy of the Social Sciences, the Society for Research into Higher Education and the Higher Education Academy conferred upon him. He has been an invited speaker in around 40 countries.

David Beckett is an Honorary Professorial Fellow in the Melbourne Graduate School of Education, The University of Melbourne, having recently retired from the Deputy Deanship. Research on the epistemological and ontological significance of innovative professional practices and formations continues, as do many doctoral supervisions and co-authorships, such as this one.

Søren S.E. Bengtsen is Associate Professor at Centre for Teaching Development and Digital Media, Aarhus University, Denmark. Also, he is Deputy Director of Centre for Higher Education Futures, same place. Dr. Bengtsen has for the last ten years researched extensively into the philosophy of higher education, educational philosophy, and researcher education and its pedagogies. He has published books and several volume chapters and journal articles on the subjects, and he was the main organiser of the world's first Philosophy of Higher Education Conference to be held at Aarhus University in 2017. Further, Dr. Bengtsen is the founder and coordinator of the national SIG-group for research and development into supervision and mentoring in higher education (within the Danish Network for Educational Development in Higher Education). His most recent work within the philosophy of higher education include the journal papers 'Confronting the Dark Side of Higher Education' (Journal of Philosophy of Education, 2017), 'Universities and Epistemology: From a Dissolution of Knowledge to the Emergence of a New Thinking' (Education Sciences, 2017), and the book chapter 'Realism and education: A philosophical examination of the 'realness' of the university' (in *A Reader in Philosophy of Education*, edited by Philip Higgs and Yusef Higgs, JUTA, 2017), all co-authored with Ronald Barnett. His recent book within the field of researcher education and supervision is *Doctoral Supervision: Organization and Dialogue* (Aarhus University Press, 2016).

Nuraan Davids is an Associate Professor of Philosophy of Education. She is the Chairperson the Department of Education Policy Studies at Stellenbosch University in South Africa. She is the recipient of a number of research and teaching awards, which includes the *NRF Research Excellence Award for Female Emerging Researcher* (2015); the Stellenbosch University Distinguished Teacher Award (2017); and the CHE/HELTASA National Excellence in Teaching and Learning Commendation (2017). Her list of international books include: *Women, cosmopolitanism, and Islamic education: On the virtues of education and belonging* (2013, New York & London: Peter Lang Publishing); *Citizenship education and violence in schools: On disrupted potentialities and becoming* (co-author, Rotterdam/Boston/Taipei: Sense Publishers); *Ethical dimensions of Muslim education* (co-author, 2016, New York & London: Palgrave Macmilllan); *Educational leadership-in-becoming: On the potential of leadership in action* (co-author, 2016, New York & London: Routledge); *Philosophy and education as action: Implications for Teacher Education* (co-author, 2017, Lanham, MD (US): Rowman & Littlefield – Lexington Series); *Tolerance and Dissent within Education: On cultivating Debate and Understanding* (co-author, 2017, New York & London: Palgrave MacMillan).

Paul Hager is Emeritus Professor of Education at the University of Technology Sydney. His major research focus has been the holistic seamless know how that characterises highly skilled performances of all kinds. This has generated research projects on topics such as informal workplace learning, professional practice ('professional' in its broadest sense), the nature of skills and competence, and group practice. Published books and journal articles include: D. Beckett and P. Hager (2002) *Life, Work and Learning: Practice in Postmodernity* (Routledge). P. Hager and J. Halliday (2006) *Recovering Informal Learning: Wisdom, Judgement and Community* (Springer). P. Hager and S. Holland (eds.) (2006) *Graduate Attributes, Learning and Employability* (Springer). P. Hager (2011) 'Refurbishing MacIntyre's Account of Practice', *Journal of Philosophy of Education*, 45(3), 545–561. P. Hager, A. Lee & A. Reich (eds.) (2012) *Practice, Learning and Change: Practice-Theory Perspectives on Professional Learning* (Springer). P. Hager (2014) 'Practice and Group Learning', *Educational Philosophy and Theory*, 46(6), 584–599. In 2013 *Educational Philosophy and Theory* published a special issue celebrating Hager's work. He is currently writing a book with David Beckett provisionally titled *The Emergence of Complexity: New Perspectives on Practice, Agency and Expertise*.

David J. Hornsby is an Associate Professor of Science in International Relations and Deputy Head of Department, Education in the Department of Science, Technology, Engineering, and Public Policy, University College London. David spent 8 years in South Africa at the University of the Witwatersrand, Johannesburg where he was an Associate Professor in International Relations and Assistant Dean of Humanities (Teaching and Learning). David's research interests pertain to the politics of science and risk in international governance, Canadian and South African foreign policy, middle power cooperation, and pedagogy in higher education. David has published in both the biological and social sciences, and is a recognized teacher having been awarded the 2013 Faculty of Humanities Teaching and Learning Award and the Vice Chancellor's Teaching Award (Individual) at Wits University. He has five books currently out including *Large Class Pedagogy: Interdisciplinary Perspectives for Quality Higher Education* (SUN Press: 2013); *Risk Regulation, Science, and Interests in Transatlantic Trade Conflicts* (Palgrave: 2014);*Universities, the Citizen Scholar, and the Future of Higher Education* (Palgrave: 2016); *South African Foreign Policy: Identities, intentions, and directions* (Routledge, 2017); and *Transforming Teaching and Learning in Higher Education: Towards a Socially Just Pedagogy in a Global Context* (Palgrave, 2017).

Thomas Karlsohn Associate professor and senior lecturer at the Department of History of Science and Ideas, Uppsala university. Karslohn specializes in the intellectual history of the university with a particular focus on the German territories at the turn of the century 1800. Karlsohn is also a regular contributor to the Swedish public debate about current developments in research and higher education. Recent works include: "The Idea of the University and the Process of Secularisation" (article, 2017); *Universitetets ide: sexton nyckeltexter* ("The Idea of the university: Sixteen Key Texts") (2016, ed., translation and introduction); "The Academic Seminar as Emotional Community" (article, 2016); "On Emotions, Knowledge and Institutions" (article, 2016); *Ensamhet och gemenskap: en brevväxling om universitetet* ("Solitude and fellowship: letters on the university") (2016, with Per Magnus Johansson); *The Humboldtian Tradition: Origins and Legacies* (2014, ed. with Peter Josephson and Johan Östling).

Jan McArthur is a Lecturer in Education and Social Justice in the Department of Educational Research at Lancaster University, UK. She has previously taught at the University of Edinburgh, UK, and Monash University, Australia. Her research interests span the nature and purposes of higher education, social justice within and through higher education and dialogue/student voice within assessment, learning and feedback. She has a particular interest in critical theory and its applications to higher education research and practice. This interest is demonstrated by her use of Adorno's work in her book *Rethinking Knowledge within Higher Education: Adorno and Social Justice.* In this book Jan McArthur argues that the university should be a special place for thinking, and involve active engagement with complex, dynamic and contested forms of knowledge. In her recent book, *Assessment for Social Justice: perspectives and practices in higher education,* she draws on the critical theory of Axel Honneth to consider socially just assessment practices.

Carl Mika is associate professor in Te Whiringa School of Educational Leadership and Policy in the Faculty of Education, University of Waikato, New Zealand. He is of the Tuhourangi and Ngati Whanaunga iwi. He has a background in law practice and legal theory, indigenous and Maori studies, and indigenous and Western philosophy. His current areas of research focus on indigenous and Western metaphysics, as well as philosophical research methods.

Rikke Toft Nørgård is Associate Professor at Centre for Teaching Development and Digital Media, Aarhus University, Denmark. She is coordinator of the MA in ICT-Based Educational Design, and steering committee member of Centre for Higher Education Futures, both at Aarhus University. Further, she is an organising committee member of the Oxford Ethnography and Education Conference. Dr. Nørgård's research focuses on the intersections between philosophy of technology, design thinking, critical pedagogy, academic citizenship and university futures. She has published research articles and given keynotes on subjects within the fields of higher education teaching and learning, philosophy of higher education, digital humanities, and learning design. Her most recent work within the field of higher education research includes the article 'Patterns of Inclusion: Fostering Digital Citizenship through Hybrid Education' (2018), 'Playful learning in higher education: Developing a signature pedagogy' (2017), 'Academic citizenship beyond the campus: a call for the placeful university' (2017), 'MOOC Design Workshop: educational innovation with empathy and intent' (2016) and 'Participatory academic communities: a transdisciplinary perspective on participation in education beyond the institution' (2015). Presently, she is leading the Aarhus University part of the Erasmus+ project *Playful Learning Experience – Enhancing adult education and learning environments with digital media* (2016-2019) in an effort to materialise educational philosophy as concrete learning designs.

Sharon Rider is Professor of Theoretical Philosophy at Uppsala University, and former vice-dean of the Faculty of Arts. In 2015, she was the first recipient of the national HumTank award for "having "with acuity and courage defended education and academic activity from external controls, short-sighted demands for utility and quality assessment exercises that fail to capture their real value." She is currently Deputy Director of *Engaging Vulnerability*, a decade-long interdisciplinary research program hosted by Uppsala University with funding from the Swedish Research Council that examines vulnerability as a productive set of relations. Rider's work belongs broadly to philosophical anthropology, with an emphasis on how epistemic issues are connected to forms of life. Recent publications include *Post-truth, Fake News: Viral Modernity and Higher Education,* eds. Michael Peters, Sharon Rider, Mats Hyvönen, Tina Besley (Springer 2018); "Coercion by Necessity or Comprehensive Responsibility? Hannah Arendt on Vulnerability, Freedom and Education", in *Phenomenology and the Primacy of the Political,* eds. Véronique Fóti & Pavlos Kontos (Springer, 2017);"Human Freedom and the Philosophical Attitude", in *Educational Philosophy and Theory,* Vol 47/3, 2015, and "Language and Mathematical Formation" in *A Companion to Wittgenstein on Education. Pedagogical Investigations*, eds. Michael A. Peters & Jeff Stickney (Springer, 2016).

Sarah Robinson is Associate Professor at Aarhus University where she works in the Centre for Teaching Development and Digital Media (CUDiM) within the Faculty of Arts. Sarah is an Educational Anthropologist whose research interests span policy in practice, curriculum reform, teacher agency (Biesta, Priestly & Robinson, 2015) and entrepreneurship education. She has published widely and is a recognized scholar in the field of entrepreneurship education having recently received an outstanding award for a publication in Emerald (Robinson, Neergaard, Tangaard & Krueger, 2017). Currently she is working closely with colleagues from CUDiM and Prof. Wesley Shumar at Drexel University (USA) on developing ideas about the purpose and future of the university.

Wesley Shumar is a cultural anthropologist and professor at Drexel University. His research has focused on cultural change in higher education, digital media, and the semiotics of mass culture. He is author of *College for Sale: A Critique of the Commodification of Higher Education*, 1997, Falmer Press, and *Inside Mathforum. org: Analysis of an Internet-based Education Community*, 2017, Cambridge University Press. He is co-editor of *Structure and Agency in the Neoliberal University*, 2008, Routledge, and co-editor of *Building Virtual Communities: Learning and Change in Cyberspace*, 2001, Cambridge University Press. Since 2014 he has been studying the craft beer community in Philadelphia and working on the role of entrepreneurship education in higher education. He is co-author, with Sarah Robinson, of the article Rethinking the Entrepreneurial University for the 21st Century, forthcoming in R. Barnett, & M. A. Peters (Eds.), *The Idea of the University: Volume 2 – Contemporary Perspectives*. New York, NY: Peter Lang.

Paul Standish is Professor and Head of the Centre for Philosophy of Education at UCL Institute of Education. He has extensive experience as a teacher in schools, colleges and universities, and he has a particular interest in higher education - with publications including: *The Universities We Need: higher education after Dearing* (1998, Kogan), co-authored with Nigel Blake and Richard Smith; *Universities Remembering Europe* (2000, Berghahn), co-edited with Francis Crawley and Paul Smeyers; and *The Philosophy of Nurse Education* (2007, Palgrave), co-edited with John Drummond. His *Beyond the Self: Wittgenstein, Heidegger, and the Limits of Language* (1992, Ashgate) indicates an interest in Wittgenstein and education that spans more than three decades. More recent books, in collaboration with Naoko Saito, are *Stanley Cavell and the Education of Grownups* (2012, Fordham), *Education and the Kyoto School of Philosophy: Pedagogy for Human Transformation* (2012, Springer), *"The Truth is Translated": Stanley Cavell and Philosophy as Translation* (2017, Rowman and Littlefield), and *Democracy and Education from Dewey to Cavell* (2018, Wiley). He is Associate Editor (2011-) and was Editor (2001–2011) of the *Journal of Philosophy of Education*, and is Chair of the Philosophy of Education Society of Great Britain.

Yusef Waghid is Distinguished Professor of Philosophy of Education in the Department of Education Policy Studies at Stellenbosch University in South Africa. He joined Stellenbosch University almost two decades ago as Director of the Centre for Educational Development and has been full Professor of Philosophy of Education in the Department of Education Policy Studies since 2002. He was also Chair and, Dean of the Faculty of Education. He holds three doctorates in the areas of Philosophy of Education (Western Cape), Education Policy Studies (Stellenbosch), and Philosophy (Stellenbosch). He is a fellow of the Academy of Science of South Africa (ASSAf), internationally acclaimed scholar, and since 2005, he is Editor-in-Chief of *South African Journal of Higher Education*. His latest books that accentuate his research foci, include, *African philosophy of education reconsidered: On being human* (London: Routledge, 2014); *Pedagogy out of bounds: Untamed variations of democratic education* (Rotterdam/Boston/Taipei: Sense Publishers, 2014); (co-editor) *International handbook for learning, teaching and leadership in faith-based schools* (Dortrecht: Springer Press, 2014); (co-author *Education, assessment and the desire for dissonance* (New York: Peter Lang, 2017); (co-editor) *International Handbook of Citizenship Education* (New York: Palgrave-MacMillan, 2017); (co-author) *Education and tolerance* (New York: Palgrave-MacMillan, 2017); and (co-editor) *African democratic citizenship education revisited* (New York: Palgrave-MacMillan, 2018).

SunInn Yun is Assistant Professor at the Department of English Language Education in Incheon National University, South Korea. Her research interests include phenomenology, existentialism, post-colonialism in literature and educational practices. The subject of her PhD thesis, which she completed at UCL Institute of Education, is the meaning of freedom in education in the light of the work of Martin Heidegger and Jean-Luc Nancy. She is the author of a number of journal articles, including publications in the *Journal of Philosophy of Education* and *Ethics and Education*. Her current research involves museum practices in relation to questions of identity and language.

Chapter 1
Introduction: Considering the Thinking University

Ronald Barnett and Søren S.E. Bengtsen

Beginnings

The university is a thinking institution. Surely, that does not need to be said but it does. In much of the contemporary world, in many kinds of nation, the university finds itself amid a climate of suspicion, a climate in which the very heart of the university, namely its interests in knowledge and thought, has been placed in the dock.

In the contemporary climate, we are being told that we live in a world of 'alternative facts' and in a post-truth age. In such a world, the university ought to be an institution that has much to offer the world. After all, the university is an institution that is particularly associated with systematic efforts to understand the world. Surely, therefore, it contains resources that can address and even overcome these contemporary challenges. Unfortunately, matters here are far from plain sailing.

There have long been 'alternative facts'. Galileo was accused of heresy in asserting – against the sure beliefs of the religious authorities - that the Earth revolved around the sun. The contemporary era of alternative facts, accordingly, may be seen in just this lineage, as a symptom of a power play over what is to count as truth. But there is a novel feature about the present situation for this undermining of the university has come in part from within itself. For the past fifty years, through a succession of intellectual waves – relativism, structuralism, ideology critiques, deconstructionism, constructivism and postmodernism – the academic world has, in effect, constructed a continuous programme of a 'hermeneutics of suspicion'

R. Barnett (✉)
University College London, Institute of Education, London, UK
e-mail: ron.barnett@ucl.ac.uk

S.S.E. Bengtsen
Centre for Teaching Development and Digital Media, Aarhus University, Aarhus, Denmark

© Springer International Publishing AG, part of Springer Nature 2018   1
S.S.E. Bengtsen, R. Barnett (eds.), *The Thinking University*,
Debating Higher Education: Philosophical Perspectives 1,
https://doi.org/10.1007/978-3-319-77667-5_1

(Ricoeur 1970) towards its own inquiries. In short, the university has played a large hand in undermining its own position as a place of considered thought in the world.

The critiques just listed spring from an internalist stance within the academic community, being tokens of an interest on the part of universities in their own epistemological foundations. Recently, however, a more externalist set of viewpoints have emerged, so as to turn the academic gaze much more towards the world. Concerns over North-South epistemologies and hegemonic practices on the part of the North, efforts to try to identify 'public goods' and the 'public good' provided by higher education, concerns that knowing efforts should promote social justice, and interests in the knowledges of indigenous communities, are together suggesting that knowledge is not to abandoned but that it should be set on a much wider base. Instead of residing in the relationship between the knower and the world, now it should be recast as a set of relationships between different kinds of knowers, especially between those in universities and the wider world.

Just this is the tack taken in this volume, which constitutes a collective effort to position the university as a place of thought in the world. That is to say, the predominant interest of the scholars on duty here is that of ferreting out connections, both actual and possible, between the university and the wider world that lie precisely in its being understood especially as an institution of thought understood *relationally*; as a thinking university that, in particular, gains its spurs through its concerns with the world. And the general claim here is that in locating the university in this way, as an institution whose thought has much to offer the world, neglected potentials of the university can be discerned and realised.

Modes of the Thinking University

The university has long enjoyed a space of thoughtfulness in society. Thought is a necessary accompaniment to serious inquiry, which must lie at the heart of the university. Serious inquiry, after all, requires thought, thought to dwell on matters, to reflect on what has been and is being thought by others and on what has come to count as knowledge in the different fields of understanding.

Thought, therefore, is an indication of thinking in motion. Thoughtfulness, in turn, is a disposition that marks out the university. However, it cannot reside solely either in individuals or in collections of individuals – whether students or professors. This thoughtfulness has also to be a collective condition, of those who are engaged in intellectual work in the university. It has to be a characteristic of the space occupied by the university. This thought is necessarily relational, characterising the inter-connections of members of the university. This is not to say that all members of the university have to be engaged in mutual thoughtful transactions but there is strong condition present here, namely that in principle any member of a university could engage in a thoughtful transaction with any other member.

But then that reflection, that thought is characteristic of connections within the university has to be extended beyond the university. For thought, once let off the hook, can have no boundaries. Disciplines themselves are worldly fields of understanding and the university is now opening itself to the world. So thought must be doubly unconfined and connected to the wider world, both the world of knowledge and understanding and the world in-itself. The thinking university is a university that is irredeemably inter-connected with the world. This inter-connection is not only about the university addressing the world, but also responding *to* the world. 'World', here, does not only mean the immediate society, but a wider world too – including other societies and cultures, and even subcultures within the present society, together with nature and all that it encompasses of species and forms of wild growth.

The Thinking University and the Thoughtful University

The thinking university and the thoughtful university: both these terms have already been sighted but they are not quite the same, although they overlap. *The thinking university* is a university in which there is a collective disposition to think deeply about matters; not to take anything for granted but to inquire into the world and all that it contains, including present understandings of the world. It is a university that has a critical disposition towards the world. It holds itself apart from the world, even as it engages with the world. *The thoughtful university* is a university that is especially contemplative. It is imaginative, it reaches out for new frameworks. It ponders matters, holding them up for examination, and seeks to place them in wider frameworks of understanding. It holds steady under fire and works at a measured pace. Thinking may be swift, sparkling, quick-witted, lively; thoughtfulness is calm, careful, considered and resolute, steadily and continuously pressing forward.

Modes of thought, therefore, are already opening here. *The thinking university* may be focused on fields of intellectual thought, its members predisposed to delving deeply into them. In research, it will gain its raw material from issues arising within the disciplines but it will seek to further the concepts and ideas in the disciplines. It will never be content to work within customary boundaries. It will seek to stretch current understandings into new places. In teaching, students will be not just encouraged to think afresh but will be pressed to do so. Their assignments and their utterances may receive such comments as 'I am not sure how your two assertions are connected' or 'I wonder where you might look for evidence for your claim' or even 'Is that not ambiguous: does it mean (a) or (b)? This is an *internalist* mode of the thinking university.

Kenneth Minogue's (1973) idea of the university was of this kind. His concept of the university rested on a sense that the world of the university and the world as such were two different worlds and never the twain should meet. The opposite view, that there was no division between the two worlds he disparagingly termed a 'Monist' view. On his view, the university was not to be concerned with the world as such. Michael Oakeshott (1989) implied a corresponding view, with his sense of the university as supplying 'the gift of the interval', a space that was separated from the world. This version of the thinking university could be termed the 'ivory-tower' idea of the university but such a pejorative ascription runs the risk of underplaying certain strengths of this internalist view, limited as it may be.

The thinking university may also be focused on the world as such; it may exhibit a more *externalist* aspect. It may take its bearings much more from the way things are in the world or, at least, from the way it perceives matters in the world. This is a university that considers that, indeed, the world matters, and that the university has resources that not only can illuminate the world but can even help to address situations that are impaired or could at least be improved. All the disciplines can throw their hats into this ring, pure as well as applied, and science-oriented as well as those veering more towards the humanities.

An obvious strength of this mode of the thinking university is that it has its feet on the ground; it does not easily give way to purposeless speculation and arcane abstraction that resides only in-itself. This thinking university is, at heart, realist and its offerings have a robustness about them. It is a kind of thinking that is likely to have ready 'impact'. But it runs the risk that its realism is rather thin and so that it only scratches the surface of the world rather than delving beneath its immediate sheen. Its thinking, accordingly, is rather shallow, taking the immediately presenting appearances of the world as the world in-itself. It does not easily turn to having a thoughtful and deeply critical gaze on the world.

The thoughtful university does not have its feet *on* the ground but has its spirit *in* the ground. The thoughtful university is old, almost one thousand years. Its roots go deep into the history and culture of the Western world, and its being goes beyond the present and timely institutions and buildings of today. It connects with them, and, still, stretches beyond them into a distant past and onto a distant future. The thoughtful university remembers. It carries with it the memories, stories, and lives of our ancestors and *their* thoughts, *their* societal engagement and visions for a higher education. The thoughtful university *is* in the mortar and bricks of some universities still; in the architecture and building structures of a different age, where the *thinking* university has different goals, leadership, and curriculum. Also, the thoughtful university is embedded within every form of the thinking university. The thoughtful university is woven into the very fibre of every present day thinking university. At the same time, it is the foundation and the spirit of the thinking university, it breathes life into the thinking university, and keeps it *thinking*.

Where the thinking university is dynamic, engaged, and involved, the thoughtful university simply is. With Heidegger's term it is 'waiting', but not 'awaiting' anything in particular (Heidegger 2010). The thoughtful university is "waitful" (Heidegger 2010, p.76), and in its waiting, it has no particular object and is not involved with any particular form of representation. As Heidegger states, "[i]n waiting we leave open that upon which we wait (…), [b]ecause waiting lets itself be involved in the open itself." (Heidegger 2010, p.75). Where the thinking university is defined by involvement, care, and societal engagement, the thoughtful university defines the openness of thought itself.

Thought and Action

In *'Thought and Action'* - one of the most important books in Western philosophy since World War II – Stuart Hampshire (1970) sought to draw connections between thought and action. 'It would be a crude metaphysics that implied that an action was necessarily a physical movement.' (p 91) Indeed, Hampshire was at pains 'to question the naïve dualism that divides ... the internal and mental from the external and physical'. That matter takes on double importance here. There is the issue as to whether the thought of academics can in itself be considered to constitute a form of action. And there is also the issue as to whether, in taking thought seriously, a university can be said to be engaging in action; the thinking university would be – to use popular modern parlance – an agentic institution. Let us take these possibilities in turn.

Thinking of any seriousness is, ultimately, a form of action. In the end, it has to yield or include an affirmation, a claim. But even thought itself, in advance of any claim being made, involves judgement, a weighing of possibilities, and choosing between this description or that. This is not to say that all serious thought must be always explicit and fully articulated. As Wittgenstein observed (2003: 52), unarticulated assumptions lie beneath both thought and action. For example, 'The assumption [that the Earth has existed for many years past] ... forms the basis of action, and therefore, naturally of thought'.

Thinking, we might say, involves, but is not exhausted by, cognitive action. It expresses values, dispositions towards the world, and human virtues. In these simple reflections, we gain, do we not, insights into the logic – if one can call it that – of despots who, in authoritarian regimes, incarcerate academics on account of their being active members of universities. Thought is dangerous to the dictators not only because its results may conflict with their beliefs and ideologies but also because thought as such is testimony to a space in which cognitive action can assert itself. But then, as implied, this thinking, understood as cognitive action, calls for particular virtues on the part of the would-be thinker; virtues such as those of courage, persistence, vigilance, and forthrightness of expression. Even further, as Roy Bhaskar points out, there is a deep emancipatory power in thinking (Bhaskar 2011), and the power of deep thinking, or "depth rationality" as Bhaskar calls it (Bhaskar 2011, p.107ff.), may even unlock powers of freedom and redemption beyond our present stated ideas and understanding. Thinking thinks more than it thinks.

But what then of the university as a thinking institution? Can it not be said to be a 'corporate agent' (List and Pettit 2011) at least partly through its powers of thought? The answer is 'yes' but only under certain *sets* of conditions. The first set of conditions is procedural. It would have to be an institution in which its major decisions were transparent to its members, carried their assent to a large extent, and in which its members felt some degree of accountability of decision-makers towards themselves. Secondly, conditions attach to the *discursive climate* of the thinking university. It would have also to be an institution in which contentious or large matters could comfortably be raised and in which those in authority were willing to engage with such debates. MacIntyre has recently suggested (2011:174) that 'the contemporary research university is … by and large a place in which certain questions go unasked or … if they are asked, it is only by individuals and in settings such that as few as possible hear them being asked'.

But there is more in front of the thinking university. For the thinking university has to be an institution that not just tolerates thinking, not just acts as a space of thought, but actively encourages thought, and at all levels of the institution. MacIntyre's suggestion – just quoted – implies that this may seldom be the case. Universities 'by and large' do not go out of their way to stimulate thinking, let alone provoke it. And this is understandable for universities, perhaps especially the research universities of which MacIntyre speaks, find themselves buffeted by swirls of forces, both national and cross-national, both overt and virtual, as their total regulatory and judgemental environment continues to intensify. As such, universities come to be risk-averse, and will act vainly to steer towards calm waters. An open discursive climate might seem to make public and even exacerbate internal conflict.

Universities are on a cusp. On the one hand, across the world, they are being enjoined to 'engage' with the wider society and to demonstrate their 'impact' upon the world; and, whatever readings there might be of such linguistic signifiers, such expectations will require thought by and within universities. On the other hand, as stated, universities find themselves in highly challenging if not hostile set of environments, where a natural response is to avoid difficulty and curtail considered thought. However, and again, perhaps especially in the research university, matters are not even-handed. An inquisitiveness about the world, and a wish to place the fruits of disciplined inquiry into the public domain, produces a collective will in favour of reflection, a will that cannot easily be silenced. One only has to recall to mind scholars – such as Gramsci and Bonhoeffer – who were cast into prison but yet could not stop themselves from continuing their reflections.

Thinking can even give voice to the ones who have not a chance to speak for themselves. As the American philosopher Alphonso Lingis points out, when we speak our thinking "we speak in the place of others. (…) We speak for the silent and for the silenced. We say what others would say if they were not absent, elsewhere, or dead. (…) Speech becomes grave and imperative when we speak for infants, for foreigners who do not speak the language. When we speak for those in a coma, for the imprisoned, the tortured, the massacred, those buried in mass graves." (Lingis 1998, p.136).

The sails of this will to reflect may well be trimmed but once present, it will difficult if not impossible to quell. A reason that this is so is that thought builds upon itself. Once it has its place in a collective disposition towards thoughtfulness, thought piles upon thought continuously. Care is needed here, certainly. Recall Heidegger's (2004: 13) warning: 'In universities especially, the danger is still very great that we misunderstand what we hear of thinking'. That the university might pride itself on its thinking is not in itself an indication that thinking is present.

Connecting Thought

Characteristically, thought reaches its apogee when it is provoked. It is set off. The thinker is disturbed to think. Provocations arise from the milieu in which thinking takes place. The thinker cannot help but think. This thinking disturbs the thinker and wells up within the thinker, with her or his *thinking-being* naturally oriented towards resolving the disturbance. This thinking is not consciously 'aimed' at resolving the disturbance but rather that is its very nature. Thinking is an excess in thought - it thinks even more than can be thought. Thinking moves beyond thought. Heidegger considered that thinking must be understood "as a listening" (Heidegger 1971, p.75), and it is when our understanding is challenged that we feel the strain of thinking, and we listen to *and struggle with* the very thinking itself.

Again, therefore, thinking becomes a form of action, to resolve a conundrum, a problem, a dilemma or an issue. But such problem resolution – of whatever kind, be it practical, empirical, theoretical, aesthetic – cannot be fully achieved by a lone thinker. For, as has become apparent, thinking has its place within collectivities. These collectivities include both the 'invisible colleges' of the disciplines but also, as indicated, the university qua institution; and, increasingly, too, they include collectivities beyond the university, in the professions, industry, the political sphere and the world of communications. David Bohm spoke (1997) of 'thought as a system' but that was a quarter of a century ago. Now, it would be better to suggest that thought is held in *multiple* systems, albeit both hazy and overlapping.

Thought is, accordingly, now necessarily relational. It is conducted in flows of thought, usually virtual and global. So just at the moment that thought experiences diminution and constraint, so too spaces open. Less 'lines of flight', we should rather speak of pools of possibility. Possibilities open for thought anew, in this interconnected age. And, in the process, spurs to the imagination prod and push. Risky thought opens here and the virtues, noticed earlier, are called upon to keep pressing thought into new spaces.

The university, as a conduit for thought, now becomes a vehicle for assisting the wider world with its thinking. And if our earlier positing of the connections between thought and agency hold water, it now emerges that the university can assist society with its own agency. The 'runaway' character of the world in the contemporary world has been remarked upon more than once and the hope, in turn, has been expressed that the world might develop learning systems that enable it to exercise at least a modicum of rational control over itself (Habermas 1987). In being intimately connected with the world, perhaps the university can – through its thought processes – provide cognitive resources that may just, at the eleventh hour, aid the wellbeing of this small planet.

Thought, to draw on Heidegger, 'gathers' what may be scattered or fragmented. It can build worlds, new worlds, make worlds possible. Thought is, or can be, worldmaking. Through its *thought processes*, the university can assist in this worldmaking. But the university has to come into itself in a new way, both to understand itself as spaces (plural) of possible thought and of its possible new connections with the world. Opening here is a sense of the ecological university in the fullest sense; not just as an assemblage of elements connecting with other assemblages in the world but also, and much more to the point, of understanding its implicatedness in the world and sensing that it has responsibilities in playing its part in repairing the world.

This is – or would be – a win-win-*win* situation. With the university understanding itself in this way, as arenas of thought for the world, the potentially open and relational character of thought is realized, the agency of the university is maximised *and* the world is enhanced. Thought takes on a new urgency, and a new mission, in coming to have a care for the world. The very *idea* of the university grows, it flourishes, in this caring. There is a growth in thinking when it acts relationally.

This stance is akin to that for which Nicholas Maxwell (1987) has passionately argued for forty years, in driving towards a university of 'wisdom', towards what is 'of value in the world'. The view here adds, though, a more heightened sense of the university as an institution subject to near-hidden layers of forces and currents in the world (its ontological aspects), and a sensitivity to the manifold forms that thought may take. Thought may be deadly serious or it can add to the gaiety of nations, of the world indeed. It can inspire, dislodge, amaze, intrigue, lead into both darkness and light, and mesmerize. The university does all of this, and can do much more, precisely through its thought processes.

Structure and Contents

This volume is in three parts. Part One, *The Thinking University – Contending with the World*, explores ways in which the university, through its thought processes, can help in forming 'a better future' and to realise potentials of the thinking university through societal action and agency.

Sharon Rider ('Truth, Democracy and the Mission of the University') unfurls the large canvas for this section, mapping a terrain across the concepts of citizenship, democracy, reason, freedom, culture and liberalism. Rider reminds us of the work of Ortega y Gasset, who not only wrote explicitly on '*The Mission of the University*' but who also wrote specifically on the matter of 'mass society'. Against this background, questions arise as to how a 'general culture' might be developed, and in what sense the 'vital system of ideas of [the] period might be discerned and sustained', and so work towards 'full humanity'. Perhaps part of the answer lies in each university understanding itself as a 'faculty of culture'. This exposition from Rider surely indicates that, as institutions of truth, universities are not merely epistemological and intellectual in nature and scope, but stand out as beacons of a new, and maybe even universal, ideal and idea for the future university.

Wesley Shumar and Sarah Robinson ('Universities as societal value drivers – entrepreneurial practices for a better future') argue for a new conception of the entrepreneurial university, one that is concerned to play its part in ushering in a new and a better world. Rather than a university that creates value for the state, or for shareholders, or for private corporations or even for the university as an economic entity, it would be a university that creates value for others in the wider world. It would not be content just to connect with social issues but would seek to identify anomalies in society and use its resources to address them and so create addition *social* value.

Sonja Arndt and Carl Mika ('Dissident Thought: A Decolonising Framework for Revolt in the University') catch and place before us that long-established – but now disappearing - idea of the oppositional university. This would be a university that uses the space granted to it by the wider society to critique the world around it. Here, thought becomes dissident and subversive, a form even of revolt, and it would take its bearings from critical sightings of disjunctions in the world. But to bring off such a stance – within the world but critical of the world – requires counter forms of thought; even forms of a-rational thought, that provoke a spirit of dissent, a 'delirium', revolt and otherness in and of thought.

Yusef Waghid and Nurraan Davids ('Towards an African University of Critique') bring this section to a close in calling for the university to hold to itself a way of 'thinking differently' about matters. It would be 'restive'; it would be 'putting into question' what it discerns around it. It would seek spaces of thought outside conventional bifurcated approaches to knowledge (bequeathed in part by colonisation). This university of critique would not just exhibit a 'condition of dissonance' but would be involved in 'deliberative engagement' with the wider world, difficult though that is.

Part Two – *Educating Thought* turns to matters of thought in relation to students and their development. The ambiguity in the title here serves to prompt the ideas both that thought can be educated *and* that thoughtfulness can aid students' education. There is a dual carefulness here, of the educator and of the student her or himself. Questions then arise as to how thinking itself could be educated; a thinking that strives to grow out of itself and reach towards ever new forms of thinking.

Robyn Barnacle ('Research Education and Care: The Care-full PhD') begins this section by dwelling on thought that is 'care-full' in the studies and thinking of doctorate students. Care-full thought cannot be aimless but has to be focused. It has to be concerned with something. Ultimately, such concerned thought will naturally lend itself to large matters, involving societal responsibility (such as ecological sustainability). Unfortunately, PhD work is increasingly narrow and taken up with technical issues. There is little encouragement towards the largeness of thinking that careful thought should properly lead.

James Arvanitakis and David Hornsby ('Citizenship and the Thinking University: Toward the Citizen Scholar') make a case for particular kinds of attributes and proficiencies associated with critical thinking, namely those likely to advance societal participation and citizenship. A central idea here is that of a 'threshold', where the immediately obvious is transcended. The thought involved at this point inhabits an 'in-between' region, 'a meeting place of domains of rational thinking, while remaining rational'. Ultimately, this would be an education that aimed to promote 'the citizen scholar', concerned to help improving society.

Thomas Karlsohn ('Bildung, Emotion and Thought') argues that serious thought has an emotional component, and develops the argument by looking at the unfolding of the Germanic idea of *Bildung*, that notoriously complex concept involving an interweaving of mind, person, culture and society and even the state. This perspective is important in offering a correction to purely cognitive, intellectual and reasoning understandings of the matter of thinking. A particular aspect at work is that of the presence of love, especially as it may be found in the pedagogical relationship between student and teacher. Such an argument has implications not just for teaching but also for educational institutions. Perhaps, as Karlsohn observes, the English (especially Newman's) liberal idea of the university may also have a part to play.

SunInn Yun and Paul Standish ('Technicising Thought: English and the Internationalisation of the University') start from reflections on the growth of instrumental reason and the 'impoverishment' of thought that could be said to characterise the university. They turn to language as potentially offering resources for thought, and go on examine, as a case study, the place of English in the internationalisation of the university, where they observe that its dominance is having an effect in constraining thought, both though its ubiquity and through the particular 'functional' characteristics of English as a language. Missing is an interest in the plurality of languages and in the prompting of thought and 'mutual intelligibility' that such an interest would sponsor. It would be 'a conception of thinking that is outward-turning and other-regarding'. An awareness along these lines may prompt 'an opening of thought that the university needs'.

Part Three – *'The Thinking University: Making Connections'* – turns to the university in-itself. The thinking university is ultimately a university that fosters connections, but of what kind and in which places? Here, we find the thinking university as a maker of worlds, a 'world-monger', holding within itself new emancipatory possibilities.

David Beckett and Paul Hager ('A Complexity Thinking Take on Thinking in the University') suggest that complexity thinking 'points to the necessary incompleteness of all theorising' and it always possesses 'emergent' properties. Within universities, certain types of group processes favour such emergent thinking, namely those that have the character of complex and open systems. These group processes 'provoke' thinking, especially through the open relationships between members of the groups concerned. Such groups are 'co-present' in universities, characteristically generating 'thought-ful' experiences. In (such) universities, learning and thinking 'emerge by doing these activities', with the groups involved exhibiting their own agency. Accordingly, the orchestration of such groups, marked by their 'thinking relationally', will aid the development of the thinking university.

Jan McArthur ('When Thought Gets Left Alone: Thinking, Recognition and Social Justice') also reminds us of the several social dimensions of thought, which look both to its internal features and its natural connectivity with the wide social realm. Ultimately, issues about thought necessarily connect with the social justice role of the university, oriented towards an emancipatory form of reason and the generation of 'a plurality of ideas'. Economics offers a test case of these ideas: it can 'contribute to the wellbeing of the social world' not least 'through its graduates' but it has been found wanting. Students in Economics have been arguing for a new kind of economics, attuned to the challenges of the world but there has been little recognition of their proposals. Thinking understood as a reaching for social justice has to be exemplified both within the university and beyond.

Rikke Toft Nørgård and Søren Bengtsen ('The Worldhood University: Design Signatures and Guild Thinking') presents a conceptual model for, what they call, 'the worldhood university'. This kind of university is deeply embedded within the societal context and the wider world. Instead of trying to be everything to everyone, this chapter argues that universities should aim for being *something* for *someone*. The chapters explores how universities focus their identity and engagement in the world, and how this creates a certain kind of higher education place and atmosphere. The worldhood university creates a signature thinking that assigns new forms of agency and to academics. The guiding metaphor for the worldhood university is the guild. In the guild academics are not just engaged and involved in the society and personal lifeworlds they become invested in. In the guild, academics are at home in the world, a thinking becomes a form of perpetual homecoming.

Ronald Barnett ('The Thinking University: Two Versions, Rival *and* Complementary') draws attention to thought being exhibited at the two levels of thought in and around the disciplines and thought about the university itself. The one form of thought looks outwards, in its concerns to understand the world; the other looks inward, with its concerns about the university and its present situation and its future possibilities. These two forms of thought have tensions between themselves: in thinking about itself, the university displays its corporate aspect and may, even if unwittingly, constrain thought in the disciplines as it seeks to advance its position in the world. However, thinking in the disciplines may and does open spaces in which the university can think anew about itself and its possibilities.

En Passant

In his (2015) book, *States of Shock: Stupidity and Knowledge in the twenty-first Century*, the French thinker, Bernard Stiegler observes that 'Western universities are in the grip of a deep malaise' (2), being complicit in an emerging general state of 'global unreason' and even 'stupidity', in which reason is regressing. This situation has arisen, Stiegler suggests, as a result of a 'technologization' of culture. However, while the position may be 'toxic', it is not one of unremitting bleakness: 'therapeutic' possibilities are opening in this new world.

But, then, if such a new stage for this Earth is to emerge, the university has to accept its share of 'responsibility'; a 'thinking responsibility' indeed. Questions arise especially for the university, 'to pose in a new way ... the question of knowing what it means to think'. (152) And Stiegler sees in the university an institution which can help usher in a thinking world, accompanied with new kinds of thoughtful associations within humanity; and doing so through the university drawing on new technologies, albeit with a concern for the world and aiming at the cultivation of new 'public spaces' (194).

However, this philosophical idea of the university will only be realised by universities across the world understanding themselves and working as a collective, united in this venture of enabling the development of global reason. *This* surely is the main task of universities in the twenty-first Century, none other than playing their part in the ushering in of a thinking world.

References

Bhaskar, R. (2011). *Reclaiming reality. A critical introduction to contemporary philosophy.* London & New York: Routledge.

Bohm, D. (1997). *Thought as a System.* London/New York: Routledge.

Habermas, J. (1987). The idea of the university: Learning processes. *New German Critique, 41,* 3–22.

Hampshire, S. (1970). *Thought and action.* London: Chatto and Windus.

Heidegger, M. (1971). *On the Way to Language* (trans Peter D. Hertz). New York: HarperCollins.

Heidegger, M. (2004/1954). *What is Called Thinking?* New York/London: Harper.

Heidegger, M. (2010). *Country Path Conversations* (trans Bret. W. Davis). Bloomington: Indiana University Press.

Lingis, A. (1998). *The imperative.* Bloomington: Indiana University Press.

List, C., & Pettit, P. (2011). *Group agency: The possibility, design, and status of corporate agents.* Oxford: Oxford University Press.

MacIntyre, A. (2011). *God, Philosophy, Universities.* Lanham, Maryland and Plymouth, UK: Rowman and Littlefield.

Maxwell, N. (1987). *From knowledge to wisdom: A revolution in the aims and methods of science.* Oxford: Blackwell.

Minogue, K. (1973). *The concept of a university.* London: Weidenfeld and Nicolson.

Oakeshott, M (1989) The voice of liberal learning. Ed by T Fuller. New Haven and London: Yale University.

Ricoeur, P. (1970). *Freud and Philosophy: An Essay on Interpretation* (trans Denis Savage). Yale University Press.

Stiegler, B. (2015). *States of Shock: Stupidity and Knowledge in the 21st Century.* Cambridge, UK/ Malden, MA: Polity.

Wittgenstein, L (2003/1969) On certainty. Malden, MA and Oxford: Blackwell

Part I
The Thinking University – Contending With the World

Chapter 2
Truth, Democracy and the Mission of the University

Sharon Rider

Introduction

John Stuart Mill opens "On Liberty" with an epigraph from Wilhelm von Humboldt's (1854) *Sphere and Duties of Government*: "The grand, leading principle, towards which every argument unfolded in these pages directly converges, is the absolute and essential importance of human development in its richest diversity" (Mill 1993). In what follows, the relationship between higher education and liberalism as a political philosophy will be examined in terms of this "essential importance of human development in its richest sense". In this essay, I consider what Ortega y Gasset considered "the mission of the university", and connect it to Arendt's notion of "institutions of truth" as necessary for the perpetuation of a liberal (democratic) form of life.

Enlightenment thinkers viewed freedom as both a means and an end of education. It was thought that intellectual inquiry and the free exchange of beliefs and ideas manifested, perpetuated and improved the exercise of human reason. A classical liberal theme is thus, on the one hand, institutionalized rights and constitutional checks on power that might inhibit that exercise; on the other, but closely related to this sine qua non of a liberal polity, is the confidence that every citizen will recognize that his right to think and speak freely is conditioned on the recognition of that right for others, and further, that he must, in a sense, actively will the possibility of disagreement as a necessary component of the free exercise of his reason, that is, as a condition for the kind of interchange that will increase the power of reason in all. The assumption that the unimpeded use of reason will lead to the attainment of universally recognized truths is now considered by many naïve, and deeply problematic, at least with regard to matters concerning the political, social and cultural

S. Rider (✉)
Uppsala University, Uppsala, Sweden
e-mail: sharon.rider@filosofi.uu.se

© Springer International Publishing AG, part of Springer Nature 2018
S.S.E. Bengtsen, R. Barnett (eds.), *The Thinking University*,
Debating Higher Education: Philosophical Perspectives 1,
https://doi.org/10.1007/978-3-319-77667-5_2

sphere. The political problem is then how to prevent the dissolution of the polity into an inchoate mass of belligerent particularism and conflicting interests.

In this regard, modern liberal democracies invest great hopes and resources into higher education. How are we to make sense of the notion that the collapse of liberalism and citizenship, i.e. of a common sense of shared civic responsibility, can be addressed and handled with enough "higher education"? To begin with, we should first try to get a hold on what we mean by "citizenship" with respect to modern liberal democracies.

The Democratic Citizen

It is standard practice to distinguish between three dimensions of citizenship: political, social and legal. These correspond, roughly, to three different institutional contexts: the legislature (political rights), welfare systems (education and health care) and the judiciary (civil liberties). This model derives in large from T.H. Marshall's highly influential "Citizenship and Social Class", published in 1950, in connection with the construction of the British postwar welfare state. Marshall defines citizenship as a "status bestowed on all those who are full members of a community", sharing rights, duties, and the protections of a common law. The bonds of modern citizenship develop first through the "struggle to win those rights," and then, once gained, by their "enjoyment." Thus modern citizenship implies also "loyalty to a civilization which is a common possession." (Marshall 2009).

But what is citizenship in a mass democracy such as the US or the EU? Who are the citizens, what is their relationship to the demos, and in what respect do they form a mass? What is the nature of the civilization that is possessed in common? For Ortega y Gasset," the masses" are neither" the working classes" nor" folk", neither" all of us", nor" the man on the Clapham omnibus". The "mass" of mass democracy as well as of "mass culture" is best understood in comparison with "mass production": it is the human being" repeating himself as a generic type: the average man thinking and behaving as such, man as undifferentiated from other men" (Ortega 1957a). In any given social, economic or ethnic group, one will find both the" mass" and the" genuine minority". Ortega defines" mass man" not in terms of being mediocre, or even commonplace, but in being what he is without reflection, in taking his moral and intellectual constitution as it is. In Ortega's view, our own epoch is characterized by the pre-dominance, even among supposed elites," of the mass" in this respect. And this massification of culture is directly related to the challenge of democracy and the point of higher education in our era.

Ideally, in well-functioning liberal democracies, whatever their inevitable flaws and deficiencies, people as collectives and as individuals can rely on the existence of specific institutions for establishing and safeguarding the basis for dependable and neutral decision-making. A liberal society is thus one built on *trust*, in which the plurality choose to live together, despite enormous challenges, on the grounds that they can count on institutions in place that will serve and secure the rights of each and the potential betterment of all.[1] By freely undersigning liberal principles and loyalty to the rule of law, the citizen takes upon himself a rigorous self-discipline in his intercourse with other citizens. In this sense, democracy and the institutions of the rule of law are synonymous: both refer to a life in common under certain constraints obtaining equally for all.

In *Revolt of the Masses*, Ortega makes the case that our century has witnessed the advent of a "hyperedemocracy", or governance by a "mass mentality", a society in which a plurality of voices is replaced by a homogenous multitude. While the solution to the challenge of mass democracy has been sought by thinkers such as Dewey in "mass education", Ortega is less confident. He notes that modern educational systems, even at elite institutions at higher levels, are designed primarily to instruct" the masses" in the techniques of modern life: students are given tools, but seldom understanding of the intellectual tradition that made possible these remarkable instruments and results, among which must be counted the institutions of democracy. The emphasis on usefulness and application without a basic grasp of what makes the cultural institution(s) of science possible, its history and its theoretical considerations and foundations, means that, strictly speaking, students do not understand what is required to think, much less to think something new or different. They leave their studies taking for granted the ideas and techniques in which they have come in contact as givens. Ortega chose the word" mass" not in the first instance to indicate a numerical multitude, but above all to suggest a static existence, the inertia of a certain attitude.

To have an idea means being capable of coming into possession of the reasons for having it, and consequently, implicitly presupposes that there is such a thing as reason, the possibility of communicating intelligibly about a common world. To have ideas, to form judgments, is to acknowledge the authority of reason in this sense. Notions in want of foundations are not really ideas at all, according to Ortega, but" desires dressed in words". Formed with the purpose of fulfilling the individual's interests, such spontanous reactions cannot be identified with the ideas and insights arrived at through a serious education, which is a laborious effort of deliberation, interrogation and cognitive self-revision. To attribute the same weight to such different phenomena as ideas and preferences means accepting that" might makes right", i.e. that it is acceptable to deny others the right to give and demand reasons as the basis for decision-making. Liberalism as a political ideal, on the other hand, requires of each citizen that she acknowledges a set of mutually binding limitations on her own liberty and the criteria for adjudicating disputes and conflicts, and respects that there are differences of opinion that are to be handled by institutions recognized by all as legitimate arbiters. If such democratic principles and rules are regarded as contingent upon convenience or convention, and therewith lacking

---

[1] Bo Rothstein has argued that without norms of trust, the "tragedy of the commons" is unavoidable. He identifies an institutional mechanism by virtue of which trust can be established "from above", that is, the trustworthiness of "efficient" institutions. He claims that this gives rise to interpersonal trust, which in its turn make the "production" of social capital in civil society possible. See Rothstein 2000.

any necessity or intrinsic value, or, alternatively, if they are viewed as inevitably partisan and biased, the ground for a democratic polity is severely undermined.

The Learned Ignoramus

Here things get difficult, especially regarding the potential of higher education to undergird a liberal, democratic and reasonable society. When Ortega seeks to identify a category of human being who would correspond to this ideal type of self-enclosed cognitive illiberalism, he finds it in the ostensibly "educated" middle class, those whom we normally associate with the survival and flourishing of liberal democracies: the professionals, specialists and experts, such as engineers, magistrates, doctors, professors and so forth.

Since scientific work and professional training in the last century have come to demand ever-increasing specialization, each new generation of scientists and professionals lose whatever contact with other disciplines was necessary for earlier generations. The narrowness of focus on one's own disciplinary apparatus and its conventions has given rise to a very specific kind of expert, namely, one who is at home in her own little corner of the universe, at the same time as she severely overestimates her knowledge and understanding of the rest, or more to the point, fails to recognize what such knowledge and understanding entails, and why it is necessary at all. The result is a new kind of human being:" the learned ignoramus". Aware of herself as" someone who knows", she considers herself entirely suited to make decisions on all matters. She is, as it were, locked up in her own preferences, instincts and representations. As Ortega puts it, she is in a state of perpetual" not listening". Thus a certain kind of specialized higher education, including, importantly, many forms of subject-specific training associated with the humanities and social sciences, can lead to intellectual isolation and even privation, rather than participation in a genuinely social sphere.

What is this social sphere from which the learned ignorami are shut out? The Latin noun *societas* indicates most broadly a union for a common purpose. In *Man and People*, Ortega insists that a union is something that is achieved, the ongoing result of a coming together, regardless of whether there is some explicit decision or contract. A society is an accomplished unity, rather than some thing that just is there for us, as a tree or a stone. And something that is achieved or done can also cease to be achieved, and can be undone. The sudden undoing of this union would likely be the result of a dramatic course of events, such as war or natural disaster. But the "ceasing to be achieved" is rather a question of negligence or pretermission. "Society" refers, therefore, not to some thing with such and such qualities, but rather works as a placeholder for the variety of things that are constantly being done and redone, modified and developed so that we can continue to "unite for a common purpose". While the State or its senate may be seen as being, in some abstract sense, a *res publica* (a public thing), the use of the term "society" simply designates the fact that human beings already at a very primitive level come together in order to accomplish things, i.e. to act (Ortega 1957b).

Unified or collective action for a common purpose requires that we on occasion refrain from acting in order to reflect, together, on what it is that we are aiming at in order to be a certain kind of society. Another way of putting the point is to say that we from time to time regard *ourselves*, our society, as a *problem*, something to be considered (and perhaps changed). Ortega takes Aristotle's claims that "man is by nature a political animal" and that "all men by nature desire to know" to be different articulations of the same view, namely, that the inclination and capacity to give and take into consideration reasoned accounts about ourselves and the world we inhabit is essential to a fully developed human form of life. But this capacity to account for our ideas and to hold each other accountable is an essentially incomplete project. (Ortega suggests that we define the human being as *homo insciens* rather than *homo sapiens*.) Thus education is fundamental for a properly human society to be attained and maintained: if society is something that is achieved only in and through our combined, considered efforts, and if thought is never complete once and for all, but always and inevitably part of our daily doings in the world in order to be what we are as a society, then the capacity for thinking itself is necessarily something that requires perpetual and vigilant sustenance.

Civilization, for Ortega, is simply the self-aware and tenacious perpetuation of the choice to live together. It means, therefore, always implicitly taking others into consideration when acting; its opposite, barbarism, is quite simply the will to disassociation. Civilization is always "liberal" in the broadest sense of the term: it assumes a certain level of generosity and hospitality, a "taking the other into account", even if that other is the opposition, or just weaker. A State, on the other hand, is quite literally a "state", i.e. a state of equilibrium, that is, a point in a dynamic process. To be a subject of a State can mean two different things. It can mean deference to a recognized (i.e. legitimate) authority, or it can be mere submission, i.e. acquiescence to force. The polity is, for Ortega, a uniting of diverse groups that, in the end, is strictly speaking *un*natural – it is, as he says, "a work of imagination". He credits Julius Ceaesar with broadening the European political imagination. Treating the State as a common *task* rather than a thing, for Caesar, there were no physical limits: there were no "natural frontiers" for the *idea* of Rome. Indeed, Ortega considers all belief in real, naturally occurring national borders along linguistic, cultural, religious or physical lines, "geographical mysticism". Frontiers and borders merely consolidate some form of unification that has already been attained through human activity. So a State is then a point of equilibrium achieved after a fusion of "us" with "others", which is to say that a State is an effect, and not a cause. It is something we have done and continue to do together (which is why its legal grounds and institutions are said to be "constituted"). Without this ongoing effort at political self-constitution by each new generation, there is no society but only atomized individuals, groups and more or less fleeting and contingent interests, without any intrinsic relation to one another. And that "state" is one of disequilibrium and dissolution. The common project of ensuring my autonomy by ensuring yours is dependent on the right sort of education, which is nothing less than the careful cultivation of the will and capacity to be part of that project.

The Mission of the University

In *Mission of the University*, Ortega follows up on his thoughts about mass democracy, and proposes a reform plan for higher education in Spain. He makes it clear, however, that the idea of the European university, in spite of great variation between countries, comes down to a few basic precepts: a university exists for the purposes of i) professionalism, i.e. the teaching of "the learned professions", that is, the ones that rest on a body of systematic theoretical knowledge; ii) scientific research as such, together with the preparation of future investigators (Ortega 1946: 41). But, he adds, there is a third task associated with universities, namely, the propagation of "general culture". This term itself, he thinks, makes clear how fundamentally the modern university misunderstands its mission: "its Philistinism betrays its insincerity" (Ortega 1946:43). What he means is that culture is by definition general, in contrast to the specificities of any given specialization or technique. By the use of the term "general culture", we think of "culture" as a kind of decoration on top of the "real stuff" of learning, rather than its very foundation. A culture is "the system of ideas concerning the world and humanity" which forms the "effective guide of existence" at any given time. To be "cultured" or "educated", then, is to have a grasp of this system in a general way. In this respect, education is something entirely different from "professional training", on the one hand, or research, on the other. Both can be conducted without "culture" in this fundamental sense, and, indeed, Ortega's worry is that this is precisely the direction that higher education has taken. "Basic distribution requirements" in the liberal arts and the like constitute a "last miserable residue of something more imposing and more meaningful". As ornamentation, it "serves no end at all" (Ortega 1946:42–43). "A vague desire for a vague culture", he says, "will lead us nowhere".

Ortega defines culture as "the vital system of ideas of a period", by which he means the ideas that are alive and in use, which characterize our ways of thinking and the grounds for our decisions and actions. While many of these ideas in our times come from science, science is not synonymous with culture or education. To the extent that universities today concern themselves primarily with scientific research and technical development, they treat the transmission of culture to the next generation at best a secondary task. Thus despite greater access than ever to higher education, the vast majority of Europeans, including those who have received a university education, remain "uncultured" in Ortega's sense, that is, "ignorant of the essential system of ideas concerning the world and man" belonging to our time.

It should be emphasized that Ortega's position is not "anti-science". To the contrary, he repeatedly refers to science as "the grandest creation of man", among its "most sublime pursuits and achievements" (Ortega 1946:60). His point is rather that its continuation requires that the scientist understands something of the nature of this formidable institution, aside from its current practical utitilty and techniques, so that this comprehension can be communicated to the next generation. Modern society needs scientists, and it needs professionals. But further, it needs competent citizens, whose exercise of judgment effects or influences others. If the university is supposed to provide training for the kind of profession that requires sound practical judgment grounded in the knowledge produced by theoretical work (research), then that training should include an education in the "general system of ideas" about the world and man as far as theoretical investigation has taken us. This, according to Ortega, is the basic function of the university, "what it must be above all else". The professional who lacks understanding of "what we now know" about the world from modern physics, genetics, history, or philosophy, and has no inkling of how "we" have come to know it, is not educated. Being uneducated, she will be a less competent doctor, judge, pharmacist, teacher or engineer, for the simple reason that she will be constrained by her limited awareness and comprehension of the world in which she is to fulfill her function. As a member of the polity, her opinions are likely to be "a torrent of drivel and bluff". It would not surprise Ortega, therefore, that we have the political climate we have today; the problem is that for all our technical and professional training, the vast majority, including the elites, have received little education.

Higher education, in Ortega's view, is enculturation. "Culture is either received, or else it is invented. He who exposes himself to the labor of inventing it for himself, accomplishing alone what thirty centuries of humanity have already accomplished, is the only man who has the right to deny the proposition that the university must undertake to impart culture" (Ortega 1946: 47). The university is modern man's best chance at avoiding the dissolution of social and individual reasons caused by specialization and professionalization. For Ortega, the basic mission of the university, in the first instance, is the transmission of culture. Beyond that, it should train professionals and perform research. But how are these duties to be combined?

The Principle of Scarcity

As a starting point, Ortega thinks that we should recognize that any kind of institution exists due to human imperfection. If adolescence were a hundred years and the ordinary citizen highly focused and extremely curious and gifted, universities would not be needed, since the youth would learn everything on their own. Universities exist not first and foremost for "excellence", but for the ordinary: "If there were none but extraordinary creatures, it is very probable that there would be no institutions, either educational or political" (Ortega 1946:49). Thus all university education should be geared not to some utopian vision of what we would ideally like to transmit to the next generation, but to *what can be learned* by the average student.

Ortega's sketch for a reform of the university is built upon the Swedish economist Gustav Cassel's "principle of scarcity". Ortega argues that human limitation with regard to the capacity to learn should be the point of departure: "It is necessary to provide for teaching precisely in proportion as the learner is unable to learn". In simpler societies, whatever little knowledge there is, is regarded as kind of valuable property and guarded by a chosen few, lest outsiders get a hold of it. This is the basis of esotercism and secret rites. In advanced societies, the opposite holds. The knowledge to be acquired is so vast and complex that the capacity to make use of stands is radically out of proportion with what there is to be learned. The principle of economy in education dictates then that higher learning be arranged and allocated such that the knowledge required actually can be acquired; "the university must be a projection of the student to the scale of an institution." (Ortega 1946:55) The two relevant dimensions of the student's education is: (i) her limited capacity for learning; (ii) what she needs to know in order to live her life fully. What Ortega is seeking here is a minimal core curriculum that any institution calling itself a university must provide to anyone seeking "higher education". This core should consist of what is strictly necessary, reduced to what is possible for the ordinary student to learn.

In order to see what is strictly necessary, says Ortega, we must first acknowledge that a profession is not a science, and that professionals are not scientists. The process of scientific discovery and the production of new knowledge are thus to be clearly distinguished from professional training. While the systematized content of numerous sciences form the foundation of many of the learned professions, the end result of research should not be confused with the investigation itself. The act of learning or teaching the content of the sciences, their methods and results, is something other than actually trying to discover something new, or to demonstrate an error. Science and research are less a body of knowledge than a tradition of inquiry, of ways and means to attain and secure knowledge. Knowledge, in turn, is the possession of the facts, routines and established techniques ("best practice") emanating from that investigation. To do research is to investigate: to formulate problems, work on them, and find solutions. One might think that Ortega here embraces a "heroic" view of science. In fact, he warns against such romanticizing of scientists. What is admirable in research is its outcomes, not the individuals performing it: "we appreciate the pearl, not the oyster that secreted it." (Ortega 1946:60).

On this account, the point of professional training ought to be to appropriate what is useful for the ends of that profession (healing the sick, building bridges, adjudicating legal conflicts, etc). That means that in taking from science whatever is efficacious for its purposes, professional training leaves the rest, including the most characteristic aspect of scientific investigation: "the cultivation of the problematic and doubtful". If research seeks to pose and solve problems, the professions seek to apply solutions (whether or not these solutions come from science). The conflation of the two undermines the integrity of each. When scientific techniques and results are integrated into professional training and practice, they should rather be organized around that profession's own principles, ideals and norms; they become what Ortega terms "professional technics". The point here is not that the professions are somehow less valuable or worthy than scientific endeavor; to the contrary, Ortega thinks that the professional schools ought to cultivate their specific excellences and exemplary forms, rather than imitate science.

Contemporary culture as a whole is saturated with the results of science. And as in the case of professional training, it is not the investigative, problematic, creative and doubtful, i.e. the characteristically scientific, which permeates the culture, but rather the results: certain axiomatic assumptions, convictions and articles of faith that constitute "what we know about the world". (Think of climate change, evolutionary genetics, the Big Bang, etc.) Public trust in such vital ideas is a matter of culture, not of investigation. Culture, Ortega writes, "borrows from science what is vitally necessary for the interpretation of our existence", whereas science itself is "indifferent to the exigencies of our life, and follows its own necessities. Accordingly, science grows constantly more diversified and specialized without limit, and is never completed." (Ortega 1946:66). Science is essentially forward-looking, that is, it is not and ought not be in the service of the here and now. That is rather the task of culture, which is what gives human beings their potential to achieve their full humanity at any given time. General education should aim to give students their bearings in the world; its purpose is to transmit culture. The making of professionals and scientists, which is absolutely necessary, is best achieved on the foundations of the former.

A Proposal for Reform

Ortega proposes that a "Faculty of Culture" be the nucleus of any university. This faculty would be responsible for transmitting the vital ideas of its time, under broad thematics such as "the physical scheme of the world". The education provided would not be the same as the one for students to become physicists or mathematicians; rather, the content of such a thematic would be a synthesis of the main ideas about the physical world as these have emerged from physics thus far, together with the study of the means by which physicists have acquired this knowledge. Such a thematic program of study would entail a history of the development of physics in terms of its conceptual apparatus and methods, which would, among other things, enable the student to envisage what "the world" must have looked like for people five hundred or two thousand years ago. More importantly, she should be able to recognize the peculiarities and characteristics of her own modern world. There is, of course, reason to worry that all this could amount to popular science and not a substantial education, if the students lack the requisite understanding of mathematics, at least enough to understand formulas. That requirement, Ortega hopes, will be satisfied if we rectify the problem of inadequate education at primary and secondary school. One might object that the mathematics necessary for a substantial understanding of the basic ideas of modern physics are so advanced, complicated, and arcane that they require formal technical training that cannot be learned by ordinary students. Ortega's response is that mastery of higher mathematics is surely essential for doing physics, but it is not for understanding its import for human life. Further, to the extent that the internal development of a science proceeds toward ideas that require technical proficiency to be understood at all, then those ideas lose their fundamental character to become instruments of the science in question, rather than its substance.

Ortega's ideal of the university is thus as

(i) the institution in society responsible for educating ordinary students for membership in that society *as well as* in a profession. Training in the latter without the former will create lesser citizens as well as lesser doctors, lawyers and teachers

(ii) an institution without pretence, i.e. one that requires of the ordinary student what can reasonably be expected

(iii) an institution that consistently acknowledges the principle of scarcity; it will not waste the student's time by pretending that she is engaged in scientific investigation. While science is and should be performed at universities, it is not the core of a university's educational mission

(iv) an institution consisting of scientific investigation, "enculturation" and professional training where the latter two are organized along pedagogical principles rather than scientific or scholarly ones. Special problems, experimentation and so forth belong to science, not culture

(v) an institution that performs both teaching and research, where the two are seen as separate activities

(vi) an institution with clear and precise requirements. By adjusting its requirements to what can realistically be achieved, it can hold firmly to those essentials.

Accepting Ortega's emphasis on the transmission of culture, one might wonder why universities should engage in research at all. The answer is that cultures and science can and in all likelhihood will stagnate without the consistent force of doubt, problematicization, criticism, correction, demands of proof and argument, and so forth that is the hallmark of research and scholarship. If modernity is the resolve to live according to reason, to think and plan and create rather than follow the course of nature and events as if these were pre-ordained or a matter of fate, then the modern university is the institutionalization of that resolve. Ortega defines intelligence or reason as "the only power which perceives its own limitations", and finds in science "the scope for its full grandeur". Scientific research is proof of the vitality of a society's resolve to keep on thinking and creating. If culture and the professions were cut off from the ferment of research, they would soon be overtaken by dogmatism and "the creeping paralysis of scholasticism". (Ortega 1946:74–75) The exertion that is research is at the base of the modern university; it must be presupposed, if culture and the professions are to remain themselves vital. In this respect, while the mission of the university is teaching, it is *also* and in addition, research.

An Institution of Truth

The intellectualist ideal of man as res cogitans, as already "thinking" insofar as he is human, presupposes that intellectual resources are just there at our disposal when we need them. The danger of this attitude, Ortega thinks, is that it leads to complacency, obliviousness and negligence. As distinct from other animals, whose lives consist of unceasing responsiveness to their current environment, and who are, in that respect, steered by it, man can from time to time withdraw "into himself", and ignore everything around him except that which is the object of his concern. He can "pay attention". To what? To himself: his ideas, thoughts, hopes, plans and aims. But, importantly, these things are not just there in the individual, but come to him from the world: talk he has heard, words he has read, patterns of social life unto which he was born, the very language he speaks. Without others, there is no "inner world" into which to retreat, and no thoughts to think. We are all every day involved in keeping up the business of achieving our language, our civilization, our knowledge, through considered common action and dialogue, through which we constitute the human world. Although thought and its manifestations (science, art, philosophy, commerce) are not the aim and purpose of human life, action in isolation from thought, is, by definition, unreflective – quite literally thoughtless (or, as Ortega says, "stupid").

In a bee society, all the bees do what they must. They have no reasons, and they don't need them. But as the animal with logos, human beings are fated to reasons, for themselves and for others. In order to decide if I have "good reasons", have thought rightly, I have to confer and compare with the reasons and thoughts of others. Yet to do that means that we have already some kind of *sensus communis*, a common ground to stand on. If we reject at the outset the possibility of achieving such common ground, we deny the possibility of living together purposefully. Every opinion or judgment about a state of affairs is a kind of movement back and forth between myself and others: in order to examine my reasons for making the judgement "X is good", I have to be able to explain or at least relate those thoughts to someone else. This is because thinking requires communicability for its performance and enlargement. Liberalism as a way of thinking and liberalism as a form of political life go hand in hand. Where there are no reasons, there are no judgments, but only expressions of something – a preference, a visceral reaction, a feeling. The very notion of judgement implies a movement into myself (my reasons) and outward (the grounds for my decision or choice), suggesting that there must be some common standard or point of reference, i.e. a shared human world. Prejudice consists in the refusal to consider seriously truth claims that don't accommodate our picture of things, or which we cannot integrate seemlessly into our previous perceptions and conceptions. There are indications that we are today witnessing the triumph of prejudice, and I will conclude with the following hypothesis: this state of affairs is in part an effect of the decline of what Hannah Arendt called our" institutions of truth"(Arendt 1961).

In Arendtian terms, institutions are enactments, achievements of the human effort to construct a world fit for human habitation through thinking and judgment. Not" naturally occurring", they are the product of patient human artifice. "Institutions of truth" are human constructions devised to uncover, unfold and preserve the common world. Universities and courts of law have been the most universally acknowledged repositories of truth, facts and knowledge, and professors and judges, their guardians. To take one of Arendt's examples, academic historians of different schools with differing interests and agendas for their research might have highly divergent accounts of the causes of WW II. But for each and every case, it is nonetheless true that Germany invaded Poland. And it is false that Poland invaded Germany. One might take a variety of stances on the explanation for and consequences of this state of affairs, but the state of affairs remains unchanged. The historian qua historian must be committed to upholding the absolute necessity of not changing the facts to fit his narrative, because if he does, then there is no such thing as history in the modern, scholarly sense, but just stories told by different people with their own reasons for telling them and for which there is no impartial adjudicator, since everyone has his own story to tell.

What are we to say about an issue such as climate change? On an Arendtian account, it would be inaccurate to call" climate change" per se a datum or fact. It is rather a short-hand term for the meticulous hardwon results of a vast intellectual effort and pooling of resources in that ongoing activity that we call the institution of science. "Climate change" is the answer to hundreds and thousands of questions and subquestions that have been posed in observations, experiments, laboratories and reports around the world. To call it a theory rather than a fact is simply to say that it, like the Big Bang theory or evolutionary genetics, is a complex "vital idea" rather than a simple state of affairs. On the other hand, to deny the results of all this conscious human labor, not just one part or element, but the whole thing all at once, is to repudiate our right to draw reasonable conclusions on the basis of our best collective efforts at thinking, understanding and knowing. "Climate change" is not a matter of opinion because it designates the outcome of decades of scientific research about which most of us are simply not expert enough to have well-founded ideas. Those who express the" opinion" that we are experiencing the meteorological effects of our form of life on the planet are manifesting confidence in the methods and practices of science, which is to say, of education and expertise. Here we arrive at the crux of the matter. Those of us who are not climatologists, whatever our" opinions" on climate change, are all on the same footing with regard to the facts. We are not in a position to assess the methods by which they are reached, or ascertain the validity of the results leading up to this conclusion. To rail against" climate denial" is in essence to argue for trust in science and expertise. Those who deny climate change, on the other hand, implicitly repudiate the value and reliability of our institutions of knowledge production and education. In this respect, the conflict is profoundly political.

A free body politic requires a public sphere in which different ideas about how things should be can come together in open confrontation and argumentation. The space that makes this possible, the *agora*, is built on the recognition of the authority of how things actually are, a common world, to which all sides may refer. In the course of discussion, it is quite right and even necessary that the facts are organized and arranged differently depending upon where the argument is supposed to lead, but that does not subtract from their authority as facts. If we renounce or waive the demand that we acknowledge authoritative "common knowledge" as our starting point, politics without force, coercion or illegitimate authority is impossible, since there is no longer a shared world about which we agree to disagree. The liberal and persuasive function of the authority of argument is entirely lost. For this reason, it is essential for any kind of genuinely public sphere that there be some agency or authority, in the institutional sense, from which all parties can obtain these" shared facts" or "common knowledge", one which has as its regulative ideal to be a repository of impartial expertise for the greater good." Arendt explicitly names the judiciary and universities as such "institutions of truth". She writes: "Very unwelcome truths have emerged from the university, and very unwelcome judgments have been handed down from the bench again and again." (Arendt 1961: 260 f). These public institutions, existing precisely for the propagation of truth have, "contrary to all political rules", been established and supported by political power. It is indeed a paradox that the State should support and defend such institutions. These refuges of truth have always been and remain today exposed to the forces of political power and social and economic interests. Nonetheless, the chances for impartiality to prevail are greatly improved by the sheer existence of such places, and the organized fraternity of "independent, supposedly disinterested scholars" associated with them.

Arendt's thought is that, as "disinterested scholars", the political function of higher learning is that it supplies knowledge from outside the political realm, where no action and no decision are, or should be, involved. The political function of the professor, like any good teacher, is to communicate the vital ideas, as Ortega put it: to say, "this is the world".[2] In teaching what is in fact the case, whether or not it meets with our approval, he teaches the habit of impartiality, which, according to Arendt, gives the faculty of judgment the opportunity to operate and develop.

Echoing the Enlightenment notion that there can be no strict distinction between the freedom to communicate and the freedom to think, Arendt stresses that the only guarantee that we judge correctly is our ability to check our reasoning and our judgments against those of others: "we think only in community."[3] It is because of human fallibility that the scholar requires an "entire reading public" to think. Opinions concern matters of fact, and factual truths are political insofar as they relate to events and circumstances requiring witnesses and testimony. But while opinions are about facts, they are never themselves facts. It is on the basis of facts

---

[2] Cf. Max Weber's remark in "Science as a Vocation" (Weber 1946) that the main duty of a university teacher is to confront students with "uncomfortable truths", that is, statements of facts which are not congenial to his political opinions.

[3] Arendt cites here Kant's vindication of freedom of speech (if limited to scholars communicating ideas as citizens not as state officials) in "Answer to the Question: What is Enlightenment?" (Kant 1996) and "What does it Mean to Orient Oneself in Thinking?" (Kant 2001). But also, for instance, Kant's famous argument for "academic freedom" (if limited to the Philosophical Faculty) (Kant 1979).

or statements of fact that opinions, inspired by interests and inclinations, are formed. If facts themselves are to be constructed arbitrarily on the basis of inclination and interest, we lose the common world in which dialogue and persuasion, the acting out of political freedom, is possible.

The legitimacy of adjudicating between a variety of opposing opinions rests on respecting the facts or "what is the case", that is, the common world. Arendt's answer to the relativist position, i.e. the claim that accounts of human affairs are nothing but assemblages of events chosen from a certain perspective to tell a certain story, the selection principle of which is itself not based on fact, is that to respect the right of arrangement from a given point of view is not the same as to respect fictionalization. And this has to do with taking responsibility for the world as it is, not as we would like it to be or as we would have it to be for our own contingent purposes at the moment. Facts are beyond agreement and consent, and, in that respect, coercive rather than persuasive. But given the common world, the "issue" upon which we deliberate in political judgments, the greater my capacity to arrange or represent the actual state of affairs for myself from different points of view, i.e. the more "enlarged" my mentality, the more subtle, adequate and accurate my judgment will be (since seeing anything from only one perspective always entails some distortion). The only way to liberate the imagination from isolation in private interest is to open it up to modification or rectification, which is to say education.

When instutions of truth absorb and integrate political agendas, however, they reproduce not only specific ideologies, but also the habit of considering all truth-seeking and truth-speaking activity as arbitrary and partisan (Arendt 1958; Beiner 1992). As such, they cannot function as repositories of facts, knowledge or ideas for public negotiations and argumentation about a common world, the sphere in which freedom can be enacted and ensured for posterity; they become part of the ephemeral politics of the now.

Conclusion

Globalisation, digitalization and new harsh economic realities constitute a genuine challenge to higher education. What Ortega and Arendt teach us is that the deeper question concerns our capacity and desire to reconstitute the common project of achieving a shared world as equals, where my freedom and capacity to think for myself is utterly dependent on yours. A prequisite for the project of a common world is that we establish and maintain institutions," safe zones", for the accretion, understanding and articulation of knowledge about the world, where the presence of personal interest and conviction have limited coercive force. Liberal democracy has an absolute need for the legitimate authority of generally recognized institutions of truth, places where argumentation brings forth all sorts of facts and ideas the future use of which is entirely unpredictable, as new facts and new arguments arise and revise what we already think we know. Without such common grounds to stand on, the risk is great that the capacity for reason, be it scientific, professional or political, will run adrift, having lost its mooring in the institutions provided by a functioning democracy.

References

Arendt, H. (1958). *The human condition*. Chicago: Chicago univ. press.
Arendt, H. (1961). *Between past and present*. New York: Viking Press.
Beiner, R. (1992). *Hannah Arendt's lectures on political philosophy*. Chicago: University of Chicago Press.
Kant, I. (1979). *Conflict of the faculties*. Lincoln: University of Nebraska.
Kant, I. (1996). *Answer to the question: What is enlightenment? What is Enlightenment? Eighteenth-century answers and twentieth-century questions*. Berkeley: University of California Press.
Kant, I. (2001). *What does it mean to orient oneself in thinking? Religion and Rational Theology*. Cambridge: Cambridge University Press.
Marshall, T.H. (2009). Citizenship and social class. Reprinted in *Inequality and Society*, eds. Jeff Manza and Michael Sauder, 148–154. New York: W.W. Norton.
Mill, John Stuart. ([1859] 1993). On liberty. *On Liberty and Utilitarianism*.New York: Random House.
Ortega y Gasset, José. (1946). *Mission of the university*. New York: Routledge.
Ortega y Gasset, José. (1957a). *Revolt of the masses*. New York: W.W. Norton & Co.
Ortega y Gasset, José. (1957b). *Man and People*. Trans. W. R. In *Trask*. New York: W.W. Norton & Co.
Rothstein, B. (2000). Trust, social dilemmas and collective memories. *Journal of Theoretical Politics, 12*(4), 477–503.
von Humboldt, Wilhelm. (1854). Sphere and duties of government (trans J. Coulthard). London: Chapman.
Weber, M. (1946). Science as a vocation. In *Max Weber: Essays in Sociology*. New York: Oxford University Press.

Chapter 3
Universities as Societal Drivers: Entrepreneurial Interventions for a Better Future

Wesley Shumar and Sarah Robinson

Introduction

This paper suggests that a re-imagined university could play a central role in the twenty-first century knowledge-based society. This reimagined vision includes an alternative view of entrepreneurship that will open up new possibilities and create a focus on new forms of value that could be centrally important to overcoming the bureaucratic and corporate structures that have come to dominate how universities are organized currently. Our vision of entrepreneurship could create a new focus on a creative thinking process that is central to the future of the university. In the following paragraphs, we discuss the context within which intellectuals and philosophers of the late 18th and early 19th centuries began to imagine the modern universities, especially those associated with the University of Berlin, the so-called Humboldt University. The imagination of the modern research university produced significant consequences for universities and the larger society.. These unintended consequences benefited the development of universities and society in that they allowed the flourishing of creative thought. We then turn our attention to the neoliberal ideology which has dominated the imagination of the university across the globe in recent years. The neoliberal is, in contrast, a narrowing and hollow vision that undermines what universities could be at their best. Further, we argue, it will have damaging unintended effects on twenty-first century society as well. Finally, we discuss a new conceptualisation of an entrepreneurial university and the power that an enlightened entrepreneurial vision could bring to universities and the larger society through a new focus in creative critical thinking.

W. Shumar (✉)
Drexel University, PA, USA
e-mail: shumarw@drexel.edu

S. Robinson
Aarhus University, Aarhus, Denmark

© Springer International Publishing AG, part of Springer Nature 2018
S.S.E. Bengtsen, R. Barnett (eds.), *The Thinking University*,
Debating Higher Education: Philosophical Perspectives 1,
https://doi.org/10.1007/978-3-319-77667-5_3

To situate this analysis we ask the reader to note that our perspective comes from a training as cultural anthropologists. One tradition in anthropology that has developed since the 1950s has been to situate a specific analysis within a large macro-structural framework (Shumar 2004). Geertz (1963) is perhaps one of the early proponents of such a framework, situating his study of two Indonesian towns within the larger context of Indonesia in the world economy. Further George Marcus (1986) looked at the local as it was situated in a global context and John and Jean Comaroff (1992, 2000) situated their work with the Tshidi within the post-colonial context of South Africa. We could mention many other examples of contemporary anthropologists situating their work within the context of globalization and neoliberalism. As such, we have situated our critique of the university in the large global political economy of neoliberalism in line with the strategy among anthropologists today.

The Humboldt Revolution

The work and thought around the development of the University of Berlin, and the modern research university in general, produced a genuine revolution. Inspired by the development of modern thought during the enlightenment, and the sense that rational thought could explore the "mechanics of the universe" and further coupled the development of the modern nation state and the hope that government could be based upon written laws and a just rationality, the modern university became the site for potential collaboration between intellectuals and the modern policy makers who were just beginning as a social group.

One cannot ignore the German notion of 'bildung' and its role in the development of the modern university (Shumar and Robinson Forthcoming). Kant, Fichte, Schelling, Schleirmacher, Humboldt and Hegel were the main thinkers who were involved in thinking through and bringing into being the modern university (Kwiek 2006:14). That imagination involved creating a context where the individual could be called to a higher purpose and higher understanding. Due to Humboldt's leadership role in bringing together the vision of German philosophers and scholars, this new modern university itself grew out of a crisis in the university and the rapid changes with the rise of the modern nation-state. There were three central features of the modern university. First, was an emphasis on the unity and teaching and research. Students and faculty were to work together in a process of creating new knowledge. Learning and knowledge production were united and were ongoing social processes. Second, was the notion of academic freedom. Academic freedom was important because knowledge could only be gained if teachers and students were able to engage in open dialogue and a free exploration of ideas. Interestingly, academic freedom was for students as well as faculty. Finally, the group of scholars imagined philosophy as the center of the university. Science, in this vision, was also imagined as consonant with philosophy and consequence of the critical exploration of the human and natural world. Within this context, scientific discourse would allow the individual to explore any and all forms of knowledge, and the university and the society would benefit from those free and unfettered explorations.

This faith in human potential, and an imagined utopia where individuals would be free, not only to explore ideas, but to call each other to task and critique weaknesses in those ideas, were the fundamental aspects of bildung, and created a kind of opening. It was about looking toward an unknown future and being open to human potential. It was an imagined way of moving beyond the limitations of thought and intellect that had, up until that point, stifled the development of modern thought. As Charles Taylor (2005) would say, it was a social imaginary, and became a new worldview that developed and was shared among philosophers, scientists, and members of the developing modern nation-state, creating in turn a collective imagination and a collective opening toward new possibilities for the development of learning and knowledge. In that imagination, the individual, the society, and the state were all tied to the same project.

This late 18th and early nineteenth century imagination of the university had unintended consequences that fueled the scientific and technological revolutions of the twentieth century. The University of Berlin and the vision of the Humboldt University became the model for modern research universities in the United States and many parts of the world. The imaginary upon which the university was based, the notion of academic freedom, the linking of teaching and research, and the idea that the liberal arts were the core of the university linked the university to critical and reflexive *thinking*. It not only helped to fuel the democratic cultures of modern societies but also inspired many scientific and technological developments that might have originally been pursued out of curiosity or what was once called basic research. Furthermore these developments also had a profound impact on the development of the modern world and the wealth of modern nations.[1] Ironically, the current call for more critical thinking in the university is, in fact, a lament about the absence of such thinking. The pressures to reify knowledge into easy transmissible packages and audit the learning process are in opposition to what is needed to foster critical thinking in the university. Today we see many progressive industries, such as aerospace, computer, and even the automobile industry moving to open up dialogue, flatten hierarchies and create more freedom to create knowledge, while at the same time we see universities, through an audit regime moving to create hierarchies and restrict free dialogue.

By way of analogy, in the *Structural Transformation of the Public Sphere*, Jurgen Habermas (1989) talks about how the early entrepreneurial businesses of consumer capitalism, such as, cafes, and newspapers, fueled the development of a bourgeois public sphere and a democratic culture. The early businesses fostered gathering in public and a public that engaged in dialogue. The printing press, over time, led to newspapers and magazine, where issues of politics and public concern were printed. This printed matter further fueled public dialogue. As capitalism continued to develop into a more modern consumer capitalism and the rise of corporations, consumer culture and the mass media, the public sphere, in Habermas's view, was diminished. In the language of Habermas, the social system originally fostered the development of a dynamic and democratic lifeworld based upon legal-rational debate. But as the social system continued to bureaucratize, the social system then begins to choke the lifeworld. For Habermas, what is lost in this process is the open rational debate that is central to a democratic culture and the development of a rational society.[2] In a parallel way, the late eighteenth century, early nineteenth century intellectual, with their vision for a modern university, also contributed to the flourishing of a democratic culture within the university. This model of the university spread to many parts of the world. What we are seeing today in universities is that same process, the social system, with its bureaucratic focus on social control and the management of problems, choking the democratic spirit of academic freedom.

If we turn to the work of the French historian Ferdinand Braudel (1977), we can see an even more nuanced view of this unfolding of a public sphere. Braudel distinguishes three layers of European economic existence, what he calls material life, the market, and the development of capitalists and capital accumulation. What is important here, is that we often see this as one smooth process in the development of capitalism. But for Braudel, there are distinct stages in the development of the material culture in Western societies. In line with Habermas, Braudel suggests that the opening of public markets brought with them not only trade and a flow of goods, but an exchange of ideas and interactions between people where democratic culture flourishes as part of the enlightenment. For Braudel, a historian, the rise of capital accumulation and the development of a capitalist class requires not free markets, but the development of private markets where there is exclusive control over trade and price etc. (Braudel 1977; Slater and Tonkiss 2001). Braudel points out that, at this time, there is not much discussion of capitalism but rather of capital and capitalists. Of course, a culture of capitalism develops later, but one interesting thing about that culture is that it is premised on the ideology that the free market made capitalism possible, which according to Braudel is not true, capitalism depended on the private market and the control of information.

We can draw some parallels between the work of Habermas and Braudel and the evolution of the modern university. The development of the modern university occurs within the larger context of the flourishing of a democratic market culture alongside the rise of the enlightenment. These parallel forces are the things that create the context for an imagined community (Anderson 1991) or a more broadly held "social imaginary" (Taylor 2005). Central to the imagination of the modern university was a democratic space where faculty and students would engage together in producing new knowledge. And while science was seen as the key discourse of the future, philosophy and the liberal arts were seen as the critical core that advanced this thinking. Therefore, the university needed to be a free space, separate from the economic and social pressures of the larger society so that knowledge could be produced in an unfettered way. In *America by Design*, historian David Noble (1977) points out that a number of the corporations of the early to mid-twentieth century knew that new products came from this free and unfettered research space. They understood that to impose their corporate discipline on university research would stem the tide of creativity and ultimately undermine what they were doing. The idea of spatial separation from the discipline of the economy, while not an overt principle of the modern research university, was very much part of the social imaginary in the dawning of the modern age.

Neoliberal Ideology

Neoliberalism is the rebirth of liberal economic philosophy, but in the twenty-first century, it became a powerful ideology as well. In fact, neoliberalism in its current form was born of the contradictions of late twentieth century consumer capitalism. Capitalism as a powerful economic system is always riddled with several basic problems, the problem of capital flowing upward and concentrating in the hands of the very wealthy, the crisis of overproduction as named by Marx, problems of debt financed growth and the potential for inflation. World War II temporarily reduced the problems of economic stagnation providing a context for vast increases in production and use of material. Furthermore, the post war period turned out to be a time of economic growth first for the U.S. the leading industrialized economy, and then later for the economies of Europe and Japan. This period, thought of as "regulation" or the "Fordist-Keynesian" system or "welfare capitalism" came into crisis in the late 1960s as the world economies reached a point of stagnation.

As many researchers have pointed out, the movements toward tax reduction, deregulation, especially of the financial system, and moving production facilities were all efforts to overcome the stagnation of the capitalist system (Harvey 2006; Strange 1986). According to Harvey (2006) labor had too large a percentage of the GDP in many industrialized nations. As long as economic growth was strong, the financial and business elites did not worry too much about the success of ordinary workers. But as the system stagnated, there was a concerted effort to increase the share of the GDP held by a small class of capitalists. The 30 year result of this effort has been the dramatic increase in the gap between wage earners and the wealthy (Pikkety 2014).

Many centrist and left-leaning economists suggest that neoliberalism is a strategy to increase the elite classes hold on wealth in a time of limited economic growth (Hickel 2012). With its ideology of limited government intervention and free markets, it allowed capitalists to begin a major effort to overcome labor's power and at the same time make money in the only arena where money could be made given the global overproduction, the financial markets. Ironically, deregulating and freeing the markets led to the rise of private and irresponsible new markets that have led to the Wall Street crises of insider trading and the most recent stock market crash of 2008. In fact, it could be argued that a genuine free market based upon rational exchange would require some regulation to make sure that there was a fair honest brokering going on. The "free" market of neoliberals opened the market up to inequities in terms of power and information that benefits a wealthier capitalist class to the disadvantage of the smaller participants in the marketplace (Braudel 1977).

However, the rise of neoliberalism had another very important impact on culture and society. It became an ideology not only for a free economy and unregulated marketplace, but also permeated other arenas of social life, based upon a metaphor of unfettered market exchange. Of course, the neoliberal view of 'free' implies an unregulated space where the wealthier and more powerful would benefit. This model has had a significant impact on various institutions, and perhaps the place where it has had the largest impact is on universities. Through notions of selling a service to a marketplace, universities in the United States, Europe, Asia and elsewhere have been greatly impacted. Further, given the size of the market and the intangible nature of the service being sold, many nations have pressed for audit and accountability strategies to guarantee the quality of the service being sold to the public.

The process of bringing neoliberal ideology to the university has had a tremendous impact on universities worldwide. As we have mentioned, the university itself had been a special sphere that was dedicated to rational debate, and where students and faculty worked together as a community producing knowledge by subjecting that knowledge to rational discussion. Academic freedom was not just a guarantee of faculty jobs, it was the culture within which this debate flourished. But as the university starts to be thought of as a business that sells a service to a group of consumers, then the idea of a protected rational debate no longer fits within this model. Rather the preferred model becomes the transfer of some service, the educational commodity, to the buying public. As Habermas (1989) notes the rise of the structuring power of the social system leads to the collapse of the public sphere. Similarly we suggest that neoliberalism reduces the sphere of debate, discussion and knowledge production from the university as well.

The model of co-constructed knowledge based in debate and collaborative work is replaced with a fragile model of knowledge transmission, where commoditized knowledge is transferred from faculty to student. In the commoditized university, knowledge that is specifically produced for transfer to the economy is marketed, and basic research, now called curiosity driven research is seen as socially unimportant because it does not make a direct contribution to the economy. Commodification is what the neoliberal university calls 'being entrepreneurial' because it serves the needs and interests of capital. Further, under this model, the university moves from being an independent institution to something of a cross between a research and development park and the headquarters of regional economic development (Clark 1998; Shumar 2008). Different universities may balance these roles differently.

The neoliberal version of the 'entrepreneurial university' suggests a few more structural shifts. First, it is important to make the professoriate part of the corporate hierarchy. Professors are still valued for their creativity, but they are part of a corporate hierarchy and are encouraged not to see themselves as independent voices, but rather employees who are ranked below the upper management. This is done through mechanisms like deficit budgeting where a unit can always be threatened with closure, even if tenured professors cannot be fired individually. It should be noted that there have been long-term moves to reduce the number of tenured professors.

In the neoliberal 'entrepreneurial university', teaching becomes a different activity under R&D and economic development. The best students get to participate in the research exercise and be junior employees while other students are taught as efficiently as possible with a knowledge-transfer model. Their tuition supports the larger economic mission of the university, supplying support for capital. To make sure that teaching happens in an efficient and profitable way, audit and accountability have become an important part of the regime of the neoliberal university (Shore and Wright 2001; Strathern 2000). Ironically, the corporate neoliberal university hires accountability experts, who then audit the faculty and assess whether their teaching is sufficient. These professionals have no experience in teaching and research, and they claim to not interfere with the content of what faculty teach. They let faculty define things like learning outcomes and program outcomes. Not understanding the collaborative and generative nature of knowledge production, these bureaucrats think knowledge is a "thing" that can pre-identified, and its transmission can be measured. These strategies will ultimately completely undermine the dynamic and creative processes that over decades have made modern universities the powerful social institutions they are. In the words of historian David Noble (personal communication), "they are destroying our national treasures."

Ironically, the effort to use the university and its resources to foster regional economic development and create new technologies for new commodities and services, is actually undermining the university's ability to benefit the economy. As the university becomes increasingly connected to economic goals, audit and accountability, its ability to be emancipating, creative and envision, as yet unknown futures, becomes less possible. What is needed is an unfettered 'entrepreneurial university' which would mean something very different than the corporate neoliberal universities we have now. We now turn our attention to thinking about a new kind of entrepreneurial university in the next two sections.

On 'Becoming'-Entrepreneurship in the University

In a short essay titled "the End of Philosophy and the Task of Thinking, delivered in 1964, Heidegger (1972) suggests that the pursuit of metaphysics found its completion in the modern sciences, and that now philosophy could turn its attention to the task of thinking. Turning to Hegel, Heidegger suggests that "opening" is that which has remained un-thought in philosophy, and further this opening, or clearing is the way in which beings can express the truth of their Being. In an almost mystical way, Heidegger points to the place where we are, to borrow from Lacan (1977:166), "we are the plaything of our thoughts." This opening points to the potential of becoming, not a random becoming but a becoming in which we participate, but where we cannot be conscious of because it is the ground upon which consciousness is formed.

If Heidegger's essay is a little opaque, Spinosa et al. (1997) build on these thoughts and develop the notion of disclosing spaces of becoming. In their book they suggest that entrepreneurship, democratic action and the cultivation of solidarity are three arenas where individuals work to make history and that this history-making process is not random nor unconscious, but rather has some specific and identifiable patterns.

They pose some important questions - How do we come to know new things and how do we come to inhabit new worlds? The old knowledge we had and the old worlds we inhabited had little in them to explain or define the knowledge of the world that would come to be. This is the central paradox that Spinosa et al. (1997) seek to explain. The authors further suggest that entrepreneurs are unique among individuals in society in that they are able to hold onto, and focus on what they call the anomalies of social life. In the current social world that we live in, elements of the culture that organize the practices in a particular arena they call a "style." The style constitutes the practices and things that exist in a particular arena of social life, and "opens a disclosive space"(Spinosa et al. 1997: 20). But the practices within a particular disclosive space always exhibit some anomalies, things that do not quite make sense or which frustrate. The authors suggest we are predisposed to ignore these anomalies in that we tend to just take them as part of the way things are. Most people do not think about our social world as something that is contingent, rather we think it is the way things are, and maybe the way things just need to be. For example, we go into a modern store and we find that there is a wealth of goods that are easy to select (style), we have shopping carts that make the gathering of many things easy even for one person to do (style) and this modern efficient comfortable shopping experience is then interrupted by long lines as we wait to pay for our goods. This long shopping line that is boring and frustrating for shoppers is an anomaly. But most of us just take it to be part of the process, we dislike it, but we do not question it.

Spinosa et al. (1997) suggest that the entrepreneur becomes fixated on this anomaly and cannot ignore it. She thinks about it, thinks about why it exists, when it occurs and how it occurs, and begins to imagine other ways of doing things, other practices and other objects that might erase the anomaly. This process of focusing on the anomaly and imagining other practices is the window to a new world, that begins the process of creating new products and services that might change the anomaly. But the authors' point is not that it just brings new things into an existing world, rather the new products and services engender new practices and a new styles that open up a new disclosive space. The world becomes transformed quite consciously, at least at one level and opens up the possibility for a new imagined world.

In several places, Spinosa Flores & Dreyfus point to the fact that there is a process to becoming aware of anomalies and hold on to them. The process begins with a personal disharmony. In a footnote, the authors clarify that there are some similarities to Kuhn's notion of anomaly, but that their concept of anomaly does not start with a puzzle, as in science, but rather a disharmony between a person's ideal and actual cultural world. If it can be determined that the disharmony is shared widely, then perhaps this is an anomaly in our social world (Spinosa et al. 1997: 193, n.25). In our above example, maybe an entrepreneur is personally very frustrated with waiting in these long lines at the shopping center. That personal frustration is a tension between the world as they think it should be, and how things actually are. If the individual in the example determined that this was a widely shared disharmony it could be said that this is an anomaly in the social world.

This vision of entrepreneurship has a lot in common with the founders of the Humboldt University. In the early nineteenth century, the social world in Europe was changing fast. Science and knowledge were growing at a rapid rate, and this knowledge was shattering old ideas. At the same time, the modern nation state was being born and ideas about the emancipation and enlightenment of the individual were linked to ideas about the democratization of society. In fact, the idea of society itself was coming into being. In that context, intellectuals and scholars felt the tension to create a university that fit the needs of the new world. The imagination of the modern university was born of the pressure to see how the university could fit into this new imagination of the modern society. Although we did not call Humboldt and the founders of the University of Berlin entrepreneurs, they were clearly creating a new institution to deal with the anomalies of learning and knowledge in their age. They not only created a new institution but a new set of values that were productive for society for two centuries.

Entrepreneurship Education in the Liberal Arts

In this section we look at how in Scandinavia entrepreneurship education is being used to both reinvigorate the liberal arts and once again make "philosophy" the center of the university. This more progressive view of entrepreneurship, rooted in practice and linked to creating openings that bring about new worlds, is shared by a number of philosophers and entrepreneurship researchers in various countries. However in Scandinavia, there seems to be a critical mass of people working in this way on entrepreneurship and entrepreneurship education which has become something of a movement. In our analysis we regard this as part of a model of the university that is linked to becoming, rather like the movement around the Humboldt University in the nineteenth century. Perhaps one difference between the nineteenth century movement and the contemporary one is that there is a level of consciousness about our role as individuals in the process of historical change and becoming that was much less clear for earlier generations (Beck et al. 1994).

Students come to the university seeking an education that equips them for life and a career. However the recent neoliberal focus has been to focus education primarily on the latter that encompassed a pre-defined definition of what a career required, namely a given set of qualifications and credentials. Entrepreneurship education at the university is typically found in the business schools and is often understood as a way of equipping students with tools to start their own business or to work with their own potential for creating new ventures and start-ups. The focus of this type of education is primarily on creating economic value. However this narrow definition of entrepreneurship, as being solely about creating economic value only appeals to particular kinds of students. For other students, in particular those from the liberal arts, focusing on creating only economic value is unmotivating.

What is missing, and what is missing from the neoliberal focus too, is the link to life and citizenship in a society where we are increasingly bound by our actions. The notion that education should take account of real life issues and problems and prepare students to tackle change is, for a growing number of students, the reason for a Higher Education (HE). For liberal arts students then a university education is about being able to create a new and better world, a world that does not yet exist and which will be shaped by their actions. In Scandinavia entrepreneurship education is gradually being defined as a way to educate to support and nurture future activist citizens, from whatever discipline they decide to study.

The focus on entrepreneurship in HE has, over the last two decades, become increasingly visible in faculties outside of the Business School. However, outside of the Business School, there is a certain amount of suspicion from both teachers and students alike who tend to question why entrepreneurship should be a part of their education as they do not see themselves starting businesses. Therefore through work at a Danish university teaching centre it has been possible to engage teachers and students in a different notion of what 'being entrepreneurial' is and what entrepreneurship involves. A model was developed at the university.

'The Aarhus Model', inspired by over a decade of work by Blenker et al. (2012) to engage all teachers and students. It draws on a broader definition of entrepreneurship which is about creating value for others that allowed them to connect their engagement with societal issues to their academic knowledge. This broader definition goes beyond a narrow focus on the economic and just for profit. Such a definition encompasses as we have noted previously, a range of values, including the economic, but which are more often focused primarily on issues concerning social justice and welfare, equity, human rights, a healthy lifestyle, sustainability and responsibility etc. The liberal arts students concerns with such issues is based on knowledge of everyday practices. Entrepreneurship education in this broad sense seeks to link their academic knowledge and competences to real life situations to create meaning for themselves and value for others. This ties into learning as meaning-making and provides a purposeful education that connects students with their own academic interests, an understanding of their competences and an ability to create a new imagined world.

The Aarhus Model is comprised of three core elements that combines research into the ways entrepreneurs think (Sarasvathy 2001) with disharmony and anomaly identification (Spinosa et al. 1997) combined with understanding one's own competences and making judgements about the ability to work and solve problems. The model is a pedagogical process that is inspired by Sarasvathy (2001). In her research into how entrepreneurs think she found that expert entrepreneur utilise a decision-making logic which differs from what she calls the normative 'causal' way to solve problems. This decision-making logic combines a focus on being able to articulate one's own competences and knowledge base, being able to communicate these for others, and bring other resources and networks into the focus area. The Aarhus model draws heavily on the work of Spinosa et al. (1997) as students are asked to define a disharmony and qualify it to an anomaly with others. The development of this model is inspired by, and shares a number of features with, other researchers as well (Steyaert and Katz 2004; Lackéus 2016). In the Danish context we describe 'entrepreneurial' students as able to articulate their own competences, collaborate with others and, through engaged involvement in real life challenges, identify potential opportunities for change to create value for others. It is this mindset that we propose to stimulate in all our students.

What Entrepreneurial Means and Could Mean

In his work on the "entrepreneurial intellectual" Clyde Barrow suggests there is a tension in modern American universities between the corporate university and the entrepreneurial university (Barrow: forthcoming). Rather as we have suggested, Barrow points out that what is often called "entrepreneurial" in the university is in fact the opposite, it is really about managing universities by the same measures and systems as modern business corporations are run. Therefore revenue centered budgeting, and systems of audit and accountability have nothing to do with entrepreneurialism but are really about corporate capitalism. While currently influenced by notions of neoliberal ideology, this corporate takeover of the university has been well documented and has been going on for a long time (Readings 1996; Slaughter and Rhodes, Slaughter and Leslie, Shumar 1997; Canaan and Shumar 2008; Newfield 2008).

Barrow suggests, drawing on the literature about the coming of the entrepreneurial state, that entrepreneurial universities should be flexible with simple administrative systems, creative and able to quickly respond to perceived needs, and they would be nimble as they would not be bogged down by lots of middle management. Barrow is beginning to think about university as a venture, or made up of units that are more like ventures. Of course modern corporate universities do have these kind of creative nimble units within them today. But they are often at odds with the more corporate and bureaucratized parts of the university. In addition these more creative units often struggle because the bureaucracy stifles them, restricting the flexibility they require to survive. Many academics and researchers of higher education collapse the corporate university, neoliberalism, and the entrepreneurial university as more or less synonymous terms. But it is important to point out that collapsing these terms makes it more difficult to understand what is going on in universities. Barrow points out, there is a significant tension between the corporate university and the entrepreneurial university. And collapsing this distinction between the two in the general literature on neoliberalism fails to understand the new ways in which entrepreneurship is being understood in some universities.

Entrepreneurship is, as we have mentioned, perhaps most often thought of as creating ventures, and while these ventures are often thought of as being creative and responding to some need, they are also thought of as wealth producing. In our discussion above, the entrepreneurial response to some anomaly often brings about a new venture that provides a product or service that changes the social world and overcomes the anomaly. Whether we are thinking about the economy or the larger society there is a natural tendency to see entrepreneurship as venture creation for economic value. This is the primary way in which Spinosa Flores and Dreyfus understand entrepreneurship. However, Lackéus (2016), following Fayolle (2007), suggests that there are three definitions of entrepreneurship, the creation of new ventures, the creation of opportunities and the creation of new forms of value. He goes on to further suggest that the creation of new value is a relatively unexplored area in entrepreneurship education.

Entrepreneurship as Value Creation

The creation of new forms of value is an important part of the entrepreneurial process and hence an important part of entrepreneurship education. Of course, value is often in this context thought of as economic value. This assumption leads back into the more traditional thinking of entrepreneurship studies. But Peters and Besley (2008) suggests that Steyaert and Katz (2004) see different forms of value extending the focus from solely economic value and see the entrepreneurial process are creating larger social values, that focus on human rights, equity issues, welfare and well-being, environmental, as well as just a basic focus on quality of life issues.. In a similar way, Blenker et al. (2012) focus on the notion that entrepreneurship is an everyday practice. Entrepreneurship is about identifying those discordant elements in one's life the researchers refer to as "disharmonies." And then the individual figures out a way to change things so that these discordant elements are overcome. This can be done by creating a new venture or helping colleagues to rearrange the office. This is what it means to see entrepreneurship as an everyday practice. Further, following Gibb (1993, 2002) Blenker et al. (2012) see a distinction between what might be called entrepreneurship (as venture creation) and enterprising behavior which is about preparing the individual, as citizen, worker, and consumer for life in the twenty-first century. As Blenker et al. (2012: 419) comment, "Enterprising behavior refers to the formation of general innovative and enterprising qualities in the individual" . From this perspective becoming entrepreneurial is about educating the individual for life in the twenty-first century and to support the creation of different kinds of value for the larger society, including economic value.

Therefore we note that writers like Peters and Besley (2008) Lackéus (2016), Steyaert and Katz (2004) and Blenker et al. (2012) are focusing specifically on entrepreneurship education and how that education is broader than learning how to create new ventures. They are articulating an important movement towards a very broad vision, and one that simultaneously addresses an anomaly in the university today. The corporate university, that the Humboldt university evolved into, is everywhere in the world in crisis. The narrow focus on wealth production, technology transfer, knowledge capitalism has left the educational core of the university hollow. The narrow focus has further undermined and even disabled its ability, as an institution, to support individuals in their ability to imagine new and better worlds. What remains is the auditing and accounting of a more limited vision of what knowledge is and conflated views of knowledge transfer. What is needed is a new imagination of what the university could be and how twenty-first century knowledge could be produced (Barnett 2013; Peters et al. 2008).

A more robust notion of enterprising behavior and entrepreneurship education could become the core of a vision for the twenty-first century university. This core, like the Humboldt University, is about supporting individuals in their ability to innovatively and creatively address social, environmental, economic, and political problems. The calling of individuals upward through this new conceptualization of bildung, will also inspire universities to, once again, become the central institutions of knowledge and learning in the twenty-first century. Peters and Besley (2008) are acutely aware of the new tensions in the era of cybernetic or cognitive or knowledge capitalism that is not just an issue of ideology but rather is a dialectical tension. In the digital era, imaginative processes are more connected to the economy and jobs. The social world and the economic world are more intertwined with each other. The movement from creative human activity to products and wealth production is often a surprising one and one that involves creativity itself. This is all the more reason why neo-bildung needs to include questions about an imagined future. If we are more aware of our process of bringing new worlds into being, we need to examine what kinds of values are being created and whether they good for people and society as a whole or whether they are only about capital accumulation.

Summary

If we return to Heidegger's notion of the opening, the clearing, we can see that the context of the twenty-first century global knowledge economy creates the possibility, and perhaps the necessity, for a new imagination of the university (Barnett 2013). In this context, value creation is perhaps the most important task of the contemporary university. Social, environmental, community values are tied to knowledge production in the twenty-first century and, just as in the 18th and nineteenth century, students and faculty need to work together in a free and open context to produce the knowledges needed. But unlike the nineteenth century, innovation in the twenty-first century knowledge society and learning economy blurs the distinctions between economic value and other social values (Lundvall 2002; Peters and Besley 2008). Entrepreneurship education is potentially a model for both learning to be innovative and creative, and produce value for society, but it can also be a model for weighing and evaluating different forms of value and for critically reflecting on what is really being added to society and what is not.

[1] The Humboldt vision was also an elite vision. These philosophers and intellectuals were not the masses and were not at this point arguing for a mass democratic institution. Rather they were arguing for the relationship between the state and the elite intellectuals of the early modern nation state. And the university, as such, would be a key institution in the development of the modern nation-state. One could argue that while a vision of an elite class, the democratic ideals embedded in

the Humboldt vision, and the philosophy of bildung, contributed to the democrati-zation of culture and the rise of the mass university. It was not a determinative force, but rather a parallel process that helped to surface some of the contradictions of modern mass institutions of higher education. So the commodification of the uni-versity was not just a result of capitalist development, but was also in part fostered by the contradictions produced by the democratization and massification of higher education which led to an increasing emphasis on credentialism and social mobility for members of the middle and lower classes.

[2] Of course, there are many criticisms of Habermas's view. It has been pointed out that this democratic culture has never been very widespread and that the bour-geois public sphere was always a limited and specialized space. There also has been debate about whether the internet has reopened the possibility of an even broader public sphere with greater potential for debate and discussion amongst a broader set of social groups.

References

Anderson, B. R. O. G. (1991). In Revised and extended (Ed.), *Imagined communities: Reflections on the origin and spread of nationalism*. New York: Verso.

Barnett, R. (2013). *Imagining the university*. Milton Park/Abingdon/Oxon/New York: Routledge.

Beck, U., Giddens, A., & Lash, S. (1994). *Reflexive modernization. Politics, tradition and aesthet-ics in the modern social order*. Cambridge: Stanford University Press.

Blenker, P., Frederiksen, S. H., Korsgaard, S., Müller, S., Neergaard, H., & Thrane, C. (2012). Entrepreneurship as everyday practice. *Industry and Higher Education, 26*(6), 417–430.

Braudel, F. (1977). *Afterthoughts on material civilization and capitalism*. Baltimore: Johns Hopkins University Press.

Canaan, J., & Shumar, W. (Eds.). (2008). *Structure and agency in the Neoliberal university*. New York: Routledge.

Clark, B. R. (1998). *Creating entrepreneurial universities: Organizational pathways of transfor-mation*. Bingley: Emerald Group Publishing Limited.

Comaroff, J., & Comaroff, J. (1992). *Ethnography and the historical imagination*. Boulder: Westview Press.

Comaroff, J., & Comaroff, J. L. (2000). Millennial capitalism: First thoughts on a second coming. *Public Culture, 12*(2), 291–343.

Fayolle, A. (2007). *Entrepreneurship and new value creation: The dynamic of the entrepreneurial process*. Cambridge: Cambridge University Press.

Geertz, C. (1963). *Peddlers and princes: Social development and economic change in two Indonesian towns*. Chicago: University of Chicago Press.

Gibb, A. A. (1993). Enterprise culture and education: Understanding enterprise education and its links with small business, entrepreneurship and wider educational goals. *International Small Business Journal, 11*(3), 11–34.

Gibb, A. (2002). 'In pursuit of a new 'enterprise' and 'entrepreneurship' paradigm for learning: creative destruction, new values, new ways of doing things and new combinations of knowl-edge'. *International Journal of Management Reviews, 4*(3), 213–233.

Habermas, J. (1989). *The structural transformation of the public sphere: An inquiry into a cat-egory of bourgeois society*. Cambridge: Polity Press.

Harvey, D. (2006). *Spaces of global capitalism: Towards a theory of uneven geographical develop-ment*. London: Verso.

Hickel, J. (2012). *A Short History of Neoliberalism* (And How We Can Fix It). New Left Project (website). First published 09 April, 2012. Accessed 19 March, 2017. http://www.newleftproject.org/index.php/site/article_comments/a_short_history_of_neoliberalism_and_how_we_can_fix_it

Kwiek, M. (2006). *The Classical German idea of the university revisited, or on the Nationalization of the modern institution* (Center for Public Policy Research Paper Series, Vol. 1). http://www.cpp.amu.edu.pl/pdf/CPP_RPS_vol.1_Kwiek.pdf

Lacan, J. (1977). Ecrits: A selection. (A. Sheridan Trans.). New York: W. W. Norton & Company.

Lackéus, M. (2016). *A 'Value' and 'Economics' grounded analysis of six value creation based entrepreneurial education initiatives*. Paper for 3E ECSB Entrepreneurship Education Conference. Leeds, UK, 11–13 May, 2016.

Lundvall, B.-Å. (2002). *Innovation, growth and social cohesion: The Danish model*. Cheltenham\Northampton: Edward Elgar Publishers.

Marcus, G. E. (1986). Contemporary problems of ethnography in the modern world system. In J. Clifford & G. E. Marcus (Eds.), *Writing culture: The poetics and politics of ethnography*. Berkeley: University of California Press.

Newfield, C. (2008). *Unmaking the public university: The forty year assault on the middle class*. Cambridge, MA: Harvard University Press.

Noble, D. F. (1977). *America by design: Science, technology, and the rise of corporate capitalism* (1st ed.). New York: Knopf.

Peters, M. A. & Besley, T. (A. C.) (2008). Academic entrepreneurship and the creative economy. In Peters, M. A., Marginson, S. & Murphy, P. (Eds.) Creativity and the global knowledge economy. New York: Peter Lang Publishing, 94, 88.

Peters, M. A., Marginson, S., & Murphy, P. (Eds.). (2008). *Creativity and the global knowledge economy*. New York: Peter Lang Publishing.

Pikkety, T. (2014). *Capital in the twenty-first Century*. Cambridge, MA: Belknap Press, Harvard University.

Readings, B. (1996). *The University in Ruins*. Cambridge, MA: Harvard University Press.

Sarasvathy, S. (2001). *What makes entrepreneurs entrepreneurial?* Washington/Seattle: University of Washington School of Business.

Shore, C., & Wright, S. (2001). Audit culture and anthropology. *Journal of the Royal Anthropological Institute, 7*(4), 759–763.

Shumar, W. (1997). *College for Sale: A critique of the commodification of higher education*. London: Falmer Press.

Shumar, W. (2004). Making strangers at home. *The Journal of Higher Education, 75*(1), 23–41.

Shumar, W. (2008). Space, place and the American University. In J. Canaan & W. Shumar (Eds.), *Structure and agency in the neoliberal university*. Routledge: New York.

Shumar, W., & Robinson, S. (Forthcoming). Rethinking the Entrepreneurial University for the 21st Century. In M. A. Peters & R. Barnett (Eds.), *The Idea of the University: Volume 2 – Contemporary Perspectives*. New York: Peter Lang.

Slater, D., & Tonkiss, F. (2001). *Market society: Markets and modern social theory*. Cambridge: Polity Press.

Spinosa, C., Flores, F., & Dreyfus, H. L. (1997). *Disclosing new worlds: Entrepreneurship, democratic action and the cultivation of solidarity*. Cambridge, MA: MIT Press.

Steyaert, C., & Katz, J. (2004). Reclaiming the space of entrepreneurship in society: Geographical, discursive and social dimensions. *Entrepreneurship and Regional Development, 16*, 179–196.

Strange, S. (1986). *Casino capitalism*. Oxford/New York: B. Blackwell.

Strathern, M. (2000). *Audit cultures: Anthropological studies in accountability, ethics, and the academy*. London/New York: Routledge.

Taylor, C. (2005). *Modern social imaginaries*. Durham/London: Duke University Press.

Chapter 4
Dissident Thought: A Decolonising Framework for Revolt in the University

Sonja Arndt and Carl Mika

Introduction

For true dissidence today is perhaps simply what it has always been: *thought* (Kristeva 1977/1986, p. 299, emphasis in the original).

True dissidence, Kristeva suggests, not only remains what it always has been: *thought*, but such thought is a critical form of inner revolt. In this chapter we conceptualise thought as a decolonising framework drawing on the notions of exile, dissidence and delirium to argue for critical encounters with thought, as inherent, and in recent times arguably disappearing, in the university. Applied through a Maori conception of thought in the historicised and localised context of New Zealand, this framework for dissent draws on the past, to rethink the present and future. It examines thinking as expressions of dissidence through elevating conceptually, ideologically, racially, culturally subjugated and marginalised ways of knowing, being and learning in the academe. We draw on Julia Kristeva's notion of revolt to argue for thought as a vital and energising confluence of knowledges, incorporating a crucial state of inner chaos, as necessary to preserving the inner life of the self and of critical thought in the university.

What is the value of thought? What is the university's proper relationship to thought? Framing the problematisations of thought throughout this book, we examine and provoke reconceptualisations of thought. If the ability to think in a deep and groundbreaking way remains the essence of the university, where and how is there space for thought that is relevant, critical, and in relationship with and in the contemporary university? Placed in relation to Kristeva's opening quote, what does this mean for the kind of thought that is valued and acknowledged, taken for granted, or rejected, ignored, or vehemently opposed, in contemporary times, of increasing

S. Arndt (✉) · C. Mika
University of Waikato, Hamilton, New Zealand
e-mail: skarndt@waikato.ac.nz; carl.mika@waikato.ac.nz

© Springer International Publishing AG, part of Springer Nature 2018   47
S.S.E. Bengtsen, R. Barnett (eds.), *The Thinking University*,
Debating Higher Education: Philosophical Perspectives 1,
https://doi.org/10.1007/978-3-319-77667-5_4

globalisation, marketisation and apparent simplification, as well as of ongoing colo-nisation, of education? This chapter explicates thought as a philosophical activity, through the conception of thought as dissident, to contest universalisable notions of thought as valuable, proper or appropriate. In a philosophical engagement with dis-sident thought itself, the chapter situates and implores a revaluing of divergent, complex, culturally situated and diverse, critical thought within the contemporary context of the university academe. Throughout this chapter, then, thought is argued as being beyond what is feasible and measurable, as also incommensurable, unknowable, uncertain and uncomfortable.

The argument for (re-)elevating the complexity of thought as 'true' dissidence explicates conceptions of thought through the work of Julia Kristeva and through Maori philosophical relationships with thought. The revelations throughout create entry points within which the incommensurability of thought, and diverse and often marginalised, subjugated ways of knowing and being of indigenous knowledges might (re-)arise and flourish within the university. Inextricably embedded within the university context of thought measurements by rateable outputs, rankings, funding and variously determined prestige, status and elevations, our response to the open-ing questions, rather than an answer, is an appeal for further questioning, and per-haps, un-knowing, both the academic and the academe (Arndt 2013). The chapter culminates in a provocation for increasing thought-ful revolt, drawing on Kristeva's (2014) conception of revolt. In this view, revolt is seen as a disturbance to the expected smoothness of the status quo, for example, of contemporary measurement and revenue raising systems and expectations. The chapter, then, opens up and responds to what often amounts to a contextual silencing, to urge subversive thought and thinking ways of being within the contemporary university.

Revolt as a Thought Culture

The void arising from any silencing of critical thought in current university trends illustrates what Kristeva (2014) laments as a contemporary lack of revolt in society. Such revolt is essential for the ongoing "evolution of society" (Sunderland 2010, p. 30). Applied to the 'thinking university', this evolutionary revolt insists on thought "that is alive and developing, not stagnating" (Kristeva 1996/2002, p. 420). In other words it seeks thought as critical, creative and complex, and it calls for a culture of revolt in the university. It promotes a thought culture that is 'alive and developing' rather than 'stagnating' or non-existent. We follow a Kristevan concep-tion of revolt not as an all out revolution, but as an essential and fundamental factor in both the ongoing evolution and re-elevation of thought from silencing and what might be seen as institutional stagnation. Further, on an individual basis, as Kristeva also asserts, we attempt "to illuminate the experiences of formal and philosophical revolt that might keep our inner lives alive" in what "we call a soul", and further to retain, reinsert, or reignite what "is no doubt the hidden side, the invisible and indispensable source of what is Beautiful" (p. 420). We propose a way of thinking as a response to Kristeva's lament and to the contemporary context.

Like Kristeva, other recent conceptions of thought as dissident complement the urgency and importance of thought as pleasure, necessity, meaning, and soul. They offer us a space in which to propose possibilities and potential openings towards reinserting intimate, personal revolt-ful thought into today's university. Dissident thought is presented for example by Peters (2016), where thought is seen amongst other things as a philosophy of non-agreement, in particular in relation to contemporary developments and expectations in and by the university, which increasingly risk sidelining and obliterating such thought. Peters (2016) portrays systems of repression and networks of hope as a foundation for subversive thought within the university, positing that

> [d]issident thought has a kinship relationship with the ecology of concepts that proceed from the concepts of dissent and the very possibility of disagreement as an inherent aspect of discourse. It has taken many different forms in relation to discourse thought and action, and encompassed and cultivated political norms associated with freedom of speech that allows the expression of opposition, protest, revolt, and the expression of anti-establishment thought that takes the form of civil disobedience, non-violent protest and sometimes revolutionary activity (p. 21).

Recognising dissidence as fundamental to such critical, or 'true' thought, as Peters and Kristeva do, strengthens our positioning in relation to a Kristevan conceptualisation of thought. Her poststructural, linguistic and philosophical work offers a possible framework for conceptualising dissident thought, through the notions of exile, dissidence and delirium. In the next section we outline a framing of these notions, followed by conceptions of indigenous Maori perspectives on thought, and the possibilities that emerge in the confluence of these ideas. Together these confluences elevate the complex thought argued for above through what simultaneously decolonises thought in the university.

A Decolonising Framework

The concepts and experiences of exile, dissidence and delirium form an orientational framework that depends on thought as philosophical and, we argue, as a form of revolt. These concepts do not follow any particular formula, or new masterdiscourse, but rather they capture the essence of philosophical thought as a creative, dissident examination of life – its beauty and ugliness. They are neither prescriptive nor directive, and they support laying bare raw inferences and undeveloped contingencies. They posit a non-linear, to and fro of elements, each of which may progress in concurrent ways and, equally, at times take unrelated tangents. They mirror how, as Kristeva states in an interview (Midttun 2006), "you see that the problems are far more complex, and through philosophy … you can render a more polyphonic and perhaps more trenchant picture" (p. 173). This chapter draws on Kristeva's conceptions of philosophical engagements with thought and life. It argues that an exile,

dissidence, delirium framework creates openings for recognising existing and opening new critical and complex thought possibilities in the university.

Exile – 'being on the inside and outside of things'

According to Kristeva, exile is critical to writing. Writing is "impossible without
some kind of exile" (as cited in Lechte 1990, p. 66), and her commitment to exile is
necessary in critically re-thinking given positions. Exile, whether self-selected or
imposed, allows a more irreverent and ruthless approach to the confrontation of
concepts, constructs, and perspectives, and therefore also to unsettling and subvert-
ing dominant discourses and practices. As Peters (2008) describes it, "[e]xile ... [is]
a profound existential condition of cultural estrangement ... that defines identity in
terms of migration, movement, departure, homelessness" (p. 592). Kristeva's own
exile for example, has been described as "*dépaysment*" (Lechte 1990, p. 66), which
means, as she says, where one stands "beside something, never in the middle of it.
One keeps a distance. A distance also to oneself as well, a kind of exile from oneself, where one in a sense is a stranger to oneself" (Midttun 2006, p. 165). In a
practical sense in the university, this underlies the necessity of exile, of academics,
or students, as an ability to remove themselves from the situations with which they
are concerned, that might be their colleagues, their educational settings, their practical realities and sensitivities, real, material or, further following Kristeva, their own
unconscious, or soul. A state of exile then evokes a more ruthless engagement with
the context, with literature and with research, treating them almost as fictive possibilities, in a way that allows an irreverent analysis and "will to subversion" (Kristeva
1977/1986, p. 299), as it is conducted from afar.

Exile from the known thus might mean a renunciation of the comfort and familiarity of being physically close to the settings with which academics or students are
concerned. It allows a more ruthless use of philosophical thinking and concern with
educational subjectivities, of the academic or student doing the thinking, or of those
about whom they are thinking. Exile requires investigating from a distance, the possible 'fleshly' experiences of life (Harré 2000), and it enables both an insider and
outsider perspective. To return to Kristeva, it is a performance of how "[t]o be able
to think, you can not stay confined to one place, because then you do not think, you
only repeat what is being said around you. To think. .. thought is a question. To be
able to ask, you must have a distance, be both on the inside and on the outside of
things" (Midttun 2006, pp. 165–166). Furthermore, place, as we will demonstrate
further below, is more than a physical location. It is a positioning milieu, a conceptual location, a "broad cultural milieu that frames our identities" (Peters 2008,
p. 595). The positioning of the university's cultural milieu through a neoliberal
focus on finances, competition, and capitalist decisions, mergers and profits (Kelsey
2015) - rather than thought and the evolution of society, civilization or sustainable
relationships and ecologies (O'Malley 2017, May 14) affects our call for exile, for
questioning, and for being 'both on the inside and on the outside of things'.

One who is exiled, then, is dis-placed, shaken (or taken) from that milieu. "Exile is an … experience based on finding oneself in another, of shoring up one's identity in other cultural terms" (Peters 2008, p. 603). The possibility of exiling themselves from the everyday university milieu offers academics and students opportunities for dis-placement, physically and metaphorically, at the same time as their own subjective encounters might fictively relate and open up to others'. From another perspective exile refers also to the foreigner, or to those who might be seen as or consider themselves as Other. It can be considered as an opening to the outside, viewing the (foreign) culture in which we might be situated, from a distance, removed and unconnected to ourselves. At the same time, if exile, and exilic thought, are also educative, the foreigner/Other is both the observer, from the outside, but also a participant in his or her own experience of the exile, of the exilic thought, and of the transformation occurring through it (Peters 2008). The transformative element that occurs through exile illustrates the point that subjects are forever in formation. It is the very transformation required in what Kristeva (1991) suggests are necessary steps for individuals to transgress the boundaries and limitations of orientations towards foreignness, enmity and alterity. Exilic thought then can be seen as a nomadic state, influenced by the strange and unfamiliar, through which the exiled academic or student travels, making meaning by transforming from the foundations of what is familiar, known, or previously thought. Arguing for exile then calls into question what seems familiar, within the milieu, and where that might lead. Exile itself, following Kristeva, like true thought, is a form of dissidence.

Dissidence – 'obnoxious disturbances'

Whereas exile may represent a physical, moral or intellectual stance in the university, dissidence can be seen to represent thought. Particular kinds of thought are crucial for philosophical work, and, according to Kristeva (1977/1986), such thought, "is already in itself a form of dissidence" (p. 298). Together exile and dissidence, then, allow for a subversion and irreverent dismantling of dominant, common thought – that which focuses on markets and drives towards measurable outcomes, for example – with more likelihood of arriving at fresh, critical insights, of diverse thought and ways of being beyond the status quo. Dissident philosophical thought demands a willingness to open oneself up to unanswered puzzles, connections and contradictions through critical analysis of what may be, or first appear to be, irresolvable, internal and logical disjunctions, as for example individuals may be experiencing in their university context.

Dissidence requires philosophical thought in examinations of Otherness and of what it means to be a thinker, academic or student, co-existing in ways that recognise, acknowledge and value each other "without ostracism or levelling" (Kristeva 1991, p. 2). Dissidence requires a critical stance, of wondering "not only about *problematic* situations but also about what is usually *taken for granted*, and to wander in alternative and as yet unexplored cognitive paths" (Papastephanou and Angeli

2007, p. 616, emphasis in the original). In the contemporary university, then, dissident thought might involve conceptualising potentialities and possibilities, to bring thought alive, by allowing, creating spaces for, different, and as we argue below decolonising, attitudes and orientations towards well established, taken for granted and possibly limiting practices.

Dissident thought makes space for a thoughtful engagement with decolonising values. Mika (2012) posits a philosophical decolonising project as one requiring careful and critical analysis, beyond a surface level acceptance of meanings and interpretations, to consider wider and unexpected possible implications. Using the Maori concept of Being, which is the totality of all things in the world, as an example, this involves not only a translation and interpretation of terms and concepts in its original language and in its colonised – and contained, narrowed - form, but a deeper investigation of harm done to the core meaning, practice and mystery of the concept. A critical, philosophical decolonising, or post colonial, critique thus complements thought as disrupting 'rigid demarcations' and opening oneself to wonder and a sense of *aporia* as proposed by Papastephanou (2009), or, following Wittgentstein (1953), it plunges one into a primeval chaos, of which one is left to make meaning and sense.

Dissident thought thus depends on a critical approach to thought. Such critical thinking, reacting to what is reified, normalised or idolised, highlights contradictions and disjunctions between the complexities, intuitions and perspectives marginalised by surface level and market oriented, or colonising thinking. Further, critical thought embodies the importance of first laying bare what is already known, and the thought that surrounds what is known, that is, its epistemological context. The importance of dissident critical thought lies in its compulsion to scrutinize, problematize and complicate thought and identity. It aims to disrupt familiarity, move language into improper, even obnoxious disturbances. Its aim of provoking a disruption of the "complacent belief that one understands one's own thoughts and the language in which one formulates one's thoughts" (Ruitenberg 2009, p. 426), is crucial, to rearticulate and rethink policies or expectations in the university and its wider milieu, that simplify and homogenize thought through their preference to remain within comfortable norms and reified practices. Disrupted already by their identification and analysis, dominant orientations, omissions and marginalisations then become unsettled rather than perpetuated through dissident thought. The chaos of dissident thought culminates in delirium.

Delirium – Climax of a Thought Process

Following Kristeva, delirium can be seen as the climax of a thought process. It represents the culmination of a succession of confusion and crises that have arisen through exile and dissident thought. In disrupting dominant thought patterns, delirium "is a discourse which has … strayed from a presumed reality" (Kristeva 1982/1986, p. 307). Delirium thus follows dissident thought, into what Kristeva calls "*an imaginary*" (p. 307, emphasis in the original), as unknown elements intertwined in interpretations produce a "perpetual interpretive creative force" (p. 307) that displaces, deforms and re-forms thought and meaning. In this philosophical thought framework, delirium represents the dimension of the interpretive and transforming force, that adds new significance through the insights gained in dissident thought. Delirium can occur at any point, as the thinker is driven to change course, think differently or re-form policy or processes. It is at the root of our concluding call for revolt.

Delirium can be experienced as a void, or a crisis, in what in a Kristevan sense appear as seemingly directionless hollows, forming intermittently throughout thought processes. Kristeva (1982/1986) explains that, "[w]ithin the nucleus of delirious construction, we must retain this hollow, this void, … as the instinctual drive's insistence, as the unsymbolizable condition of the desire to speak and to know" (p. 307). The desire to 'speak and know' aroused in or forced through dissident thought and the crisis of delirium, is the desire that pushes enquiry to fresh insights from what is laid bare in an analysis. Differentiated from what might be seen as a dominant need for knowledge in the university (solutions, answers, measurable outcomes, for example), delirium resulting from the unsettling, critical, ethical and transformative process of exile and dissident thought exposes the lack in the contemporary desire for clarity and measurable knowledge. The desire for knowledge thus appears as premature and empty, rather than fruitful recognitions of meaningful understandings, and perpetuates the marginalizing effect of calls for quantifiable, knowable outputs in the contemporary university context.

Delirious voids and crises are critical points in the thought process. Connections and insights might present seemingly plausible positions, "making distinctions" or "proofs", as Feinberg (2014, p. 4) suggests. However, other forms of truths, non-totalising, contingent constructions of complex discursive truths, in a Foucauldian sense (Kritzman 2006), for example, might argue further for renewing theory, renewing the discourse, rejoining the cycle, opening the analysis once more, to further unsettle what appear as 'proofs' or logical ways forward. The desire for what Kristeva (1982/1986) calls the *jouissance* of delirium, moving beyond frustration out of the transitoriness of exile, provides interim points of meaning (Huri 2006). They occur when the analysis moves through chaos, towards contextual and conceptual realisations that either did not previously exist, or were not previously evident, and may not have occurred without transcending the crisis of delirium. Transcending and re-forming the ontological and conceptual boundaries through emerging intermittent insights at various points, is the philosophical role of delirium. It contributes in important ways to the decolonisation of thought in the university.

Decolonising Thought in the University

Applying the conceptions of exile, dissidence and delirium to thought in the university, implicates minority and marginalised thought, knowledges and ways of being. In this sense it implicates those universities and contexts where the common language and articulation of thought is the language of the colonisers. The context then remains one permeated by Othernesses, in indigenous people, refugees, migrants, visitors, tourists. Papastephanou's (2015) cautionary warning against unconditionally accepting, desiring and enabling linguistic de-territorialisations exacerbates our argument for more than a mere multiplicity, or cosmopolitanism, of thought. Rather than a testing of boundaries, crossing borders, paradigms or disciplines, the framework of exile, dissidence and delirium re-views and re-places thought in the university to re-insert complexity and meaning into thought, refocusing not only on what Kristeva calls for as beauty, but on what Papastephanou calls the 'ugliness' of contemporary complexities, in relation to language, and for us in this chapter, of thought. The following section interweaves the concepts of exile, dissidence and delirium through a Maori indigenous presence in the New Zealand university context.

What follows is a Maori thinking with Kristeva, but with some key Maori metaphysical tenets as necessary guides. To begin with: Maori have a view of a primordial substance *within which* one acts even as one moves about *upon* it (Mika 2017). Discourses and modes of describing things are similarly entities – including colonisation. Everything that derives from that substance is thus also acted upon/within by the Maori self – including the Maori academic. Thought in the academy, however, is not material for the Maori thinker and is self-derived. The delimiting of thought that Maori must encounter – and indeed, that they often adopt in order to meet the rationalism of the university's episteme – calls for counter measures that are sourced in resistant thinking. But this necessarily destructive thinking or philosophical inquiry, which does indeed draw on exile, dissidence and delirium, must be understood as culturally bound, and thus the three components of transformation that Kristeva invokes are reconfigurable so that they reflect a careful but not thoroughgoing rationalism. We identify here that the banal discourse that Kristeva warns against is not necessarily the various offshoots of rational thought, but rational thought itself. To that extent, our default to exile, dissidence and delirium must comprise two approaches: it must ensure that those three predispositions are not themselves immediately preferential towards rationalism (and thus replicate a placement of objects so that they meet the 'truth correspondence' of dominant Western thought, and then amount to a pedestrian account of those objects); and it seeks to formulate them so that they can be reiterated as relevant for a Maori, counter-colonial (and a-rational) approach to thought, where thinking is necessarily always cognizant of colonisation and proposes a way that does not automatically configure with rationalism. For example, being aware of how rational thought tries to align objects according to their clarity and deliberately invoking various modes of thinking that destabilise that linearity, demonstrates a dual approach to an object or concept.

The stated aim of this Maori response to Kristeva is not to formulate such an a-rational response as a basis for all perception but instead to explore how exile, dissidence and delirium can unfold in a Maori understanding that will necessarily take account of a holistic metaphysics. There is a danger in assuming that it is the human self that is sole agent in thought for a Maori account, for instance, and while Kristeva is not overly anxious about maintaining that anthropocentric approach, neither does she explicitly take it to task. When left implicit, anthropocentrism extends its reach throughout the critical endeavor – often to the detriment of Maori philosophy, which along with other indigenous thought tends to emphasise the non-human world in the act of thinking (Mika 2017). Our call for reconceptualising and decolonising thought in the university responds to the problems caused by its colonisation.

Colonisation of Maori Thought

Western disciplines and practices have long had a difficult relationship with Maori, who have throughout history been labelled rebels or dissidents in one form or another. Sometimes, these determinedly pejorative labels come to the fore quite clearly, such as in statutes that were designed to deal with wayward Maori action: the New Zealand Settlements Act 1863 and Suppression of Rebellion Act 1863, for instance, set about first designating Maori as insidious Other and then confiscating land from the tribes at which the statutes were aimed. Another example lies in the Tohunga [knowledgeable expert] Suppression Act 1907, which sought to prevent the practice of supernatural methods to ensure wellbeing, the transmission of knowledge, and so forth. These laws are well-known and described in the literature and will not be discussed further here, but we do offer a speculative observation that is based on the general aim of colonisation to civilize (see Simon and Smith 2001): that those laws, and others, aimed in the first instance not to deprive Maori of land or traditional practices as such, but to obliterate the ontological relationships that Maori had with deeper notions of land and the external world, and hence to undermine the thinking process that relates to those phenomena. If the thinking process is indeed weakened, then so is access to a traditional mode of critique. But just as problematically, through policies that restricted Maori access in education to learning the more 'concrete' disciplines (Office of the Auditor General 2012), funneling them into learning that would set them up for trades or unskilled work, their recourse to more conventional practices of abstract Western critique would be hampered.

In a sense, then, Maori have long retained an intimacy with the discomfort that comes with inheriting a colonising set of beliefs. Colonisation, the Maori self's closeness to it, and the ensuing divorce of the self from the self – in many cases, for survival's sake – may be especially identifiable to the Maori student and scholar because a Maori experience of colonial history still obstructs the 'distance' that Kristeva refers to in the notion of exile. In other words, the implicancy of colonised practices and policies pervades Maori experience, with interesting and unforeseen repercussions for all of Kristeva's components of philosophical revolt. Not quite incidentally, Kristeva seems to be asking non-indigenous scholars and students to cease thinking of themselves as uncolonised, and instead to understand that being situated within static thinking is a form of dysfunctional existence. In both Maori and non-indigenous approaches, then, the speculation on the harm imposed by expected results and well-worn methods for research, becomes especially important as an intimate colonising companion.

Reconfiguring Exile, Dissidence and Delirium

In relation to Maori students and scholars in the academe, it seems that there is a particular responsibility to engage with the discomfort of colonisation as a close phenomenon. First, the Maori scholar is tasked with keeping the needs of his or her community at the forefront (Mane 2009) whilst making a proposition of any kind – whether this be through funded or empirical research or through formulating a speculative concept. *Keeping* something *at the forefront* is not simply an abstract process; in Maori thought, as a whole it forms a materiality that integrates with the Maori scholar's being, evident in the genealogical link between thought-as-entity in traditional Maori philosophy and the human self (Mika 2017). Moreover, even if the Maori scholar managed to somehow rationalize their concern for their communities, he or she is crowded by *ideas* themselves (see Mika 2017). Herein lies another particular Maori metaphysics – that the idea is material. The Maori scholar is hence never completely alone in the sense of being hermetic. S/he may be *exiled* to the extent that there is no-one else apparently around, or that there is no administration to be seen to, but the materiality of both expectation (i.e. keeping at the forefront) and idea (what crowds him or her as a material relation) is emotional and substantial.

In their simultaneous solitude-community, Maori academics' (and here we include students as much as scholars) contemplation of colonisation must embrace objectifying it whilst also resisting it as something that inflicts emotional and spiritual harm on Maori communities and, indeed, on the contemplating self. Returning to our introductory comments about Maori metaphysics for this section: Maori academics come to realize that colonisation is not simply a matter for contemplation but a phenomenon *within which* they act. They are both transcendent and immanent to colonisation. Novalis stated in relation to the proximity of the invisible that "[w]hat is thinking sensing etc. here – is burning, fermenting, thrusting etc. yonder" (Wood 2007, p. 24); with relevance to Maori philosophy, any meditation on a harm, as if it is cognitively thrown before the self, seems to immediately evidence the real harm – or, at least, illuminate it as always-already manifesting – in the academic self: What emerges over there, is immediately internal and enfolding. Maori dissidence and delirium must always consider the twists and turns, the assumptions and tendrils of, for instance, fragmenting thought as an external event, even as the Maori academic tries to holistically keep objects, including him- or herself, in the world as one. Any excavation into any apparently innocent, uncolonised thing, must also account for a possible colonised interpretation as both within and external. It must therefore **be** cognizant of the patience of colonisation as it waits to manifest in Maori thought – delirium from a Maori view would understand this as the gradual coming-to-being of a phenomenon through an idea.

To reiterate, then: it is mythical to believe that the Maori self can truly distance or completely implicate a thing through one's thinking. In traditional times, it is likely that the latter was privileged in Maori expression (the thing itself would have been *presented* within an utterance or art forms) (Whitt et al. 2001), but this collapse of the thing with the self's experience is continuously threatened with the need to throw the thing before the self. It is that mode of representation that is clearly endorsed by the academe. Thus, the Maori academic is always brought to write about something as if it is nothing more than an idea – unrelated to the self apart from how he or she understands it. It is perhaps this strong idealism that is, for Maori, most in need of dissidence – the academic idea that something is important only insofar as it can be idealised needs to be challenged. Maori philosophy, if it is to truly follow the Kristevan conceptions would need to undertake a complete dis-interment of the assumptions of Western philosophy and thought *even as it acts within that Maori critique.*

But the Maori scholar can take action to some extent, and can constantly answer back to the attempts and drives of idealism to render thinking static in the academe. Maori thought can undertake a deeply subjective interpretation of coloni-sation, as Hokowhitu and Cooper have carried out. Hokowhitu (2009) challenges the essentialising of the Maori self, for instance, and asks the Maori self to recon-sider traditionalist thinking, and Cooper (2012) urges Maori to think deeply beneath assumptions that are provided by colonisation. These encounters with the unmoving, leviathan categories of selfhood and thinghood that the academe encourages are quite possibly destabilising – not just for the discipline but for the Maori self. In this sense another approach that Mika (2017) has argued for is to reclaim the mystery of a thing.

This reclaiming involves recapturing the possibility that the thing-in-itself is inti-mately connected to the self as a constitutive force. In this act that posits something as 'romanticised' (Novalis 1960, p.545), concepts and phenomena are lifted from the pedestrian to the obscure. Their hiddenness develops in the self a thrilling sense of closeness and draws the Maori academic self on to contemplate why the thing is fundamentally hidden from conceptual view. It is this reflection on the self's limita-tions in respect of the 'thatness' of something that is a philosophical discipline (Mika 2016), not any certain utterances in relation to that thing. The point of delir-ium here is the outcome of not-knowing, and the journey to that point. This instance then opens up Maori thought for further contemplation, ensuring that the self is forever incorporated into the power of the object. The Maori academic self is hence no longer trotting out the research; instead, he or she is confounding not only its outcomes but also the way in which it is produced. It comprises a research method that always implodes back on itself, because it brings into question the nature of a formalized approach even as it adopts a determined approach to a phenomenon, and to the thought surrounding it.

The reflection on the self's limitations at various stages of research and thought involves some fascinating corollaries with the objectified/intimate 'thing' being considered. The self must be understood as a facsimile of a colonised reality – 'out there', considered in perhaps the same way as Freire (1970) encouraged the oppressed self to see his or her reality through viewing themselves as a distant member participating in a colonised activity. In a sense, the Maori academic self is an archetype that, in self-reflective mode, moves throughout a colonised world, accruing layers of colonised thought and matter – a Maori possibility for *Bildung* which is not dissimilar to Novalis' version (see Mika 2015). But the self also conceives of him- or herself as a fundamentally obscure entity, much as the object is, who happens to write on a segment of a thing at any one time (but who, still mysteriously, might be formulating the All in his or her work). This movement between strong and weak selfhood in the face of the world is an existential reality for Maori – it is indeed 'nomadic' and represents the dual reality of responsibility for reproducing thought that can be taken to task by others and by the self, and, it seems, of this decolonising framework of thought and revolt.

Thought and Revolt

A Maori philosophy that overturns static and colonising representation is dependent on the self's feeling of incompleteness in relation to all other things in the world; at some point, nothing more can be said about the problem-as-entity. Silence on those matters in one's academic work forms spaces for other people to step in and address where the original Maori thinker left the discussion. Kristeva's illuminations around these concepts from her own philosophising are relevant, because the silent gaps that one cannot fill – perhaps themselves formed by the dark obscurity of the object (colonisation) being contemplated as well as the self's limitations in respect of thinking about that object and also the self – draw other scholars' thinking into the maelstrom.

Challenging a simple dominant need to know that normalises what counts as thought and knowledge in the university explicates and elevates forms of indigenous Maori and marginalised thought. The framework of exile, dissidence and delirium furthermore elevates the validity of non-knowing, and the possibility of knowledges or ways of being as co-existing, in equally valid ways, yet inaccessible to each other, as a confluence of knowledges and thought within the university. It challenges what risks becoming an "annihilation of differences" that "neatly situates everyone on the linear path that we call progress" (Söderbäck 2012, p. 306), and creates space for a vitality of thought and thinking, that cannot be prescribed, but instead is a critical, creative and meaningful response to particularities in time, space, beings and realities.

Yet, thought as a reaction, dissent, philosophy of non-agreement, or dissidence is not an argument for any kind of rootless or meaningless response to contemporary confines or restrictions, merely for the sake of change, difference or unsettling. Papastephanou (2015) cautions in what she describes as a "parody of the rhizome" (p. 1493), against the glaring ironies of merely domesticating, celebrating, divergences, "minor writing" and sacrificing it "the very moment that it is domesticated as educationally digestible material … on the altar of a new, faddish uni(formi)ty and simplicity" (p. 1493). Exile dissidence and delirium respond to the questions underlying this book, by questioning the nature of thought, or what thought ought to be, in the university, by calling for transformations beyond these questions. They create a culture of revolt, as they call for critical, creative, and complex thought – not a revolution, but a transformation, elevating thought possibilities from stasis to life, from marginalised and silenced, to alive and developing.

Concluding Comments

This chapter is our response to the unsettling call for rethinking thought in the contemporary university. A decolonising philosophical framework for thought and revolt, we have argued, challenges the dominant pressures to measure, quantify and to know. By positing thought on a precipice of a 'hollow' or 'void' upon which Kristeva insists, of dominant and marginalised thought, we have explicated exile, dissidence and delirium as a framework of essential constructions of thought. The thought confluence in this philosophical framework and its response to a Kristevan call for revolt open thought in the academe up to understandings of ways that might otherwise not be achieved. It opens unparalleled thought possibilities and puzzles that arise because of, and are messily entangled with, the language by which thought is articulated, clarified, aligned and resolved. Philosophical thought in this view reaffirms thinking as a complex undertaking, informing, and illuminated by, but also recognising the nuanced entanglements of the everyday – and the colonised – contemporary university. Revolt, as argued here through a Kristevan – Maori confluence, represents not only a desirable but a crucial state of inner chaos and transformation, necessary to preserving the inner life of the self and of thought and thinking in the university.

References

Arndt, S. (2013). Ignorance in a knowledge economy: Unknowing the foreigner in the neoliberal condition. In T. A. C. Besley & M. A. Peters (Eds.), *Re-imagining the creative university for the 21st century* (pp. 123–133). Rotterdam: Sense Publishers.

Cooper, G. (2012). Kaupapa Māori research: Epistemic wilderness as freedom? *New Zealand Journal of Education Studies, 47*(2), 64–73.

Feinberg, J. (2014). *Doing philosophy* (5th ed.). Boston: Wadsworth, Cengage Learning.

Freire, P. (1970). *Pedagogy of the oppressed*. London: Penguin.

Harré, R. (2000). *One thousand years of philosophy: From Ramanuja to Wittgenstein*. Oxford: Blackwell Publishers Ltd.

Hokowhitu, B. (2009). Indigenous existentialism and the body. *Cultural Studies Review, 15*(2), 101–118.

Huri, Y. (2006). Who am I without exile?: On mahmûd darwîsh's later poetics of exile. *Domes, 15*(2), 56–68.

Kelsey, J. (2015). *The fire economy: New Zealand's reckoning*. Wellington: Bridget Williams Books.

Kristeva, J. (1982). *Powers of horror: An essay on abjection* (L. S. Roudiez, Trans.). New York: Columbia University Press.

Kristeva, J. (1977/1986). A new type of intellectual: The dissident. In T. Moi (Ed.), *The Kristeva reader* (pp. 292–300). Oxford: Blackwell Publishers.

Kristeva, J. (1996/2002). The sense and non-sense of revolt. In K. Oliver (Ed.), The portable Kristeva (pp. 413–434). New York: Columbia University Press.

Kristeva, J. (1991). *Strangers to ourselves*. New York: Columbia University Press.

Kristeva, J. (2014). *New forms of revolt*. Paper presented at the the Kristeva circle, Nashville, TN.

Kritzman, L. D. (2006). Michel Foucault. In L. D. Kritzman (Ed.), *The Columbia history of twentieth-century French thought*. New York: Columbia University Press.

Lechte, J. (1990). *Julia Kristeva*. London: Routledge.

Mane, J. (2009). Kaupapa Māori: A community approach. *MAI Review, 3*, 1–9.

Midttun, B. H. (2006). Crossing the borders: An interview with Julia Kristeva. *Hypatia, 21*(4), 164–177.

Mika, C. (2012). Overcoming 'being' in favour of knowledge: The fixing effect of 'mātauranga'. *Educational Philosophy and Theory, 44*(10), 1080–1092.

Mika, C. (2015). Novalis' poetic uncertainty: A Bildung with the absolute. *Educational Philosophy and Theory, 48*, 621. https://doi.org/10.1080/00131857.2015.1068681.

Mika, C. (2016). Worlded object and its presentation: A Māori philosophy of language. *AlterNative, 12*(2), 165–176.

Mika, C. (2017). *Indigenous education and the metaphysics of presence: A worlded philosophy*. Oxon: Routledge.

Novalis. (1960). Vorarbeiten zu verschiedenen Fragmentsammlungen. In P. Kluckhohn & R. Samuel (Eds.), *Schriften: Das philosophische Werk I* (Vol. 2, pp. 507–651). Stuttgart: W. Kohlhammer.

Office of the Auditor-General. (2012). *Education for Māori: Context for our proposed audit work until 2017*. Wellington: Office of the Auditor-General. Retrieved from http://www.oag.govt.nz/2012/education-for-maori/part3.htm.

O'Malley, B. (2017, May 14). Purdue and kaplan venture is a bizarre muddle of very different institutions, *University World News: The global window on higher education*. Retrieved from http://www.universityworldnews.com/

Papastephanou, M., & Angeli, C. (2007). Critical thinking beyond skill. *Educational Philosophy and Theory, 39*(6), 604–621. https://doi.org/10.1111/j.1469-5812.2007.00311.x.

Papastephanou, M. (2009). Method, philosophy of education and the sphere of the practico-inert. *Journal of Philosophy of Education, 43*(3), 451–470.

Papastephanou, M. (2015). On ugliness in words, in politics, in tour-ism. *Educational Philosophy and Theory, 47*(13–14), 1493–1515. https://doi.org/10.1080/00131857.2014.963493.

Peters, M. A. (2008). Wittgenstein as exile: A philosophical topography. *Educational Philosophy and Theory, 40*(5), 591–605. https://doi.org/10.1111/j.1469-5812.2008.00448.x.

Peters, M. A. (2016). Dissident thought: Systems of repression, networks of hope. *Contemporary Readings in Law and Social Justice, 8*(1), 20–36.

Simon, J., & Smith, L. (Eds.). (2001). *A civilising mission? Perceptions and representations of the New Zealand native schools system*. Auckland: Auckland University Press.

Ruitenberg, C. (2009). Distance and defamiliarisation: Translation as philosophical method. *Journal of Philosophy of Education, 43*(3), 421–435.

Söderbäck, F. (2012). Revolutionary time: Revolt as temporal return. *Signs, 37*(2, Special issue on Unfinished revolutions), 301–324.

Sunderland, L. (2010). The art of revolt. *Comparative Literature, 62*(1), 22–40. https://doi.org/10.1215/00104124-2009-030.

Whitt, L., Roberts, M., Norman, W., & Grieves, V. (2001). Belonging to land: Indigenous knowledge systems and the natural world. *Oklahoma City University Law Review, 26*, 701–743.

Wittgenstein, L. (1953). *Philosophical investigations*. London: The Macmillan Company.

Wood, D. (Ed.). (2007). *Novalis: Notes for a romantic encyclopaedia*. Albany: State University of New York Press.

Chapter 5
Towards an African University of Critique

Yusef Waghid and Nuraan Davids

Introduction

The recent #FeesMustFall campaign in South Africa has once again brought higher education into the spotlight. Protesting students demanded that the South African government implement a policy of equal access to higher education for all students. In addition, university authorities should be more responsive to students' aspirations instead of relying on police intervention and brutality to quell their demands for free and equal higher education. What was very evident from the violent disruptions witnessed at institutions of higher learning, was a tangible lack of plausible engagement between students and institutional authorities. In this chapter, we argue that although (South) African universities, since the first democratic elections, have mainly been designated as places for deliberative engagement and the cultivation of decolonised pedagogical knowledge spaces, the recent predicament highlighted a marked absence of critique. The latter is so on the grounds that students and institutional authorities (including government) blame one another for the violence that has permeated South African universities. As a corollary of an apparent lack of critique, we discuss why the idea of an African university with its intent to engender dissonance and just human relations, seems to be under threat. We further argue that, unless (South) African higher education reclaims the notion of critique, the possibility of a thinking university on the African continent would be dealt a heavy blow. Put differently, if African universities are not gong to be more responsive to restiveness (that is dissonance) it would be alienated from practicing thinking that is reflective, critical, and uncomfortable. By implication, the latter situation would not contribute towards decolonising knowledge on the African continent.

Y. Waghid (✉) · N. Davids
Stellenbosch University, Stellenbosch, South Africa
e-mail: YW@sun.ac.za; nur@sun.ac.za

© Springer International Publishing AG, part of Springer Nature 2018
S.S.E. Bengtsen, R. Barnett (eds.), *The Thinking University*,
Debating Higher Education: Philosophical Perspectives 1,
https://doi.org/10.1007/978-3-319-77667-5_5

South African Universities and the Yearning
for Transformation: A Brief Look

Accompanying the emergence of a post-apartheid democracy in 1994 was the rapid production of a series of White Papers, Acts and Plans. These policy texts would seemingly set higher education on a track, not only transforming itself into an integrated knowledge power base, but which would also speak to the research, development, social and economic needs of a society in deep political flux. Central to the *National Plan for Higher Education* (NPHE) (DoE 2001), was the proposal of sixteen outcomes, which included increasing black student access into the university sector, and enhancing students' cognitive abilities with respect to technical and professional competences. The latter would not only ensure greater competitiveness in an ever-evolving labour market economy, but will hopefully also ensure increased participation of students as democratic citizens in service of the 'public good'.

Underscoring the aforementioned three key policy drives was a dual attempt to redress an apartheid-induced, widely disparate legacy of higher education institutions (HEIs). Simultaneously these policies are trying to pave the way for a marriage between knowledge production and socio-economic growth. Critical to the redressing agenda was the highly contentious merging programme which, by 2001, saw either the closure or the merging of colleges of education into universities and technikons (polytechnics), as well as the dissolution or merging of 36 HEIs into 26. From the perspective of Higher Education South Africa (HESA 2014), the closure and merging of particular institutions were critical to restructuring a diverse higher education system that would resonate with the knowledge and development needs of South Africa and the imperative of achieving social justice. As a corollary of mergers, the migration of black students to historically white and better-resourced spaces has had serious financial implications for already constrained institutions. Government's funding formula subsidises institutions according to student enrolments, graduation rates and recognised or accredited research publications; fewer students therefore means less money. Indeed, while student numbers have doubled since 1994, black students comprise the vast majority of the student body, 'the block grant to universities, however, has declined in real terms, and therefore, so, too, the per capita contribution per student' (Badat 2016: 3). Consequently, Badat (2010: 7) explains that the extent to which government and universities have sought to pursue social equity and redress and quality in higher education simultaneously, has resulted in difficult political and social dilemmas. Primary among these dilemmas – as is alarmingly clear in the recent #FeesMustFall campaign – is inadequate public finances and academic development initiatives to support under-prepared students, who tend to be largely black, and/or of working class or rural poor social origins.

Subsumed in the afore-mentioned discussions is the ever-lingering tension of decolonisation. By decolonisation is meant an attempt to think about knowledge in an integrated way. The latter implies that knowledge produced elsewhere, for instance, in the dominant western countries like the UK, US, Canada, Europe and Australasia, should be considered together with knowledge indigenous to local and national communities. And, countries on the African continent should not merely uncritically endorse knowledge produced elsewhere. Rather, knowledge produced locally on the continent should be brought into conversation with knowledge produced elsewhere. Such a situation in turn, would give rise to a possible decolonisation of knowledge. Moreover, the weight of the legacy of colonialism was, perhaps, made most explicit in the removal of the statue of Cecil John Rhodes at the University of Cape Town – commonly referred to as the #RhodesMustFall campaign. Similarly, a video, entitled 'Luister' (Listen) vividly depicted the pervading 'whiteness' of Stellenbosch University, as black students recalled humiliating experiences of exclusion, discrimination and racism. Unsurprisingly, the desire for decolonised post-apartheid HEIs is not limited to the academic or residential experiences of students. More recently available statistics from 2012 reveal that, although whites constitute 8% of the South African population, white academics constitute 53% of full-time permanent staff, of which 55% are male (HESA 2014). Although gradually shifting, the poor representation of black academics in higher education is exacerbated by the insufficient cohort of PhD graduates. In this regard, South African universities, according to the HESA report (2014), are confronted with two challenges. The first pertains to the production and retention of the next generation of academics. The second challenge relates to transforming the social composition of the academic workforce through measures that advance social equity and redress for black people and women of all races.

Thus far, we have shown briefly that the transformation agenda of higher education is embedded in deep social, economic and political challenges. Next, we turn our attention to the realisation that, although higher education policies create the impression of inviting deliberative engagement and the cultivation of decolonised pedagogical knowledge spaces, the recent – and increasingly violent – spates of student protests suggest that this in fact might not be the case.

Students and why the Violence

One of the deepest concerns about the recent student protests in the #FeesMustFall campaign, is the intense levels of violence, which have not only seen the wanton destruction of university libraries, administration buildings and lecture halls, but also arson and violent attacks on individuals. And while it might be easy merely to condemn violence (as one should), it is more important to make sense of why students have resorted to the types of measures that they have, and then, what the implications are for universities on the African continent. On the one hand, we know that the issues at stake here are more than just a call for free higher education. The #FeesMustFall campaign intersects with a depleting state-funded National Student Financial Aid Scheme (NSFAS) inasmuch as it collides with issues of race and social inequality. In this regard, even if students are academically eligible to access universities, the NSFAS cannot provide the necessary financial support to all students as they might require it. Badat (2016: 4) explains:

It is not that the state is unaware of the challenges or the measures that are required to ensure that higher education addresses effectively equity, quality, and development problems, or that the higher education budget has not increased, or that funds have not been provided to address important issues and areas. The simple reality is that state funding has been inadequate to support universities to discharge their critical purposes of producing knowledge, cultivating high quality graduates, and engaging meaningfully with diverse communities.

On the other hand, the #FeesMustFall campaign cannot be divorced, says Du Toit (2000: 93), from the prospect of large debt, high drop-out rates, poor throughput rates, inadequate facilities and accommodation. In addition, the aforementioned campaign cannot be uncritical to largely unreconstructed epistemologies and ontologies, questionable quality of learning and teaching to ensure meaningful opportunities and success, and alienating and disempowering academic and institutional cultures that are suffused by 'whiteness', and which are products of the historical 'legacies of intellectual colonisation and racialization' (Du Toit 2000: 93). In agreement with Du Toit (2000), Suttner (2016) states that key features of the structural architecture of South African society have remained the same, despite gains that have been made. To this end, says Suttner (2016), the experiences of many black people in South Africa remain troubling continuities of the apartheid era and its racism. To Suttner (2016), the #FeesMustFall and #RhodesMustFall campaigns may raise wider questions that go beyond the educational realm and offer a prism through which we can look at post-1994 South Africa and ask troubling questions about the nature of this society. Primary among these, on which we will now focus our attention, is what Suttner (2016) describes as the 'readiness of some to resort to violence or the rhetoric of violence-as-solution'.

In continuing, therefore, one has to make sense of the complex facets, which have given rise to the student protests and violence. First among these is the all too evident economic facet, which as Badat (2016: 3) assesses it, resides in the reality that South African higher education is inadequately funded by the state. In turn, inadequate funding is exacerbated by insufficient resources, which ought to be devoted to academic development programmes in light of the support many students require to ensure that there is meaningful equity of opportunity and outcomes (Badat 2016). The cripplingly high cost of higher education is not unique to South Africa. As Calitz and Fourie (2016: 3) point out, in just the last three years, students have publicly protested against fee increases in Australia, Brazil, Germany, the Netherlands, the United Kingdom, as well as Finland, Thailand, Poland, New Zealand and Turkey.

The second facet might be considered in relation to notions of transformation. And here it is important to recognise that collective calls for the transformation of higher education have not always enjoyed collective understandings of what transformation entails. Thus far, the transformation agenda in higher education has been overwhelmingly couched in the oppositional politics of historical advantage and disadvantage. In turn, constructions of advantage versus disadvantage have ensured that policies of transformation remain trapped in discourses of race and racism. Consequently, university students, as well as South African society, continue to operate and relate to the other on the basis of an us-and-them dichotomy. The continuing use of oppositional politics in transformation is not only embedded in the historical role of higher education in countering apartheid, but also in the post-apartheid government's motivation that higher education ought to play a socially transformative role. In other words, government – as made explicit in the aforementioned policies – expects university students to continue the unfinished business that gave shape to the struggle against apartheid. But, what does transformation mean? And does transformation stop when an institution has seemingly been transformed? And, in any case, how would one know when transformation has been reached? To date, racial demographics of students have been used as an indicator of transformation. But, does, an increase of black students at historically advantaged institutions mean that the institution has been transformed? As we might be well aware, physical access neither determines nor implies practices of inclusion and participation. Consequently, the contestations attached to notions of transformation raise particular questions not only about the implications of transformation, but also whether transformation will actually facilitate the democratic agenda of South Africa.

According to *White Paper 3* (DoE 1997: 3), in the context of present-day South Africa, higher education 'must contribute to and support the process of societal transformation outlined in the Reconstruction and Development Programme (RDP), with its compelling vision of people-driven development leading to the building of a better quality of life for all'. For Reddy (2004: 6–7), the post-apartheid South African government holds high developmentalist expectations for HEIs: 'In the main the state hopes that higher education institutions will contribute towards overcoming the legacies of the country's racialised development, transform the society along democratic and more equitable lines, and make the country more competitive in the global economic system.' The problem with this particular ongoing expectation and narrative is that it is unequivocally entrenched in protest forms that are violent. It is therefore unsurprising that students involved in the #RhodesMustFall and the #FeesMustFall campaigns justify the destruction of buildings and resources by comparing their protests to those of the 1976 Soweto Uprisings, or to the student resistance of the 1980s. To their minds, the types of student protests that have come to define the #FeesMustFall campaign are exactly what led to the downfall of apartheid. It is therefore implicit to how student protests ought to unfold, and how these protests will presumably achieve the same outcome – albeit a different type of freedom, namely freedom from paying fees.

Because protests are always in response to something, and therefore entirely dialogical, the third facet, in fact, relates to the unfinished business of government. Certain post-apartheid promises were made that speak not only to the use of higher education in furthering the democratisation agenda of a new democracy, but also to higher education as a means towards the cultivation of equality, equity, social justice and a public good. To this end, if students are expected to enact the democratisation agenda that will cultivate a vibrant, critical and engaging democratic society, then government needs to complete the unfinished business of not only providing free higher education, but also to deliver on the promises, which access and completion of an education ought to yield – that is, to fulfil the purpose of a public good. *White Paper 3* (DoE 1997: 4) states –

> Higher education equips individuals to make the best use of their talents and of the opportunities offered by society for self-fulfilment. It is thus a key allocator of life chances considered as 'an important vehicle for achieving equity in the distribution of opportunity and achievement among South African citizens.

The concern of the third facet differs from the economic facet of inadequate funding. The facet of unfinished business hinges on the propagation of the democratisation agenda as a realisation of equality, equity and social justice. In this regard, has government met its end of the bargain by sustaining its own democratisation agenda by cultivating the political and social climate conducive to higher education, thereby fulfilling its mandate of equality and equity? Stated differently, has government held itself accountable in relation to the democratisation agenda, which it propagates through its higher education policies?

In sum, the three facets of economic deficiency, the contested terrain of transformation, and the paralysis of a democratisation agenda have to be taken into account for two primary reasons. Firstly, it assists one in understanding that the expression of violence through student protests (while being condemned) emanates from a particular context. Secondly, now that we have identified at least three facets that might be playing a role in the levels of student frustration, anger and violence, it becomes necessary to consider why universities in South Africa have not (yet) fulfilled their designation as spaces for deliberative engagement and the cultivation of decolonised pedagogical knowledge spaces. It is to this discussion that this chapter will next turn the attention.

Cultivating Deliberative Engagement through Critique

The question is, what constitutes an African university of critique? Put differently, how should such a university deal with the notion of critique in relation to matters of concern to African HEIs? Clearly, the idea of critique as just finding fault with human action in the face of challenges that confront universities on the continent, seems to be untenable. For too long have we heard that the fault lies with unresponsive university management, or with excessive student revolts – as if the dilemma about university access and retention is just a matter of blaming each another. Such a notion of critique is indefensible in the sense that casting blame has not always resolved challenges. This is the problem, which confronted higher education and its predicament of, say, the contestations surrounding student tuition or accommodation fees. The South African example of excessive police interference and the apparent and persistent student intransigence is just one case in point in which critique as an articulation of blameworthy action fails to be responsive to the university predicament that is, #FeesMustFall. Critique is not meant to constrain or coerce human action of the kind associated with the afore-mentioned campaign. Instead, critique is meant to resolve the predicament university management and students happened to find themselves perpetuating and practising through an implausible meaning of the concept. In the latter sense, critique is a form of thinking that invokes, what Foucault (1988) refers to as sudden upheavals of thought whereby one is provoked to think differently about matters. In other words, critique as a form of dissonant thinking brings a discomfort in one's reflection about something, yet, simultaneously stimulates one to reflect freely and in opposition to forms of coercion and domination. For instance, critiquing higher education would involve taking issue with the dominant forces of management and control that envisage the university to be run according to market conditions that favour that of running a corporate enterprise. Together with the latter way of thinking on the basis of which one shows dissonance, people could also think differently about university access in the sense that students should not be entirely exonerated from paying tuition fees. That is, the idea that students pay some fees cannot also be dismissed completely. Consequently, we turn to the seminal thoughts of Michael Foucault (1998) and Jacques Rancière (2011) to ascertain whether critique can be looked at differently. In other words, in reference to the afore-mentioned theorists' conception of critique, we want to examine whether dilemmas in higher education on the African continent can be meaningfully addressed without necessarily the exchange of reproach.

First, Foucault (1998: 154) articulates critique as 'neither [the] subjection nor total acceptance' of people's points of view about societal matters that concern them. If one does not subject oneself to another's point of view, one is not drawn to that view uncritically. In other words, one recognises that 'one may work with it and yet be restive' (Foucault 1998: 154). To work with a particular view, the possibility exists that one might recognise that there is something in that view to which one is drawn. That is, one is persuaded by some authenticity in the view espoused and considers it feasible enough to work with it. For instance, university management might offer a response to student protestations that their budgetary restrictions do not permit the university to reduce fees unconditionally in the middle of an academic year. Inasmuch as such a view and explanation for that matter is perceived as reasonable by students, this does not mean that students should in their entirety remain subjected to the view espoused in defence of the actions of university management vis-à-vis the institution's financial constraints. By implication, students could 'work with' such an explanation but yet remain 'restive' about it – that is they are prepared to work with it, yet their uneasiness about the claim does not result in them fully endorsing it. Put differently, students remain in a state of discomfort about a university management's decision regarding paying tuition fees. Yet, students do not outright reject the institution's decision as they might see some merit in the decision later on – that is, that they (students) have to compensate for some tuition fees. In other words, following Foucault, being restive about something does not amount to a complete agreement with a decision, yet, simultaneously one also does not reject the decision completely. And, when students embark on critique, they merely point out 'what kinds of assumptions, what kinds of familiar, unchallenged, unconsidered modes of thought' (Foucault 1998: 154) the practices with which they deal, present. In this regard, students can show that mere talk of budgetary restrictions is in line with a particular understanding of financial responsibility, which considers student income as a necessary component of the budgetary process of the institution. Similarly, university management can articulate to students some of their reasons for strictly adhering to a corporate mode of financial accountability and why less affluent economies on the continent perhaps could not completely embrace a market economy similar to that of a welfare state in Europe, for instance.

The point we are making, is that being 'restive' remains a condition of critique whereby participants in the discourse – on the basis that discourse engages people in encounters – articulate their readiness to take issue with one another. In other words, being engaged in critique implies that humans show the propensity to take into controversy one another's claims to truth and simultaneously show a willingness to listen reflectively to one another's different justifications. By implication, engaging in critique does not merely amount to shutting down the views of others or instantaneously opposing others' views for the sake of showing one's dissatisfaction with another's point of view. Rather, in Foucauldian terms, one articulates one's reasons 'in a free atmosphere, one constantly agitated by a permanent criticism' (Foucault 1998: 155) and simultaneously recognises 'cracks, silent shocks, malfunctionings' (Foucault 1998: 156) in others' claims without just rejecting or accepting what one encounters. The point we are making is that being restive implies a condition of dissonance in which people can agree to consider one another's points of view. Simultaneously, they also take issue with one another's perspectives, that is, without endorsing such views in its entirety.

Second, in relation to understanding politics and society, Rancière (2011: 4), explains critique as a practice that 'consists in blurring the boundaries ... between the political from the social or the public from the domestic'. Thus for Rancière (2011: 4), critique is to 'put into question' but not to unravel this or that matter or event continuously. Rancière (2011: 10) elucidates 'putting into question' without continuously unravelling matters of public and domestic concern as a matter of breaking away from 'the grand narrative of the victim', for instance, blameworthy action and, to 'reframing it [thoughts] ... in order to make a new use of it'. So, looking at critique differently implies giving it 'a meaning that perhaps was not there and certainly was not obvious at the beginning' – referred to as 'the radical disagreement [dissensus] of sense and thought' (Rancière 2011: 10). For Rancière (2011: 11), critique as dissensus means a kind of thinking that breaks away from considering something as absolutely wrong or disastrous. As he puts it, 'to practice critique as disagreement [dissensus]' is to think of 'the wrong that cannot be settled but can be processed all the time' (Rancière 2011: 11). If one were to think of a wrong in such a way that it cannot be resolved, it implies that one should always be open to new ideas or ways of coming to understand the wrong in question. And, because this putting into question of a wrong or disaster for that matter ought to happen all the time, this implies that there is no end to thinking about resolving the wrong in light of new thoughts and conceptualisation. The point is, when one embarks on such a critique of dissensus, one traces back understandings of a concept ontologically – that is, in relation to the history, politics and societal contexts of such a concept. And, simultaneously one looks poetically at the descriptions, narrations, metaphors and symbols that make concepts what they are – a matter of making sense of concepts interrelatedly. Put differently, what Rancière (2011: 15) purports of critique as dissensus is tantamount to a disclosure of an *arkhê* of the *arkhê* – that is, 'an authority of the authority' (Rancière 2011: 15). This means that meanings of concepts ought to be considered both in relation to existing and agreed-upon meanings of concepts (established meanings) together with looking again at such agreed-upon meanings. When one uses critique to verify meanings continuously – that is, on the basis of established meanings and simultaneously looking for new meanings (descriptions, narrations, metaphors and symbols) as one verifies continuously, one embarks upon reflexive meaning making, also known as a critique of disagreement.

A critique of disagreement, following Rancière (2011: 15), is a two-pronged approach: to look at established meanings and then simultaneously bringing such meanings into contestation with 'otherness'. In relation to the concept #FeesMustFall, following Rancière, such a concept could refer to making what is understood about the practice happen. So, many might think that the slogan #FeesMustFall is merely associated with its ontological understandings, which might include the reasons why university fees must be abandoned. Yet, simultaneously, looking again at the very ontological meanings of the concept one might be opened up to other meanings in relation to the narrations and metaphors used by the proponents (such as, students) of the concept. And, it could be that students have now initiated what Rancière (2011: 15) refers to as 'a specific battlefield' in relation to which the funding of universities in the country should no longer adhere to a corporatised, neoliberal agenda. For once, the absolutication of the wrong of university fees in the eyes of students would be subjected to more authoritative verification or tracing back and disclosure of meanings not yet thought of before.

This brings us to our next question: Following on the espoused ideas of both Foucault and Rancière, what does the decolonisation of knowledge mean?

Decolonisation as an Instance of Critique

Knowledge is both universally and locally situated. A local understanding of knowledge could influence a global understanding and vice versa. The idea of global knowledge thus makes sense because of the interrelationship between knowledge produced locally – that is indigenously – and knowledge that is produced elsewhere. For instance, knowledge produced in a local fishing community in Africa could be of relevance for global use. Similarly, knowledge produced globally could be used to guide local practices of say, fishing. It is in such a context, that we concur with Masolo (2003) that knowledge in Africa has been informed both by local indigenous understandings and universal notions of knowledge. Our advocacy for a non-bifurcationist view of knowledge stems from a particular procedure of knowledge construction rather than the specific context in which knowledge is produced. By a non-bifurcationist view of knowledge we mean that knowledge produced globally and locally are both situated and framed according to their indigenous contexts. Put differently, knowledge produced universally is indigenous to its global context. Whereas, knowledge produced locally is indigenous to its own situational context. Together such an understanding of global and local knowledges that are interrelated we refer to as being non-bifurcationist or non-separationist. Our view is that knowledge is non-bifurcationist as local understandings of knowledge has an inherently universal dimension and versa a versa.

Of course we are not denying that knowledge produced in Europe, for instance, might be different from knowledge produced in Africa because knowledge in itself is context-specific in the sense that it is related to situational circumstances and conditions. So, producing knowledge about the fishing industry in an indigenous local African community might not be of relevance to a European fishing industry in its entirety, although some aspects of both communities might equally affect fishing in both contexts. However, the point about knowledge construction and production is that the relevance of knowledge is determined by the situational contexts in which such knowledge is/was constructed and produced. However, if knowledge was used to exclude indigenous communities en masse as if nothing could be learnt from such communities, then such understandings of knowledge ought to be subjected to scrutiny. This is the problem with colonisation of knowledge, as such knowledge, often produced and imposed by colonialist powers, was aimed it hegemonising 'colonial' knowledge to the illegitimate exclusion of indigenous knowledge as if knowledge from elsewhere is of exclusive significance. The problem with colonisation of knowledge was not only meant to alienate indigenous communities but also to subjugate them into slavish action whereby people were coerced to serve the imperialist interests of only their colonisers. In other words, to act slavishly implies that one does not or is not permitted to question and challenge existing views, in particular those of the dominant powers. And, when one envisages to decolonise knowledge one endeavours to bring back the criticality that was denied previous constructions of knowledge. Knowledge that has not been subjected to critical scrutiny in itself is pernicious in the sense that indigenous thoughts and practices are subsumed under dominant traditions of others that might not be responsive to local situations. For example, African higher education still encounters remnants of its previous colonised education system, which propelled inequality of access and learning. Yet, by far the most devastating effect that colonialism bequeathed African higher education, is the lack of criticality that was considered a means to subjugate indigenous people into advancing only what they were obliged to do without any form of critical interrogation. Olukoshi and Zeleza (2004: 4) posit that African universities still suffer from a lack of criticality and autonomy in expediting their social responsiveness and responsibility on the continent. If criticality and autonomy remain at large and institutions do not produce knowledge according to such modes of human action, then it seems unlikely that knowledge will ever be decolonised.

In our view, decolonisation of knowledge is not a replacement of one tradition of knowledge with another, for instance, exchanging everything produced in Europe and Britain with only what is produced in Africa. Rather, decolonisation is a philosophical procedure of critique whereby, first, one neither subjects to inconclusive scrutiny nor completely accepts different understandings of knowledge. Put differently, decolonisation is a kind of restive or dissonant thinking; and second, one puts into question and reframes something retrospectively (both ontologically and poetically) in order to make new use of it. Subjecting knowledges to scrutiny with the possibility that one could temporarily suspend one's over-zealous criticality makes sense. This in itself would prevent one from completely accepting or rejecting knowledges as they are presented. Decolonisation implies that one remains 'restive' about that which one encounters irrespective of whether the knowledges originated in Europe or Africa. Likewise, one endeavours to weigh up contradictory or conflictual thoughts with the aim to find a new use for it, particularly in relation to addressing pertinent issues say, on the African continent. For instance, considering that advanced knowledge about the HIV and AIDS pandemic is produced in the US, does not mean that Africans should simply reject such knowledge. If such knowledge produced in the US is combined with knowledge produced locally on how more appropriately to care for HIV infected patients, this non-exclusivist conception of knowledge should not be abandoned too prematurely. It might just be that a potential cure for HIV and AIDS patients might emanate from such a non-bifurcationist understanding of knowledge co-construction.

What follows from the aforementioned argument in defence of decolonisation of knowledge as a procedure of knowledge construction and production, is that knowledge, irrespective of where it emanates from cannot summarily be dismissed or just accepted. This also implies that knowledge of colonising interests is in itself a way of insulating particular understandings of knowledge and also privileging one form of knowledge over another. Such practices in themselves are too parochial and exclusivist and do not commensurate with the construction of knowledge in itself. The latter procedure of knowledge is most appropriate if pursued along the lines of critique, for such a process of knowledge construction would not be oblivious of the pitfalls and advantages of knowledges in order to be responsive to societal challenges. Instead, such a decolonised account of knowledge construction would examine knowledge responsibly and as of relevance to societal changes, particularly in relation to Africa's political, economic and societal advancement. We cannot see how knowledge reframed and reconstituted for the purposes of societal change cannot be of relevance to the complex and ever-evolving changes that occur on the continent if such knowledge remains subjected to a critique of dissensus and autonomy. That is, criticisms of knowledge that do not in their entirety accept or abandon understandings of knowledge from elsewhere, and reconstitutionalised knowledge that looks at its ensuing use in response to what is yet to come.

Conclusion

In relation to advancing the *National Plan for Higher Education* (NPHE) (DoE 2001) in which South African university students are encouraged to enhance their cognitive competence, we contend that using critique in both a Foucauldian and Rancièrean way would not only oblige students to put into question what they encounter restively, but also to be open ontologically and poetically to that which is still to come. Such practices are commensurate with deliberative engagement itself because people would be invited to critique – that is, to put into question and look for other ways of constructing thoughts and practices. Democratic engagement is often truncated as a consequence of a lack of critique as is evident in the #FeesMustFall negotiations or a lack thereof among university staff and students in South Africa. If the decolonisation of knowledge were to be taken seriously, critique should invariably be invoked. If the latter happens, the democratisation of education would be a much more likely possibility than perhaps is currently the case. In the main, it is an African university of critique that will deal more poignantly and trans-formatively with higher educational matters, conflicts and concerns. And this is far more inspiring than to constantly make hollow claims for the decolonisation of knowledge and the democratisation of higher education. Critique in itself invites participants in higher education to confront one another in an atmosphere of non-subjection and restiveness – that is, dissonance, which augurs well for looking at things both ontologically and poetically.

References

Badat, S. (2010). *The challenges of transformation in higher education and training institutions in South Africa*. Paper commissioned by the Development Bank of Southern Africa.. Retrieved from https://www.ru.ac.za/.../The%20Challenges%20of%20Transformation%20in%20High

Badat, S. (2016). *Deciphering the meanings, and explaining the South African higher education student protests of 2015–16*. Retrieved from wiser.wits.ac.za/.../Saleem%20Badat%20%20 Deciphering%20the%20Meanings,%20a...

Calitz, E., & Fourie, J. (2016). *The historically high cost of tertiary education in South Africa.* Stellenbosch Economic Working Papers 02/16.

Department of Education. (1997). Education White Paper No. 3: A Programme on the Transformation of Higher Education Transformation. Pretoria: Government Printers.

Department of Education. (2001). *National Plan for higher education*. Pretoria: Government Printers.

Du Toit, A. (2000). Critic and citizen: The intellectual, transformation and academic freedom. *Pretexts: Literary and Cultural Studies, 9*(1), 91–104.

Foucault, M. (1988). In L. D. Kritzman (Ed.), *Politics, Philosophy, Culture: Interviews and Other Writings 1977–1984*. London: Routledge.

Foucault, M. (1998). *Politics, philosophy, culture: Interviews and other writings (1977–1984)*. New York: Routledge.

HESA (Higher Education South Africa). (2014). South African higher education in the 20th year of democracy: Context, achievements and key challenges. HESA presentation to the Portfolio Committee on Higher Education and Training in Parliament, 5 March, .Cape Town. Retrieved from   http://www.hesa.org.za/hesa-presentation-portfolio-committee-higher-education-and-training (Accessed 18 Sept 2015).

Masolo, D. A. (2003). Philosophy and indigenous knowledge: An African perspective. *Africa Today, 50*(2), 21–38.

Olukoshi, A., & Zeleza, P. T. (Eds.). (2004). *African universities in the twenty-first century. Volume 1: Liberalisation and internationalisation.* Dakar: Council for the Development of Social Science Research in Africa.

Rancière, J. (2011). The thinking of dissensus: Politics and aesthetics. In P. Bowman & R. Stamp (Eds.), *Reading Rancière: Critical dissensus* (pp. 1–17). London: Continuum.

Reddy, T. (2004). Higher education and social transformation: South Africa case study. Report for the Council on Higher Education.

Suttner,   R.   (2016,   February   11).   Op-Ed: Student   protests,   an   indictment   of   "post-apartheid"   South   Africa.Retrieved   from   www.dailymaverick.co.za/.../2016-02-11-op-ed-student-protests-an-indictment-of-po.

Part II
Educating Thought

Chapter 6
Research Education and Care: The Care-Full PhD

Robyn Barnacle

Introduction

University researchers face numerous challenges, including to expertise, the reproducibility of knowledge and the effects of performativity measures (Grundmann 2016). In the research training context, there is a widely held view that PhD training is overly narrow and theoretical in scope leaving graduates poorly equipped with employability skills for work beyond academia. Such issues raise the question of what high level expertise means and the value and distinctiveness of a PhD. Drawing on the work of Nel Noddings, this chapter explores the PhD through the lens of care (Noddings 2001, 2005, 2009). Noddings argues for education to develop a capacity to care, drawing on Martin Heidegger's (1927/1962) notion of care. A capacity to care is not intended in the narrow sense of a skill but as a mark of personhood. This chapter investigates how such a notion of care might extend or enrich existing conceptions of what PhD training is all about.

> "That's why we feel compelled to go out and clear the air and put alternative facts out there." Kellyanne Conway responding to press questioning over claims of inflated numbers at Donald Trump's US presidential inauguration in 2017.

As this quotation aptly conveys, an abiding distrust of authority – as well as expertise – has rendered the status of science and knowledge in the twenty first century decidedly bleak. And it's not all due to the manipulations of unscrupulous media and politicians. While slogans like 'post truth' capture headlines, technological disruption is changing the world of work and learning. For example, new 'democratising' technologies are challenging the traditional role of knowledge-

R. Barnacle (✉)
RMIT University, Melbourne, Australia
e-mail: robyn.barnacle@rmit.edu.au

© Springer International Publishing AG, part of Springer Nature 2018
S.S.E. Bengtsen, R. Barnett (eds.), *The Thinking University*,
Debating Higher Education: Philosophical Perspectives 1,
https://doi.org/10.1007/978-3-319-77667-5_6

based institutions by sorting and distilling expertise from wherever it resides, with the potential to result in new institutional forms - such as collaborative institutions. Some see a great opportunity for more participatory forms of democracy as well as knowledge and learning. In the words of Beth Simone Noveck:

> By divorcing the concept of expertise from elite social institutions and creating tools to enable neutral identification of talent and ability— whether of those inside or outside of government, with credentials or craft knowledge—technology is democratizing expertise. (Noveck 2016).

Face-book, Linked-in and micro-credentialing are all disruptive in the sense that they are unbundling expertise from universities and challenging their formerly monopolistic role as arbiters of knowledge and learning.

Assaults on the status of university credentials and expertise are not just coming from outside the academy. As what has come to be known as the 'reproducibility crisis' attests, systemic issues within science also gnaw away at its heels (Baker 2015). Performance based research metrics in the contemporary neo-liberal environment can unwittingly promote perverse or aberrant behaviour and careerism among scholars. When tenure, promotion and a job *per se* hinge on volume of publications and 'positive' findings people will respond accordingly. In practical terms, this can undermine the independence of researchers resulting in game playing. As Kathleen Lynch argues in relation to the effects of performativity within higher education:

> Those committed to independent scholarship and education are asked to live a lie, to sign up to values and practices which they believe are morally abhorrent and scholastically futile. (2010, 55)

I situate this discussion in the context of contemporary challenges to the expertise, authority and independence of scholars to make the point that these issues present challenges to universities as well as the individuals who work and study in them (see also Macfarlane 2015, 2017; Barnett 2004). Such issues raise questions to do with the role and value of research and what it means to be a researcher.

Issues to do with expertise and work are never far from contemporary debates on the value of the PhD. Such issues are at the heart of a 'crisis' debate that has been raging over the last few years – notably in advanced economies such as the US, the UK and Australia – over the suitability of PhD's for diverse workplaces and whether there is an oversupply of graduates (Cuthbert and Molla 2015; Cyranoski et al. 2011). While this is largely an employability debate it reveals an underlying tension in contemporary discourse on the PhD between an instrumental conception, in which the PhD is seen primarily in the service of knowledge societies and economic and social prosperity, and an older conception in which the value of the PhD is located in the service of the disciplines, truth and knowledge (Clark 2006). At the heart of this employability debate is a question about expertise and particularly the idea that the knowledge acquired through the PhD is of little value to society more broadly. There is a concern, that is, that it is overly narrow and theoretical in scope leaving graduates poorly equipped with employability and other skills for industries and sectors beyond academia (Cuthbert and Molla 2015; Maldonado et. al. 2013; Mowbray and Halse 2010; Nerad 2009).

The notion that *what you can do and who you are* has a role to play in what it means to be a researcher or scholar is not new. It is there in the ancient conception of philosophical inquiry as *philosophia* - love of wisdom. The PhD – although multi-disciplinary – is a Doctor of Philosophy after all. Although arcane in this formulation, even in the contemporary environment there's potentially much going for an educational program dedicated to wisdom. The capacity for critical judgement and independent thinking offer a handy compass in this supposedly 'post-truth' age. There is little doubt, however, that if we are looking to locate the value of the PhD today the notion of the 'love of wisdom' sounds not only arcane but somewhat supercilious. Alternative, more prosaic alternatives are available, however, as Frances Kelly has charted through her work on the PhD imaginary, including representations of research in fiction (2012, 2017). For example, it is not uncommon today for the PhD scholar to be conceived as a detective, painstakingly amassing clues toward the discovery of truth.

What I want to do here is imagine the role and value of the PhD through the lens of care. This conception picks up threads from these other images of the PhD – truth sleuth and lover of wisdom – but foregrounds the relational aspects of care. My question is this: what if research education and specifically the PhD were conceived as learning care: to think care-fully? I'm deliberately formulating this as 'care-full thought' rather than 'care-for-thought' because I want to allow sufficient scope for the idea of thought itself as care. The online etymology dictionary tells us that care and research are closely related. For example, research is from the French *recherché* which means 'carefully sought out' past participle of *rechercher* 'to seek out.' *Chercher* 'to search,' is from Latin *circare*, meaning 'to wander hither and thither,' from circus 'circle' – reflecting the repeated activity of researching. A connection between care and research can also be found in related terms such as curious, from the Latin *curiosus*, meaning 'careful, diligent; inquiring eagerly', and also, 'meddlesome' is akin to the Latin *cura*, meaning 'care, concern' and 'trouble.' As this suggests, care carries with it an ethical and affective dimension – as well as risk – that contrasts with the neutrality and disinterest that is usually associated with scientific research.

In exploring these ideas this chapter draws on earlier research with Gloria Dall'Alba (2007, 2011, 2017) and the work of Nel Noddings who argues for education to develop a capacity to care, drawing on notions of care from Martin Heidegger (1927/1962) and Carol Gilligan (1982). A capacity to care for Noddings is not intended in the narrow sense of a 'skill' but 'as a mark of personhood' (Noddings 2005, 24). This work can be situated in the broader context of an 'ontological turn' for higher education, building on the work of Ronald Barnett (2004) and others whereby higher education is understood ontologically in terms of *who* students *are* as well as who they are *becoming*.

Care and the PhD

Care is not a new concept in the research education space. Indeed, much of what might be considered standard supervisory practice could be described in broad terms as aimed at providing guidance to the PhD candidate on what they should care *about* and *for* as researchers. Even a cursory glance the literature – from scholarly articles to handbooks and policy statements – reveals wide-ranging matters for which candidates are encouraged to care. This includes practical issues such as research methods, writing and publishing but also concern for broader issues such as the discipline, institutional objectives, research integrity requirements and the needs of potential end users, as well as national social and economic agendas (Barnacle and Dall'Alba 2013; Lee 2012; Wisker 2012; Aitchison et al. 2010; Delamont et al. 2004).

Given ongoing challenges to research and researchers – as discussed above – it is unsurprising that questions to do with the overarching purpose of the PhD have also attracted the attention of scholars. Notable in this regard is a large US project, the Carnegie initiative on the doctorate, led by Chris Golde and George Walker. It set out to "…reframe the educational mission in a more constructivist direction than the current unexamined default that defines success as securing an academic position or tenure"(Golde and Walker 2006: 12). Through the notion of 'stewards of the discipline' Golde and Walker make care the centrepiece of their approach with the aim of re-directing the overall purpose of the doctorate away from self-interest.

> By invoking the term steward, we intend to convey the sense of purpose that guides action. Self-identifying as a steward implies adopting a sense of purpose that is larger than oneself. One is a steward of the discipline, not simply a manager of one's own career. By adopting as a touchstone the care of the discipline and understanding that one has been entrusted with that care by those in the field, on behalf of those in and beyond the discipline, the individual steward embraces a larger sense of purpose. The scale is both temporally large (looking to the past and the future) and broad in scope (considering the entire discipline, as well as intellectual neighbours). (Golde and Walker 2006: 13)

The notion of disciplinary stewardship is appealing in a number of ways. Notably, it promotes a sense of purpose for research and research education that clearly extends well beyond mere career or self-interest concerns. Stewardship invokes a broad set of concerns in that the steward cares for the discipline, or recognises and takes ethical responsibility for the discipline and beyond – particularly to cognate disciplines – and a community of scholars more broadly. But other aspects of this notion are less appealing. While Gold and Walker recognise in their formulation that disciplinary boundaries overlap, my concern is that the discipline is nonetheless a discrete and potentially insular unit. Many important contemporary research problems, such as climate change, often get described as 'wicked' in the sense that they defy easy conceptualisation or solution within a single or cognate disciplinary frame. Highly complex social, economic and cultural problems don't necessarily sit comfortably within a disciplinary frame at all.

The complex nature of contemporary problems and the need to build relationships between researchers and the broader community invites greater scrutiny of the scope of disciplinary based knowledge (Hancock et al. 2015). This calls for a broader conception of what researchers might care about – and the potential of thought itself – that can include but also extend beyond primarily disciplinary oriented concerns. This is where I hope Noddings can help through her account of education and care.

Noddings' and Care

Noddings' account of care draws its ontological foundation from the work of Martin Heidegger as developed in *Being and Time* (1927/1962, 155–159) and his all-encompassing conceptualisation of care as fundamental to being human. As I have explored elsewhere (see Barnacle and Dall'Alba 2017) for Heidegger, 'all aware humans care' in the sense that caring is part of what he calls the *concernfulness* of being-in-the-world. This idea is intended to describe the way that we as humans are permanently bound up with, engrossed or entwined with others and things in our day to day tasks and activities. The world, for Heidegger, 'is always the one that I share with others' (155), enmeshed in projects and activities. To care, therefore, refers to this enmeshment with others and things as we are always recruiting others and things into our projects and activities and in turn are ourselves endlessly recruited by others and things. But care can take numerous different forms. For Heidegger, there's care 'that leaps in and dominates, and that which leaps further and liberates' (1927/1962, 159). Care, therefore, has to be harnessed and directed away from deficient modes, such as domination. When solicitude manifests as leaping *in* for others it in effect takes away the others' own care, leading to domination and dependency. For Heidegger, this manifests as 'being for, against or without one another, passing one another by, [and] not mattering to one another' (159). An alternative, collaborative, form of solicitude involves - conversely - leaping *ahead* of the other and assisting them to shape their own becoming.

It is this latter form of care that interests Noddings. This conception of care is distinctive and important for learning because it involves a genuine openness to an other and the situation in which they find themselves. In her words, 'a caring relation is, in its most basic form, a connection or encounter between two human beings – a carer and a recipient of care, or cared-for' (2005, 15). When a carer engages with the cared-for, they do so with what Noddings calls full, attentive receptivity. Using the example of an exchange in which someone asks for – and is provided with – directions, Noddings makes the point that such encounters require the full attention of the person who is being asked for directions. In doing so, the carers' own motives are displaced in favour of those of the other who is in need; the cared for. Openness or 'motivational displacement' such as this means caring in the sense intended by

Noddings can be neither detached nor dispassionate. This introduces the first of three key aspects of Noddings' account of care that I want to highlight: the directedness or orientation of care. Care, for Noddings, is not dispassionate. The carer is 'seized' by the needs of the other and takes on their project or need as if it were their own: 'I receive what the other conveys, and I want to respond in a way that furthers the other's purpose or project' (2005, 16).

Related to this is the second aspect of Noddings' account of care that I want to highlight: the mutuality of care. Genuine caring for Noddings is mutual in that both the carer and cared-for must participate and feel caring and cared for. Mutuality sets a caring relation apart from other kinds of inter-personal encounter. As Noddings says: 'everyone wants to be received, to elicit a response that is congruent with an underlying need or desire' (17). This doesn't mean, however, that there is necessarily congruence in the caring relation. For Noddings, there is no 'care recipe' on which we can depend to gauge an appropriate response and this is why genuine openness to others is so important in her account of caring. It is only through full, attentive receptivity that the would-be carer can distinguish an appropriate response to the would-be cared-for, eliciting what Dall'Alba and I have described elsewhere as 'attuned responsiveness' (2009, 68).

This brings me to the third and last feature of Noddings' account of care that I want to highlight: its ubiquity yet non-transferability. Care is ubiquitous in the sense that we are capable of a caring relation with all things – other people, ideas, inanimate objects etc. However, Noddings clearly privileges the type of care involved in the caring relation between people: 'caring for ideas and objects is different from caring for people and other living things' (2005, 20). This is particularly due to the mutuality necessary for what Noddings considers a genuine caring encounter as discussed above. But although we are capable of entering a caring relation with all things this does not mean caring relations are transferable. As she points out, capacity to care in one domain does not necessarily translate into sensitivity to enter what Noddings would call a caring relation with another person or thing. For instance, a teachers' passion for a particular subject does not ensure they take care to address this passion to the interests or capacities of their students, which would be required in a teaching relation imbued with care for students. The directedness of care means that although we have the capacity to care for all things the act of caring is specific rather than generalised. We care for this or that in this time and place. And, moreover, being adept at caring for one thing does not necessarily make us good at caring for an other thing. We see this in everyday examples of care whereby someone may be excessively devoted to caring for their vintage car collection, or rose garden, but show little regard for other people and things. There is something paradoxical about care, then, in the sense that to care allot here can mean to care less there. This final point about the non-transferability of care clearly echoes criticisms of PhD programs as too specialised leading to overly narrow minded PhD graduates - I'll return to this point below.

Noddings, Care and the PhD

Now let's turn to consider the implications of Noddings' account of care for the PhD. How might it extend or add to existing conceptions of what PhD education is all about? The relational nature of care for Noddings suggests that care has relevance not just for what we think *about* but also *how* we think. One way to begin to unpack this is in terms of the directionality and mutuality of care. If care is directional and mutual then care-full thought must always be *about* something. Indeed, it becomes necessary to ask in which directions care-full thought might be oriented. As discussed above, although Noddings' account of care privileges the reciprocal nature of inter-human care, she also recognises that an element of reciprocity is conceivable in human to non-human care as well. A caring relation, for Noddings, can extend to all things: people, non-human life, as well as ideas. This is not surprising on one level given it is commonplace to think of people as caring for pets, the environment etc. But the idea of reciprocity means, in Noddings' words: 'the care we exert induces something like a response from fields of ideas and from inanimate objects' (2005, 20). In other words, by caring for the ideas and things that hold our interest, those things themselves somehow 'act back'. In my view, this echoes the notion of love of wisdom and the intrinsic attraction of ideas, and other beings and entities: that they can draw us in and hold us enthralled. Interest in a particular topic or area of enquiry, therefore, is not simply reducible to projection for Noddings - as the notion of being 'seized by' a call to care suggests. Care-full thought would be responsive and attentive to that which it is about.

Understanding what this means requires addressing the question of language, of course, which requires a far deeper examination than this chapter allows. Heidegger, for example, examines the relationship between language and being and the capacity – or indeed decrepitude – of thinking in our own time (1968). We could also look to feminist philosophers such as Donna Haraway and the idea of knowledge creation as a relational practice (2007). But even everyday notions like that of a 'living language' offer insight into the interconnectedness of language and world. A language is not considered living simply because it is actively spoken; weasel words and acronym laden public discourse are testimony to that (Watson 2005). Rather, as John Berger puts it: "language is a body, a living creature ... and enfolded in a language is the speaker and world which live through it" (2016). The idea of a living language provides one way of conceptualising thought in terms of a mutual, two-way relation between ideas and things.

If thought can be care-full, however, then it also follows that it can be care-less. If care-full thought is necessarily oriented and therefore *interested* it also follows that it is always partial – or perspectival, to borrow from phenomenology (Gadamer 1988). This raises the question of how to avoid deficient forms of care or carelessness in how we think. In exploring learning how to care, Noddings explores an 'ethic of care,' drawing particularly on the work of Carol Gilligan (1982) and the idea that: 'we have to show how to care in our own relations with the cared-for' (Noddings 2005, 22). When it comes to care-full thought there are a number of ways that this could be modelled. Noddings' uses the example of a maths lecture in which the lecturer doesn't simply explain the rules and concepts of mathematics but demonstrates *how* to think like a mathematician by, for example, enacting the thinking process – what might be called 'thinking out loud'. In the context of research education the task falls to the supervisor or advisor to embody for the PhD candidate how to think and act like a researcher in the field by actively modelling the research processes and practices of the particular disciplinary community. Carefull writing, for example, would include not only the craft and skill of writing but also extend to supporting the candidate to develop a scholarly identity by recognising and adopting the symbolic and other practices of the field. An example of this kind of comprehensive approach can be found in the body of work by Barbara Kamler and Pat Thomson on doctoral writing (2014).

For Noddings' account of care, however, the disciplinary frame is too narrow. Noddings invites us to think beyond learning how to care for the discipline to a broader set of concerns. For Noddings, as for other education scholars, preparing graduates for a complex and challenging world is one of the key roles of education (Nussbaum 2006; Noddings 2005; Barnett 2000). Given her interest in care, however, Noddings emphasises the role of education in creating a more just and caring world. The distinctiveness of Noddings' approach, therefore, is that it foregrounds care for others. In Noddings' view, this would be achieved by organising educational programs around themes of care, such as ecological sustainability and social responsibility, rather than formal domains of learning, such as disciplines.

We see elements of this in university strategic research frameworks and national policy imperatives which often highlight broader social and environmental objectives. It is unclear, however, the extent to which such objectives are reflected in PhD programs in terms of curricular and graduate outcomes. Moreover, as others have identified, attempting to reconcile competing institutional, policy and disciplinary objectives can present challenges for PhD candidates (Hancock et al. 2015; Mars et al. 2014). This is little wonder given the polarising tendency in the debate regarding the role and purpose of the PhD. As Cuthbert and Molla argue:

> The policy discourse is also essentially silent on the importance of striking a balance between immediate economic significance of the doctoral qualification and its value as preparation for scholars. In the current debate about the PhD, there appears to be a tension between universities' traditional role of cultivating stewardship—preparing candidates to become scholars who discover, disseminate, and apply knowledge in their disciplines (Golde and Walker 2006), and new expectations for 'knowledge workers.' (2015: 48)

Organising the PhD around themes of care, such as ecological sustainability and social responsibility, offers one way of potentially striking such a balance.

Conclusion

I began this discussion with reference to contemporary challenges to the expertise, authority and independence of scholars, and in the context of PhD's, questions regarding the value of in-depth disciplinary knowledge. As this discussion has touched on, thinking care-fully is challenging and also carries risks for thought which highlight the limitations of knowledge. However, Noddings' account of care challenges us to develop a more expansive conception of the purpose of the PhD by reaching through and beyond the discipline to caring for others, things and ideas. In some ways this is nothing new, evoking as it does the ancient conception of philosophy as the love of wisdom. But Noddings also provides a more contemporary imperative: the need to make the world a better place. Anthropocentric climate change has consequences for life on earth that eclipse disciplinary boundaries. This doesn't render disciplinary knowledge and practice obsolete but it does suggest a need to question what is served by disciplines and educational programs. The notion of care-fully oriented thought highlights the need to direct thinking toward a more just and caring world. Given the context of contemporary challenges to universities, re-thinking the value of the PhD in these terms offers a fruitful way forward.

References

Aitchison, C., Kamler, B., & Lee, A. (Eds.). (2010). *Publishing pedagogies for the doctorate and beyond*. London: Routledge.

Barnett, R. (2004). Learning for an unknown future. *Higher Education Research and Development, 23*(3), 247–260.

Barnett, R. (2000). University knowledge in an age of supercomplexity. *Higher Education, 40*, 409. https://doi.org/10.1023/A:1004159513741.

Barker, M. (2015). Irreproducible research costs put at $28 billion per year. *Nature*. https://doi.org/10.1038/nature.2015.17711.

Barnacle, R., & Dall'Alba, G. (2017). Committed to learn: Student engagement and care in higher education. *Higher Education Research & Development, 36*, 1326. https://doi.org/10.1080/07294360.2017.1326879.

Barnacle, R., & Dall'Alba, G. (2013). Beyond skills: Embodying writerly practices through the doctorate. *Studies in Higher Education*. https://doi.org/10.1080/03075079.2013.777405.

Berger, J. (2016). *Confabulations*. London: Penguin.

Carol Gilligan (1982). *In a different voice*. Cambridge: Harvard University Press.

Clark, W. (2006). *Academic charisma and the origins of the research university*. Chicago: University of Chicago Press.

Cuthbert, D., & Molla, T. (2015). PhD crisis discourse: A critical approach to the framing of the problem and some Australian 'solutions'. *Higher Education, 69*(1), 33–53. https://doi.org/10.1007/s10734-014-9760-y.

Cyranoski, D., Gilbert, N., Ledford, H., Nayar, A., & Yahia, M. (2011). The PhD factory: The world isproducing more PhDs than ever before. Is it time to stop? *Nature, 472*, 276–279. https://doi.org/10.1038/472276a.

Dall'Alba, G. (2011). Re-imagining the university: Developing a capacity to care. In R. Barnett (Ed.), *The future university. Ideas and possibilities* (pp. 112–122). London/New York: Routledge.

Dall'Alba, G., & Barnacle, R. (2007). An ontological turn for higher education. *Studies in Higher Education*. https://doi.org/10.1080/03075070701685130.

Delamont, S., Atkinson, P., & Parry, O. (2004). *Supervising the doctorate. A guide to success*. Berkshire: The Open University Press.

Gadamer, H. G. (1988). *Truth and method* (2nd ed.). London: Sheed and Ward.

Golde, C. M., & Walker, G. E. (2006). *Envisioning the future of doctoral education: Preparing stewards of the discipline - Carnegie essays on the doctorate*. San Francisco: Wiley.

Grundmann, R. (2016). The problem of expertise in knowledge societies. *Minerva, 55*, 25. https://doi.org/10.1007/s11024-016-9308-7.

Hancock, S., Hughes, G., & Walsh, E. (2015). Purist or pragmatist? UK doctoral scientists' moral positions on the knowledge economy. *Studies in Higher Education, 42*, 1244. https://doi.org/10.1080/03075079.2015.1087994.

Haraway, D. (2007). *When species meet*. Minneapolis: University of Minnesota Press.

Heidegger, M. (1927/1962). Being and Time (trans: J. Macquarrie and E. Robinson). New York: SCM Press.

Heidegger, M. (1968). *What is called thinking?* (trans: T.F.D. Wieck and J.G. Gray). New York: Harper Row.

Kamler, B., & Thomson, P. (2014). *Helping doctoral students write: Pedagogies for supervision*. Abingdon: Routledge.

Kelly, F. J. (2017). *The idea of the PhD: the doctorate in the twenty-first-century imagination*. Abingdon: Routledge.

Kelly, F. J. (2012). Seekers after truth? Images of postgraduate research and researchers in the twenty-first century. *Discourse: Studies in the Cultural Politics of Education, 33*(4), 517–528. https://doi.org/10.1080/01596306.2012.692959.

Lee, A. (2012). *Successful research supervision. Advising students doing research*. London/New York: Routledge.

Lynch, K. (2010). Carelessness: A hidden doxa of higher education. *Arts and Humanities in Higher Education, 9*(1), 54–67. https://doi.org/10.1177/1474022209350104.

Macfarlane, B. (2017). *Freedom to learn*. Abingdon: Routledge.

Macfarlane, B. (2015). Student performativity in higher education: Converting learning as a private space into a public performance. *Higher Education Research & Development, 34*(2), 338–350. https://doi.org/10.1080/07294360.2014.956697.

Maldonado, V., Wiggers, R., & Arnold, C. (2013). *So you want to earn a PhD? The attraction, realities, and outcomes of pursuing a doctorate*. Toronto: Higher Education Quality Council of Ontario.

Mars, M. M., Bresonis, K., & Szelényi, K. (2014). Science and engineering doctoral student socialization, logics, and the National Economic Agenda: Alignment or disconnect? *Minerva, 52*(3), 351–379.

Mowbray, S., & Halse, C. (2010). The purpose of the PhD: Theorising the skills acquired by students. *Higher Education Research & Development, 29*, 653–664. https://doi.org/10.1080/07294360.2010.487199.

Nerad, M. (2009). Confronting common assumptions: Designing future-oriented doctoral education. In R. G. Ehrenberg & C. V. Kuh (Eds.), *Doctoral education and the faculty of the future* (pp. 80–89). Ithaca: Cornell University Press.

Noddings, N. (2009). All our students thinking. In M. Scherer (Ed.), *Engaging the whole child: Reflections on best practices in learning, teaching and leadership*. ASCD: Virginia.

Noddings, N. (2005). *The challenge to care in schools: An alternative approach to education* (2nd ed.). New York: Teachers College Press.

Noddings, N. (2001). Care and coercion in school reform. *Journal of Educational Change, 2*, 35. https://doi.org/10.1023/A:1011514928048.

Noveck, B. S. (2016). Enough of experts? Data, democracy and the future of expertise. *Published: November, 28*, 2016. http://www.socialsciencespace.com/2016/11/enough-experts-data-democracy-future-expertise/.

Nussbaum, M. (2006). Education and democratic citizenship: Capabilities and quality education. *Journal of Human Development, 7*, 385–395. https://doi.org/10.1080/14649880600815974.

Watson, D. (2005). Watson's dictionary of weasel words, contemporary cliches, cant & management jargon. Random House Australia.

Wisker, G. (2012). *The good supervisor*. New York: Palgrave Macmillan.

Chapter 7
Citizenship and the *Thinking* University: Toward the Citizen Scholar

James Arvanitakis and David J. Hornsby

Introduction

As academics, teachers, researchers and lecturers, we work inside institutions whose twin goals sit comfortably together: knowledge production and knowledge translation. That is, we not only produce knowledge, but ensure we can communicate it to both our student body and the communities we interact with (be they local, regional, national or global). Translation does not stop there, however, it includes how our research can be applied and by who. The production and translation requires a specific type of labour – the labour of thought.

Despite this, we should be wary to draw simple and straightforward conclusions about our labour and thinking. This is why the editors of this volume have set an interesting task: to consider what constitutes a '*thinking* university'. Such a question maintains conceptual and normative dimensions that necessitate a re-imagination of what a university should look like and how *thought* is treated in this arena.

As such, this question at first glance seems odd – are universities not naturally spaces where thought results in the production or mobilisation of knowledge?

It is here that this chapter makes its contribution: how we can produce and transmit knowledge that is transformational to both the students we encounter and the communities we engage with. Our argument is that the role of the contemporary university is not only to produce and transmit knowledge – which we broadly define

J. Arvanitakis (✉)
Western Sydney University, Sydney, NSW, Australia
e-mail: J.Arvanitakis@westernsydney.edu.au

D. J. Hornsby
University College London, London, United Kingdom
e-mail: d.hornsby@ucl.ac.uk

© Springer International Publishing AG, part of Springer Nature 2018
S.S.E. Bengtsen, R. Barnett (eds.), *The Thinking University*,
Debating Higher Education: Philosophical Perspectives 1,
https://doi.org/10.1007/978-3-319-77667-5_7

as scholarship – but to empower those we engage with to promote active citizenship. Combing the philosophical postulation of Martin Heidegger's (1927) 'threshold' and Paulo Freire's (1972) liberation pedagogy, our position is that we can create an environment that our students discover their own agency (or empowerment) and the tools to employ it – or citizenship. As such, the aim of the thinking university should be the promotion of the citizen scholar (Arvanitakis and Hornsby 2016).

Such an approach is fundamental because, regardless of context, the utility and benefit of the university is being questioned and institutions of higher education are struggling to demonstrate their continued relevance as centres for thinking. In part this stems from changes to how higher education is considered: neo-liberal logics, debates over the private and public benefits of higher education (*The Economist* 2012), massification and credentialism have all had significant impacts on the form and practice of universities. For example, rapid changes in tuition, enrolment (TES 2017), diversity of student populations, and medium of instruction have changed how universities act and relate to society (Christensen et al. 2001). But universities are also struggling to keep up with the pace of change in information and knowledge. The advent of the internet and its proliferation as a site for information has raised fundamental questions as to how degree programs position universities as central to thought and prepare students to be *thinking*.

In a context where disciplinary relevant information is produced and disseminated outside of university spaces, an uncomfortable reality comes to bare – universities are no longer the keepers and producers of knowledge and information that then get transferred to students. Disciplines are no longer the primary sites where thought occurs and is disseminated, and disciplinary focused approaches to teaching, disconnected from societal problems, are viewed as less and less relevant as information changes so rapidly and complexity is the new norm. Further, it appears that university education as a pathway to employment is no longer as clearly linked as it may have been in the past (Ortlieb 2015).

The context and space in which thinking occurs has changed. But does this mean that universities as sites of thought are redundant? We consider that university education still maintains a space in this changing environment. And emphasising thinking is a key way to reinforce relevance of institutions of higher education to society. That said, the way in which *thinking* is defined in university spaces needs to be modified and reformed.

We most frequently consider thinking to be about providing the space and time to reason and reflect. Rarely is thinking framed as a skill that universities inculcate in individuals and contribute to society. As ten Dam and Volman (2004 p. 32) argue, thinking, in particular critical thinking, is a crucial competency that citizens need to participate in society:

"Learning to think critically is conceptualized as the acquisition of the competence to participate critically in the communities and social practices of which a person is a member."

Thus, thought – in particular the capacity to engage in critical thought – is a desired competency that individuals need in order to contribute and participate in society. Critical thought is defined here as the

"independence of thought, fairness, insight into the personal and public level, humble intellect, spiritual courage, integrity, perseverance, self-confidence, research interest considerations not only behind the feelings and emotions but also behind the thoughts and curiosity"
(Paul 1995).

By framing thought as central to community engagement and societal participation, we propose that a *thinking university* is in fact one that places citizenship at its
core. Indeed, community engagement and societal participation are important civic
virtues (Honohan 2002, p.145). It seems logical that a *thinking university* is also a
space where attributes and proficiencies that enable societal participation and foster
good citizenship are inculcated alongside the traditional university mission of disciplinary thinking.

Accepting that rapid change in information and knowledge is the new norm,
focusing solely on the transfer of disciplinary knowledge at university does not
prepare graduates well to be thoughtful and engaged citizens once they leave.
Disciplinary information and knowledge changes, but students armed with only disciplinary content, do not. In order to prepare students for this context, universities
need to foster thinking graduates capable of adapting, deciphering, and analysing
changing information and knowledge towards societal betterment. This is not to
suggest that disciplinary thinking is irrelevant – on the contrary – it is important, but
it needs to be contextualised and enhanced through a set of attributes and proficiencies that frame universities as sites where *thinking* towards societal betterment and
citizenship are central.

To this end, we argue that if universities wish to be *of and for thought* it is necessary to appreciate that a *thinking* university is also a space that places fostering good
citizenship at its core. A thinking university creates thinking citizens and scholars
not only through its curriculum, but in the way this curriculum is delivered as well
as in the way both the institution and its educators act. In other words, academics
must be what they expect of their students.

In moving forward, this builds on our argument that the aim of a thinking university must be to create 'citizen scholars'. To this end, this chapter is constituted by
three sections: firstly, we draw on Freire's pedagogy of the oppressed and Heidegger's
concept of the *threshold* to describe how the university creates the thinking graduate; second, we elaborate on the relationship between citizenship and education; and
finally, we offer a way forward in bringing the idea of thoughtful graduates to frui-
tion by examining/advancing/pressing the concept of the citizen scholar.

Crossing the Threshold for Thought

As educators, a fundamental challenge is to work with our students towards thinking as transformation. That is, create an environment whereby educational engagement with our students is not simply about transmitting knowledge, but challenges
their preconceived concept and transforms the way they understand the world
around them. To achieve this, we work to create conditions of belonging and

support in our classrooms that release the creative and critical thinking energies of our students. This means that as educators, we are not satisfied with scholarship alone – which remains at the core of the university – but also promoting citizenship: that is, empowering them to transform their own lives and reshape society.

Lecturers aim to do this in many different ways: from the way classes are structured to the assessment criteria set. The pedagogical environment and tools available to us – from assessment to curriculum – are used with a specific end in mind: to take our students on a journey of discovery. Expanding on our argument in the above paragraph, this journey can be multidimensional: promoting disciplinary knowledge, critical thinking, civic engagement, social betterment and personal transformation. While different curricula may prioritise these goals differently, they are not mutually exclusive.

To theorise this, we draw on the ideas of Brazilian critical educator Paulo Freire (1972) and German philosopher Martin Heidegger (1927). It may appear that the work of Freire (who dealt with illiterate Brazilian peasants in the 1940s) and Heidegger are dramatically removed from the challenges we face in the twenty-first century classroom, but their work remains both relevant and insightful even decades later. Despite any perceived distance, both theorists raise important issues around student engagement, critical thinking and, central for our argument here, transformation.

To begin with, Freire focused on both skills development and consciousness-raising, two aspects that he saw as complementary in achieving individual empowerment. Importantly, and a key reason why Freire's work continues to resonate, is that he argued that any 'engagement' must be two-way: that is, rather than taking a 'deficit' approach towards our students and treating them as passive containers to be filled by the knowledge of the educator, any classroom engagement is one that also informs and potentially transforms the 'teacher'. That is, lecturers or those tasked with constructing the learning environment can learn from the experience, insights and knowledge of our students. For example, the young Aboriginal student who may have suffered discrimination and exclusion may not be armed with Edward Said's (1979) insights captured in *Orientalism,* but has a lived experience both the teachers and other students can all learn from.

Freire (1972, p. 69) argued this by beginning with the world of his students as they understood it: this was their 'thematic universe'. This is the starting point for a 'thinking' journey: allowing us as educators to reflect on the experiences of both the students and communities we engage with, as well as creating an environment to safely share that knowledge, exchange our ideas and move beyond our everyday experiences to create what C Wright Mills (1959) called for when describing the 'sociological imagination'. That is, thinking critically about societal issues in different ways by removing biases, approaching them from different perspectives and making links between personal troubles and public issues. This can be achieved by creating an education environment whereby the 'thinking' of both ourselves and our students to be informed but not constrained by past experiences.

We can think of this occurring through 'concentric circles' (Hodge 2014). That is, we start from particular to general, move from local to global – undertaking a journey that all parties involved took together. The journey is likely to be very different for the educator and the students, but they take this together. But at the core or centre of these concentric circles is *learning by thinking.*

For example, in focusing on the experiences of racism and stereotypes, students can be encouraged to reflect on understanding how others perceive them based on their own physical characteristics: skin colour, eye shape, hair and so on. What starts as a broad and theoretical discussion on the subject of race and racism, moves to the local by discussing contemporary and localised examples, to the very personal as students are asked to reflect on the following question: what stereotypes do people perceive about you and how many are true?

As educators, we are inspired by the work of Paulo Freire which has two complimentary aspects: skills development and critical consciousness-raising. The development of skills or proficiencies is something that we outline below but this is at the core of our own work in developing the idea of the citizen scholar (Arvanitakis and Hornsby 2016).

The second part of Freire's equation is 'critical consciousness-raising'. Here Freire argued it was important that as educators we not only pass on the disciplinary knowledge, but also ensure those we work with develop the ability to perceive social, political, and economic oppression and to take action against the oppressive elements of society. These are twin aims that take our students through the concentric circles described above: understanding the global, the impacts on the local and how they can respond personally and by working together. This linking between global and the personal provides insights that allows students to cross into an educational 'threshold' whereby they can never look back.

To do this, we draw on Martin Heidegger's (1927) phenomenological concept of the 'threshold'. While this concept of 'threshold' represents a relative small fraction of Heidegger's work, it is both powerful and significant. What Heidegger is identifying here are the moments of change when we realise something about the world around us that moves us from ignorance to a state of reflection. It is that moment we encounter the world with fresh eyes. This moves us beyond a sense of wonder, to understanding, being inquisitive, willing to question, and possibly challenge established power relations. This learning 'journey' is undertaken together by both educator and students. For Heidegger, artists created the threshold moment. At universities, it is the educators: lecturers, teachers, tutors. This is because the changes we are attempting to promote through education are not simply 'acts' of teaching, but the culture and consciousness of thinking and learning: this is the act of learning by thinking at the core of the concentric journey.

This is relevant for education engagement because we, as both individuals and educators, are interested in deep change: that is, to change the way our students see the world and be in the world. By giving them insights into the world and encouraging them cross the threshold, through self-discovery and a sense of citizenship. The proficiencies we work towards enhancing in the classroom is only one step, the other is working towards *cultural change*: that is, how the students see themselves and their place in the world. To achieve this, we aim to ensure our students are both engaged and empowered in their life journeys.

Drawing on both our own interpretations as well as Freire's, we begin with the concept of humans *being* in the world: our 'being' and 'world' must always be thought of together and cannot be separated (Hayes et al. 2010, p. 517). The way we humans relate to this being in the world varies significantly, however: we may feel at home, indifferent, empowered or even alienated.

The challenge that we must confront, both as researchers and educators, is: can this sense of being be influenced by some kind of transformation through education? When discussing the concept of the threshold, Heidegger argues transformation can occur when we transcend the ordinary and every day, and venture into an unfamiliar domain – something which requires us to reflect *and* think. This is a moment that is both transitory and transformational.

It is here that the concept and metaphor of 'the threshold' can inform our practices as educators. The threshold is the place of passage supporting this transformation between the radically different and the familiarity of our everyday lives. For example, in teaching students in the outer western suburbs of Sydney and in South Africa (where the authors have spent much of their time teaching), we interrogate the way that economic structures are seen to influence their lives. Many of these students have low socio-economic status backgrounds and a vast majority in both contexts are 'first in family' to attend university. In initial discussions, many of the students argue that there are no systemic limitations to prevent them from achieving economic success. By journeying with them through looking at where economic capital sits and how political elites are selected, they gain insights into the class structures that shape modern and emerging capitalist societies. Combined with other such insights, the students cross a threshold by coming to understand the hierarchies they have experienced but all too often ignored. The threshold both defines and sustains the uniting difference between two domains: between the familiar everyday experience that is common up to this point, and where the purely sensible and obvious are transcended. The threshold establishes an 'in-between region'; a meeting place of different domains of understanding: the before and the after.

Our challenge is to achieve this through our teaching: to work with our students to create moments of reflecting and thinking that sees them move from their everyday experiences and cross a threshold. For Heidegger, it was the role of the artists to create such an environment: be it the poet, musician or painter. They have the ability to take us out of the everyday through their work to create moments that disorientate – forcing us to think and reflect on our being in the world. As educators, we have the same potential.

This moment of disorientation forces both us as educators and our students, to enter into two simultaneous domains of thinking: seeing and relating to the everyday while also perceiving the *potential* for social change. This is a transitionary thinking because it does not disconnect us from every day calculative and objective thought, but nevertheless ruptures the habitual and addresses its limits. As highlighted in the above examples relating to both class structures and stereotypes, the constrained logic of everyday familiarity is ruptured.

Freire and Heidegger's thinking around 'thresholds' and changes in 'consciousness' come from different theoretical traditions, but we have found this difference gives them importance. We have applied these approaches to our educational programs that not only promote a sense of agency amongst our students but also attempts to achieve this by facilitating them to see the world in a different manner: a world where they have potential to reflect, think, make change and have agency. That is, to cross a Heideggerean threshold and see their own potential in changing the world.

This we aim to achieve within a Freirean approach that promotes practical skills and strategies as outlined in the proficiency clusters outlined below. This is done while simultaneously unpacking the structural challenges confronting our contemporary society – be they economic, social (such as racism) or cultural – as well as providing the tools to build the agency in which citizenship thrives upon. That is, we create an environment that encourages our students to cross the threshold. While they may only cross this line for a short period, Heidegger argues that even if they cross back, they are forever transformed.

The transformation that is sought in pedagogical approaches is one where students take a journey along a pathway of promoting the citizen scholar. It is this journey that we turn to next.

Contextualising Citizenship with Education

When discussing citizenship within the education context it is often understood within the frame of 'civics'. Civics is meant to focus on education as a kind of student 'self-government': that is, promoting the ability for students to be actively involved in their own governance, challenging what they are taught and confronting power structures. This more radical approach to pedagogy is at the forefront of the work of cultural theorist Henry Giroux (1981) – who also draws heavily on Paolo Freire when formulating his arguments. Such an approach is meant, ideally, to be embedded across the curriculum encouraging students to both critically reflect on the education institution which they are attending – be it secondary or higher education – and even challenge it as part of their educational journey.

All too often, however, civics is reduced to an individual subject that is taught 'in addition' to the main curriculum. This means that the students simply see it as something that is 'added onto' their curriculum and secondary to key disciplinary subjects. In this way, civics is seen as something that is separate from the core disciplinary knowledge that they are learning in their journey. The consequences are both an under-developed pedagogical environment, low educator engagement and poor student response.

This has been the case in the Australian context where both federal and state governments have spent many millions of dollars attempting to teach civics and citizenship – with most attempts clearly failing. While recognising that civics education is an integral part of a 'healthy' democracy, providing for citizens who are knowledgeable and keen to participate (Joint Standing Committee on Electoral

Matters 2007), the implementation into the curriculum has been poor and the response from students likewise.

At a secondary school level, for example, the federal government spent AUD$31 million between 1997 and 2004 to implement a national civics and citizenship education program (Department of Education, Science and Training 2007). Realised through the Discovering Democracy program, one of the key objectives was to create "active citizens" able to "discharge the formal obligations of citizenship [and] make an informed judgement about the extent of their civic engagement" (Civics Expert Group 1997: 6). While 'citizenship' entails both rights and responsibilities, the curriculum support materials issued to all schools in Australia promote the former over the obligations that young people have, leading to a narrow and individualistic presentation of the concept of citizenship. This individualism is further entrenched as the responsibilities are framed in terms of economic achievement than in broader social context.

Furthermore, this was neither taught as a stand-alone subject not appropriately embedded within the curriculum. Incorporated into the existing syllabi with History at the secondary level, civics competed for space in an already crowded curriculum. This reflects one of the key failings of the federal government when attempting to reinvigorate civics education: it was believed that if young people were simply taught about the nature of citizenship in Australia, then somehow the connections between participation and change would be apparent to them. The 2004 national testing of students demonstrates otherwise: 92 percent of Year 6 students and 60 percent of Year 10 students failed to acquire the minimum proficiency levels required (MCTEEYA 2004). While the study of Citizenship and Education in Twenty-Eight Countries (Torney-Purta and Schwille 2001) showed that ninety-one percent of Australian teachers surveyed believed that civic education is of tremendous importance to our nation (Mellor et al. 2001), teachers did not feel competent or confident to teach many of the concepts, and current curriculum structure is not conducive to integrating alternative forms of knowledge (Mellor 2008).

This is not unique to the Australian context. Within the United States, similar challenges are emerging. The National Centre for Education Statistics in Washington reports that only 27 percent of final year secondary-year students were proficient in civics and government in 2006 (NCES 2015). The Centre identified a growing "civic achievement gap" between white, wealthy, native-born youths who consistently outperform and poorer, non-white and immigrant young people (NCES 2015). This exasperates established political disadvantage. Results released in 2015 looking at trends in 2010 and 2014 found "no significant change" (NCES 2015).

The response has been both predictable and unfortunate. In 2015 it was reported that a number of States in the US would be requiring high school students to pass a civics test in order to receive their diploma. The article quoted Professor Brian Dille, from the political science department at Mesa Community College (United States) who noted that while there was a high burden placed on the educators and school system, it remained unfunded, noting that, "because it's a requirement and a burden, it's going to be done poorly (Bowling 2015)."

If we turn our attention to university level education, we can see a dispute over the way that civics is also approached within the United States. The conservative think tank, the National Association of Scholars (NAS) released a report arguing for a 'return' to the traditional approach to civics education within higher education institutes: that is, a focus on understanding the civic institutions and structures, as rather than the current approach which they argue have been overrun by the progressive politics (NAS 2017). The current approach criticised by the NAS puts students through service learning – a process that encourages students to be actively engaged with community organisations to operationalise their learning objectives.

While the NAS report has a very clear conservative political and educational agenda, it is worth considering the key criticisms they put forward: that service learning and other such experiences need to be better embedded within the curriculum and more clearly articulated. As the service learning currently sits, there is an assumption that students will simply draw the desired conclusions together (Smith et al. 2013).

In the Australian context, a focus on disciplinary outcomes and ensuring students are work ready leave little room for civics. It is an often-neglected area of education and certainly not integrated into the curriculum. Liberal arts departments, where civics traditionally resides, are increasingly under financial pressure. As such, an ongoing fear is that civics as a concept of inquiry, at once challenging and questioning, which we would argue should be at the very core of a university education, is under threat.

Citizenship and the *Thinking* University: Toward the Citizen Scholar

Any university that wishes to be of and for thought needs to consider how teaching and learning is fostered. Based on the considerations of Heidegger and Freire discussed above, we contend that it is necessary for a *thinking* university to develop curricula and pedagogical stances that challenge students to apply their knowledge, to innovate, and makes them aware and interested in understanding and changing the societal structure in which they live. Universities need to create space to inculcate skills and cultural practices that pushes students to think beyond their disciplinary knowledge, enabling them to address societal problems and needs; they need to foster citizen scholars (Arvanitakis and Hornsby 2016).

The citizen scholar encapsulates the idea that the role of universities is both to promote scholarship as well as active and engaged citizens who think about the society around them (Arvanitakis and Hornsby 2016). Citizen scholars aim to live an ethical and fulfilled life, continue in the pursuit of knowledge, and are prepared to question the status quo, and engage with the community. They treat information and knowledge critically and aim to improve society. In short, they think.

By maintaining curricula or teaching that narrowly focuses on the content of disciplines, universities only enhance disciplinary knowledge and reinforce disciplinary boundaries. This narrows thinking as opposed to inculcating an understanding across disciplines and the importance of gaining not only knowledge but also cultivating wisdom.[1] By advocating learning environments that place at their core particular proficiencies and attributes that the learning environment is meant to foster, it is suggested that the place of thinking in higher education can be renewed and reinvigorated.

To do this we suggest a pedagogical stance that moves us towards a practice of developing graduate attributes and proficiencies, in addition to disciplinary knowledge.

We have identified a number of proficiencies and attributes inherent in the citizen scholar, which are proposed to be essential in establishing the *thinking* university. For conceptual clarity, these are separated into four 'Proficiency Clusters' with underlying or relevant attributes.

Proficiency Cluster 1: Creativity and Innovation

Any *thinking* university should hold creativity and innovation as central, but this is not always the case in practice according to recent research (Kim 2011). This cluster is integral to generating new and unique ideas and ways of doing things. It is readily accepted that creativity and innovation are required for research but they should also be held paramount in learning environments. Indeed, focusing on fostering creative and innovative thinking in the classroom results in a learning space that enables all involved to contribute different, interesting, and unexpected ideas.

Under such a proficiency cluster, six specific attributes are immediately apparent. The first, critical thinking, is often defined as clear and reasoned thinking, "independence of thought, fairness, insight into the personal and public level, humble intellect, spiritual courage, integrity, perseverance, self-confidence, research interest considerations not only behind the feelings and emotions but also behind the thoughts and curiosity" (Paul 1995). This concept also includes challenging perceptions and conceptions through the application of novel or different ideas. The second is problem-solving, where students develop an orientation towards finding solutions to problems through innovative thinking. The third is reflection, here student reflects on the information provided and considers alternative ways to address it. Fourth is entrepreneurship where students find ways to innovate and be creative, taking new ideas and turning them into actions. Fifth is process-driven, where students learn to focus on the process associated with a problem as a means to consider ways of solving it rather than purely on the content of the problem. Finally systems

---

[1] By cultivating wisdom, we refer here to the process of gaining experience, knowledge and good judgement.

thinking, when students think about how different elements influence each other or are related by breaking down component parts of a system.

Proficiency Cluster 2: Resilience

Resilience is an important factor in student success at university (McIntosh and Shaw 2017). Here we mean resilience in the sense of a capacity of students to adapt, be nimble and flexible to change, adopt and even anticipate innovations, maintain a real capacity to learn from mistakes and to persevere. Indeed, learning is at its most pure when we make mistakes. We often do not recognize resilience as a necessary attribute for graduates, but it is important to foster particularly in the process of social change. Sometime ideas work, and others do not, but we do not want our students or graduates to become discouraged. But, like other attributes, we argue that resilience can be acquired through practice. Two attributes are suggested to be relevant here: first is adaptability, when a student is nimble and flexible, capable of anticipating change and innovation, and also of adapting; the second is perseverance or what can also be referred to as mistakability, where mistakes and errors are treated as part of the learning process and students are encouraged to learn from these moments, as opposed to necessarily being penalised.

Proficiency Cluster 3: Working across Teams and across Experiences

Teamwork is another important proficiency for a *thinking* university and is a normal activity in today's world. That said, teamwork is often eschewed in university environments which privilege learning as an individualistic endeavour. However, teamwork is important to thinking, innovation and the advancement of ideas. Indeed, the notion that ideas are generated in a vacuum seems almost preposterous, yet in higher education environments we remain rooted in an individualistic approach to learning, often penalising students who collaborate with each other. We need to break this mould and recognize that by encouraging students to work together, we are assisting them in developing an important attribute associated with thinking, innovation, and knowledge creation. We need to create a culture where individual and collective success are synonymous.

Equally important is the need to recognise and accommodate the growing interconnectedness of our societies. The massification of education has brought with it increasing access to groups previously excluded from higher education (Hornsby and Osman 2014; Arvanitakis 2014). Additionally, our classrooms are becoming inherently more international with students from abroad or exchange programs becoming more commonplace. This means that our learning environments need to be more attuned to fostering students' ability to work across diverse experiences because the demographic make-up of universities is dramatically different from ten or even five years ago. To this end five specific attributes appear immediately relevant here. The first is interdisciplinarity which means an ability to work across disciplines in pursuit of more holistic problem-solving. The second attribute is cross-cultural understanding where the ability to appreciate that different cultures bring different ideas and thinking is considered integral to advancing understanding. Third is developing new literacies, which implies not just advanced reading, writing and advocacy skills, but understanding literacy within the new and changing technological environment. The fourth is internationalisation which is considered to be the ability to work in different cultural contexts. The fifth and final attribute in this cluster is inclusivity, which recognises that societies are diverse and with this comes different ways of thinking that can be important in innovation.

Proficiency Cluster 4: Design Thinking

Design thinking ultimately places people at the centre of our decision-making. Those adopting this approach emphasize accounting for people's needs and desires as well as the relationships around them when solving problems. Inherent in design thinking is the need for aesthetics: that is, a pleasing environment. The desire for beauty and refinement is part and parcel of our working and social lives. Just think of the last time we purchased something that was functional but ugly: from mobile phones to cars, from our work environments to our homes, aesthetics plays a role.

Ethical leadership is also an important element in design thinking which espouses an ethos of relationships across individuals rather than a hierarchy between employers and employees. Indeed, the way educators treat students is indicative of leadership, and it is important to remove the hierarchical pedagogies of the past and make way for a more symbiotic relationship between members of university communities. The relationship between lecturers and students can no longer being limited and unidirectional but, rather a dynamic exchange where each bring their own experiences to bear on the information. There are a number of pedagogical approaches that can be used to achieve this aspiration. Enquiry-based learning (EBL) is an approach that would fit well here (for more information on EBL see: Summerlee and Murray 2010). Here, three specific attributes appear most relevant. First, placing people and their needs must be at the centre of work. Thus, people-centred thinking is an important attribute to foster. The second is aesthetics where the importance of functionality and beauty are appreciated (Satell 2014). The third attribute under this cluster is ethical leadership. This requires building a frame of reference in which to reflect on moral and confronting challenges and understanding that leadership is a process not a hierarchy.

The four proficiencies presented here with their underlying attributes are meant to enhance the role of thought in university spaces. No longer can we simply provide students with disciplinary knowledge. Rapid change to knowledge and increased flow of information means that disciplinary content is evolving faster than it ever used too, and in ways over which universities have little control. As such, if we wish to ensure that universities continue to remain of and for thought, we need to shift and give consideration to how to ensure thinking is fostered. The proficiencies and attributes considered here are by no means meant to be an exhaustive list, but rather are presented to provide indications from which to stimulate thinking around what a *thinking* university might prioritise as the place and space for thought.

Conclusion

Our chapter has sought explicitly to link the teaching and learning space to the notion of a *thinking* university. We explored the relationship between citizenship and education and advanced the idea of the citizen scholar as a key mechanism through which to organise and provide space for thinking to take place. The citizen scholar concept takes both academics and students across a threshold – ultimately with the aim of ensuring universities and students are prepared for the needs of tomorrow and inherently oriented to improving society.

In effect, the argument advanced in this chapter is about promoting thinking as a way of developing citizenship at the core of university education. Whilst the suggestion that a *thinking* university should give more attention to citizenship rather than just disciplinary content, may seem radical, it is based in a number of realities. First, universities are no longer as central in knowledge production or transference as they once were, so they need to adapt and consider what is that they might contribute to society. Second, knowledge changes so quickly that the capacity to adapt to evolving knowledges and understandings requires that we treat thinking and different approaches to thinking as qualities and/or dispositions. Third, society has changed in a way that we need citizens able to think broadly and deeply and who are not confined to one disciplinary perspective.

Indeed, a *thinking university* is a space where attributes and proficiencies that enable societal participation and promote good citizenship are inculcated alongside disciplinary thinking. A *thinking* university is a place where fostering citizen scholars is at its core.

References

Arvanitakis, J. (2014). Massification and the large lecture theatre: from panic to excitement. *Higher Education, 67*, 735–745.

Arvanitakis, J., & Hornsby, D. J. (2016). Are Universities Redundant? In J. Arvanitakis & D. J. Hornsby (Eds.), *Universities, citizen scholars, and the future of higher education*. Palgrave MacMillan Publishers: Critical University Studies Series.

Bowling, J. (2015). High school students now required to pass civics test. Mesa Legend 02/02/2015. Available from: http://mesalegend.com/high-school-students-now-required-pass-civics-test/ [Accessed 18 Nov 2017].

Christensen, C. M., Aaron, S., & Clark, W. (2001). Disruption in education. *The internet and the university: Forum 2001*. Educause. Available at https://net.educause.edu/ir/library/pdf/ffpiu013.pdf [Accessed 23 July 2015].

Civics Expert Group. (1997). *Whereas the people: civics and citizenship education. Report of the civics expert group*. Canberra: AGPS.

Department of Education, Science and Training (DEST). (2007). *School education: Civics and citizenship education for the future. national civics and citizenship education forum report*. Canberra: DEST.

Freire, P. (1972). *Pedagogy of the oppressed*. Harmondsworth: Penguin.

Giroux, H. A. (1981). *Ideology, culture and the process of schooling*. Philadelphia: Temple University Press.

Hayes, M., Watson, F., Oviawe, J., & Saul, M. (2010). The citizen of empire. *Citizenship Studies, 14*(5), 511–525.

Heidegger, M. (1927). *Being and time, trans. J Macquarrie & E Robinson* (p. 1967). New York: Harper & Row.

Hodge, B. (2014). *Teaching as communication*. New York: Routledge.

Honohan, I. (2002). *Civic republicanism*. London: Routledge.

Hornsby, D. J., & Osman, R. (2014). Massification in higher education: Large classes and student learning. *Higher Education., 67*(6), 711–719.

Joint Standing Committee on Electoral Matters. (2007). *Civics and electoral education*. Canberra: AGPS.

Kim, K. H. (2011). The creativity crisis: The decrease in creative thinking scores on the torrance test of creative thinking. *Creativity Research Journal, 23*(4), 285–295. Available at http://innovators-guide.ch/wp-content/uploads/2012/12/Kim_Creativity-Crisis.pdf [Accessed 23 July 2015].

MCEETYA - Ministerial Council on Education, Employment, Training and Youth Affairs. (2004). *National report on schooling in Australia*. Available from: http://www.mceetya.edu.au/mceetya/anr2004/index.htm [Accessed 18 Nov 2017].

McIntosh, E., & Shaw, J. (2017). Student resilience: Exploring the positive case for resilience. Student Unite. Accessed from: http://www.unite-group.co.uk/sites/default/files/2017-05/student-resilience.pdf [16 Nov 2017].

Mellor, S. (2008). *The national assessment program – Civics and citizenship: Reflections on practices in primary and secondary schools*. Conference proceedings, Australian Council for Educational Research (ACER). Available from: http://www.acer.edu.au/documents/RC2008_ConfProceedings.pdf [Accessed 18 2017].

Mellor, S., Kennedy, K., & Greenwood, L. (2001). *Citizenship and democracy. Student's knowledge and beliefs: Australian 14 year olds and the civic education study*. Canberra: ACER.

Mills, C. W. (1959). *The sociological imagination*. London: Oxford University Press.

National Association of Scholars. (2017). *Making citizens: How American universities teach civics*. Available from: https://www.nas.org/projects/making_citizens_report [Accessed 18 Nov 2017].

NCES (National Center for Education Statistics). (2015). The Nation's report card: Civics 20101. United States Department of Education. Available from: https://nces.ed.gov/nationsreportcard/pdf/main2010/2011466.pdf. Accessed 18 Nov 2017.

Ortlieb, E. (2015). Just graduating from university is no longer enough to get a job. *The Conversation. February, 11*, 2015. Available from: https://theconversation.com/just-graduating-from-university-is-no-longer-enough-to-get-a-job-36906 [Accessed 13 Nov 2017].

Paul, R. W. (1995). *Critical thinking: How prepare students for a rapidly changing world*. Santa Rosa: Foundation for Critical Thinking.

Said, E. (1979). *Orientalism*. London: Penguin.

Satell, G. (2014). Design is eating the world. *The creativity post* October 21, 2014. Available at http://www.creativitypost.com/technology/design_is_eating_the_world [Accessed 23 July 2015].

Smith, K. L., Meah, Y., Reininger, B., Farr, M., Zeidman, J., & Thomas, D. C. (2013). Integrating service learning into the curriculum: lessons from the field. *Med Teach, 35*(5), e1139–e1148.

Summerlee, A., & Murray, J. (2010). The impact of enquiry-based learning on academic performance and student engagement. *Canadian Journal of Higher Education, 40*, 78–94.

ten Dam, G., & Volman, M. (2004). Critical thinking as a citizenship competence: Teaching strategies. *Learning and Instruction, 14*(4), 359–379. Available from: https://eric.ed.gov/?id=EJ731629 [Accessed 13 Nov 2017].

TES. (2017). Number of pupils planning to go to university 'at lowest level in 8 years'. *TES August, 10*, 2017. Available from: https://uk.finance.yahoo.com/news/number-pupils-planning-university-lowest-230101124.html [Accessed 13 November 13, 2017].

The Economist. (2012) Not what it used to be: American universities represent declining value for money to their students. *The Economist*. December 12, 2012. Available from: https://www.economist.com/news/united-states/21567373-american-universities-represent-declining-value-money-their-students-not-what-it [Accessed 13 Nov 2017].

Torney-Purta, J., & Schwille, J. (2001). *Civic education across countries: 24 National case studies from the IEA civic education project*. Amsterdam: IEA.

Chapter 8
Bildung, Emotion and Thought

Thomas Karlsohn

Introduction

The way in which people relate emotionally to the university as an institution has gone through various historical phases. The era of radicalization from the mid-sixties and onwards was for example to a high degree characterized by notions of loss and alienation. This was the background against which students actively and publicly attacked the contemporary emotional state of academic institutions (see for instance Draper 1965). Subsequently the dominant position in many countries often became one of melancholy. Criticism assumed a more resigned, distanced tone; greater space was given to varieties of academic nostalgia (see, for instance, Gadamer 1988; Readings 1996; also Ylijoki 2005). During recent decades, the university has often been presented as an emotionally indifferent, even apathetic milieu, without any real ability to encompass and encourage human desire (cf. for instance Hörisch 2006; Hörisch 2009). Sometimes portrayals of the university's emotional inner life have also depicted an institution which is emotionally loaded but socially degenerate. Such pictures have been particularly common within the North American debates, in descriptions of conflicts surrounding *political correctness*, *free speech* and *conduct on campus*.

There are in university history innumerable testimonies to the warying ways of expressing and handling emotions within academic institutions. One could furnish multiple instances from different periods and geographical locations, and contunied empirical mapping of these testimonies is whithout doubt a necessary precondition for detailed analysis and an important research task in its own right. My own discussion below, however, follows a different path. In part one of the chapter, I begin by discussing —briefly, and in general terms—the importance of the fact that we

T. Karlsohn (✉)
Uppsala university, Uppsala, Sweden
e-mail: thomas.karlsohn@idehist.uu.se

© Springer International Publishing AG, part of Springer Nature 2018   103
S.S.E. Bengtsen, R. Barnett (eds.), *The Thinking University*,
Debating Higher Education: Philosophical Perspectives 1,
https://doi.org/10.1007/978-3-319-77667-5_8

academics have paid insufficient attention to the emotional aspects in our atempts to systematic reflection over the institution we inhabit. I believe that this inadequacy has negatively affected both our own self-conceptions and the public understanding of what we do, and I also believe it thereby has harmed the university's ability to be a genuinely thinking institution.

After briefly sketching the limitations of our own time's reflections on the university, I hope to make a constructive contribution. This is presented in parts two and three Here I return to the history of ideas and to a concept that played a decisive role during the establishment of the modern research university, which began in the German countries at the turn of the century 1800: *Bildung*, translated into English as cultivation, self-cultivation, formation, self-formation et cetera. The role of *Bildung* in relation to research and higher education has been debated ever since, and for many the concept retains its significance and attraction, even if it today has an increasingly insecure position both within internal academic self-reflection and in external debates.

My discussion of *Bildung* is grounded in the conviction that it is meaningful and necessary to return to the past in order to reactivate both conceptual means and historical experiences. Public discussion on science and higher education have, in most most countries—albeit to varying degrees—been characterized by ahistoricism and presentism. When researchers have turned to ideas from earlier epochs, they have to often detached them from their historical context. The concepts have sometimes been used as if they existed independently of all real-life situations. Clear examples of this line of reasoning are the references in our own time to Wilhelm von Humboldt and his ideas of the universality (exemples of uses and misuses are discussed in several of the contributions to Josephson et al. 2014).

The following account is marked by the conviction that if we are to draw historical lessons of enduring contemporary importance, they must be securely anchored in the multi-faceted realities of the past. My discussion will, therefore, present a rather detailed and wide-ranging account of the circumstances and intellectual preconditions that informed the period during which the concept of *Bildung* first entered the discussion of pedagogy and university policies. Here i draw on earlier scholarship on the the conceptual history of *Bildung* and of German university history around the turn of the century 1800. At the same time I also delve into primary sources—mainly programatic philosophical texts written by leading idealists and discussing education and the fate of the university—in search for content pertinent to our own time. By focusing on German idealism I deliberatly exclude other pertinent sources in French and English Enlightenment culture and among its crititics (obvious examples are Rousseau and Hume).

In my reactivating of the historical texts I first and foremost focus on the emotional dimension of *Bildung*. It is worth pointing out that this aspect of the concept has often been passed over in silence when *Bildung* is mobilized in today's debate. Rather, the concept usually has been associated with particular forms of personally based acquisition of knowledge and with the cultivation of generic intellectual abilities. Nonetheless, *Bildung* was originally marked by the inclusion of emotions as a medium for both individual and collective human development. This can be explained by examining how ideas concerning *Bildung* had connections to the religious sphere. Such connections affected both ideas concerning the individual learning subject, and ideas concerning the importance of *Bildung* for societal institutions. And, what is more: the individual and the institutional aspects invested in *Bildung* were eventually moved to a position of tension-filled opposition. I believe that this tension furnishes material for thought and for a deeper reflection on the fate of the university today.

The historical narrative in the chapter's parts two and three constitutes the bulk of the investigation. Part two focuses on the concept of *Bildung* in relation to the individual subject to be educated. Part three discusses the concept on the institutional level, in connection with the growth of the modern research university. In the fourth and final part of the text I briefly approach our own day and discuss how the historical account of the concept of *Bildung* can broaden our understanding of the role of emotions in academic life. I further believe that the concept, used in this way, can contribute to the development of the university as a genuinely thinking institution.

Before we continue it must be added that I abstain from any elaborated definition of the central concept of emotion. It is my conviction that such a procedure would ad little to my argument and direct the attention away from what I concider most important. By emotion i simply mean affective aspects of consciousness in general, and I use the word—well aware of the potential theoretical complexity—as synonymous with feeling, passion and so on.

Entrance: Absence in the Present

Despite the fact that emotions play a central role in the university's self-understanding and self-presentation, they have as mentioned been relatively invisible in researchers' efforts to understand the institution (for further reflections on this topic, see Karlsohn 2016a, b). This is probably to no small degree due to the fact that the modern research university during its entire existence has—with good reason—celebrated various ideals of objectivity and disinterestedness (cf. for instance, Merton 1973, Dear 1992; Ziman 2004). These ideals are usually presented as emotionally neutral, and this, in turn, has helped create the impression that academic life has no room for the existential concerns and desires of the subjectively experienced life-world. Such feelings have, so to say, been roped off, bleached out, and kept in place by institutional norms and codes of behavior. This situation has in turn led to academic emotions—also often with good reason—being rendered either wholly invisible or being canalized into well-regulated, discreet, temperate and socially encapsulated forms of expression.

The under-emphasis on emotions has also characterized both the literature on the history of the university and the various analyses within the social sciences and humanities of how academic institutions function today. To be sure, a number of studies with different directions of inquiry have been published (examples of this are Bellas 1999; Widdowfield 2000; Di Leo 2006; Beard et al. 2007; Ehn and

Löfgren 2007; Knouf 2010; Bloch 2012). Within the history of science, a field that lies close to university history, the role of emotion has gained increasing attention during recent decades (see the summary in Dror et al. 2016). But there remain—as is regularly mentioned by researchers in the area—a good number of tasks still to do if our understanding of the theme is to deepen. To summarize, the university as arena for human emotional life is palpably present when we talk or argue about the institution. At the same time, emotional life is often missing from the research we do on the institution and its past.

One effect of this deficit is the tendency of reflections on the actual conditions of the university's intellectual life to remain one-sided. Discussants have traditionally emphasized the cognitive side of the issue. The university has often been presented as bodiless, a purely cerebral establishment, or as a fortress of unemotional rationality, situated at a secure distance from the immediate every-day of complex, emotional realities. This situation has not only ensured insufficient internal self-reflection, it has also affected the university's external relations. One example from our own time is the hope, currently flourishing, that research and higher education through their pure objectivity and rationality will play a major role in reason's retaking of the public sphere, an arena at present dangerously beleaguered by *fake news* and irrational populism. According to this mode of thought, public opinion can only be led back onto the right path—and be guided, once more, along the road of modernization and progress, towards ever-brightening horizons—with the aid of infallible scientific methods and reliance on the persuasive power of results based solely on reason and logical arguments.

Such hopes are nourished both within and outside the university. They were openly expressed, in a contemporary example attracting much attention during Spring 2017, namely in the events taking place under the umbrella designation of March for Science. In the wake of President Trump's anti-research initiatives, action groups were created throughout the world to celebrate their—as they put it—"passion for science" (Yong 2017). Despite this emotional key note, however, many of the demands presented by the demonstrators postulated a pure, neutral science, which—were it only freed from its chains—would be capable of righting most of what is wrong in society. For instance, many demonstrators advocated evidence-based politics as promoting progress and diminishing conflicts (see Jewett 2017).

Such hopeful faith in the potential accomplishments of academic institutions has to be considered naive from the perspective of sociology of science, and without foundation in the history of the university. Those who hold such hopes badly underestimate—despite their own declared passion for science—the significance of passions as components in inter-human communication and intellectual work. Such hopes show, along with many similar ideas circulating at present, how impoverished our understanding of the preconditions for thinking and intellectual work has become. In their more elaborated forms, such hopes are also problematic in that they show a fundamental lack of understanding of the university's social role and of how politics function. The task of science is not, nor can it be, easily and simply to judge public debates or solve political or social conflicts once and for all.

One possible escape from this unsatisfactory situation is—I would argue—to turn to the past. The history of ideas concerning the university is too seldom used as a genuine resource in discussions of the politics of education; all too seldom are the debates of former times treated as sources of a living, mutable tradition with implications for the present. One reason for this is probably that it has become increasingly difficult to feel, relate to and experience what it means to be linked to the past, given the radical, fast-paced rate of post-war change. A number of commentators have indeed asked themselves if it is not, in fact, a mistake to presuppose much institutional continuity at all. Perhaps, they postulate, the university's supposed chronological continuum is nothing more than a rhetorical product, without foundation in institutional realities (see, for instance, Scott 2004). Perhaps our difficulties in clarifying the identity of the modern university are caused by the fact that the institution we speak of today is so unlike all the prototypes provided us by history. When historicizing language seems to be eradicated in many exchanges of opinion concerning university politics, past traditions may survive only in the form of a few loose-floating historical fragments. Such fragments may at the most be vaguely adduced during speeches held on solemn academic occasions, when, for a fleeting moment, those present are allowed to feel a soon passing relationship to something that precedes them.

The fact that the ties that bind us to the past have become thin and flimsy, however, gives us some advantages compared to earlier times. When the past is no longer believed to hold up a clear, irrefutable ideal or binding norm, opportunities emerge for a more dynamic relationship to tradition. History's diminished normative power does not, necessarily affect its potential ability to speak to the present. On the contrary, in a certain sense the current situation improves the conditions for fruitful historical re-interpretations and changes in emphasis. That which formerly existed can become alive, in the present, in a new way, and as i hope to show this is particularly true in the case of *Bildung*.

Bildung, Emotion and Individual in the Past

It makes a good deal of sense to start a historically oriented discussion on the importance of emotions in the individual acquisition of knowledge with the thinkers of antiquity, and not least with Plato's concept of *eros* (see for instance Gordon 2012). Plato's concept certainly encompasses insights that are valid and relevant today. A number of attempts have, in fact, been made to launch eros as an intellectual resource in today's debates on the politics of education, as well as in concrete pedagogical practices (Burch 1999; Tushnet 1999; Hull 2002; Kroflic 2003; Bell and Sinclair 2014). Indeed, the spread of insights on the importance and relevance of the concept of eros would entail a number of positive changes.

Despite this fact, I would like to argue that the concept of *Bildung* has an important advantage over that of eros in discussions concerning the universities' ways of thinking about, relating to, and handling emotions. The modern variant of the concept was formed, at least in part, in conjunction with the emergence of the modern research university as social institution. Hence it contains conceptual components that have bearing not only on the individual, but on the institutional situations that developed during the modern era.

I will develop my argument concerning the institutional perspective below. First, however, I would like to define further the meaning of *Bildung* and emotions in relation to the specific individual. The concept has, to be sure, many meanings and a rich history (for further discussions see, for instance, Horlacher 2017; Danner 1994; Koselleck 1990; Dohmen 1978; Froese 1978; Vierhaus 1972; Lichtenstein 1971; Pleines 1971; Rauhut 1965; Scharschmidt 1965). But regardless of its complexity and rich variety, I will dwell upon one central aspect: namely, the way in which the concept refers to the combined intellectual and emotional process of development, as rooted in the individual subject.

This process is—right from the beginning in the last decades of the eighteenth century when *Bildung* became a secular pedagogical concept—seen as being free, and yet at the same time completely integrated into the individual's own personal existence, springing forth from an individual's own capacities. This means that man has the ability to direct himself beyond himself. He can, by starting from within himself, proceed beyond and advance towards everhigher levels. Man is thus able to—while retaining his own individuality—lift himself out of the particular and to place himself in the universal. Thus all individual subjects of *Bildung*, with their different experiences and types of knowledge, can be fused together into a differentiated whole. The regulative goal for this movement is, in the final perspective, the full realization of the truly human. *Bildung* thus stands in polar opposition to all forms of instrumental learning where knowledge is used without close ties to what the learning student experiences as his or her own existence.

On the other hand, *Bildung*, when it was first established as a key philosophical concept within education and politics, did not include the notion that the individual's acquisition of knowledge and abilities of purely practical value was unnecessary or harmful (see in this context, for instance, the arguments in Mendelssohn 1784). Rather, the important point was that the two types of knowledge—intellectual and practical—must be integrated into a specific subjective whole. Later, however, a shift in meaning occurred: increasingly, *Bildung* came to denote purely intellectual development (see Bollenbeck 1996). Regardless of which ideals of knowledge it is associated with, however, the concept has always included the notion of striving to transcend one's limited, intimate situation in order to reach a larger existential, social and cultural community. *Bildung,* thus, is a concept that ties together and mediates between the particular and the general, and between the private and the mutually shared culture.

Despite the emphasis on the purely intellectual aspects within the German tradition, *Bildung* has always also been associated with an emotional register. In order to understand this, it is important to examine a specific aspect of *Bildung*'s origin as a concept: its roots in the theological sphere and in ideas concerning the formation of the soul (see, in this context, for instance Lichtenstein 1971; Vierhaus 1972; Koselleck 1990). Allready in the middle ages, when the word *Bildung* first began to circulate in the German language, it was associated with conceptualizations of the individual's emotionally tinted process of turning towards the transcendent and giving him- of herself to God. This, in turn, was linked to the cultivation of the spirit, to be realized through practices that entailed much more than a neutral mastery of the stuff of knowledge.

One indication of this religious ancestry can be found in the word's etymology. "Bild" is German for *picture*, and *Bildung* originally referred to the process whereby a person, by internalizing a picture of Christ, sought to live in *imitatio Christi*. The process of *Bildung* was, thus, deeply imprinted with desire, and stimulating, regulating and canalizing this desire correctly was regarded as an essential human ability. In other words, the individual already from the beginning harbored an emotional reservoir in which all knowledge was accomodated. Such conceptualizations of *Bildung* with time became closely associated with contemporary ideas on the formation of *die schöne Seele*, the beautiful soul. These ideas, in turn, were inspired by classical and premodern thought as inherited and developed in pietist milieus (cf. Norton 1995).

The evolution of the relationship between *Bildung* and ideas of the beautiful soul was only one aspect of the general process that made *Bildung* into an independent concept, removed from its original religious context (cf. Vierhaus 1972). During the second half of the eighteenth century, the concept was increasingly cut of from its explicit Christian roots and instead it became interwoven with contemporary pedagogical discussions. One example of this development, very important for contemporaries, can be found in Friedrich Schiller. That is especially the case in a central text from 1795 called *Über die ästhetische Erziehung des Menschen in einer Reihe von Briefen* (Schiller 1963/1795), translated into English as *On the Aesthetic Education of Man*. This text was a fertile source of ideas for the growing movement of early Romantics. It established—although it used the exact word rather infrequent and mixed it with *Erziehung* (fostering)—ways of thinking about *Bildung* that were soon to seem virtually self-evident. Schiller's text presented a series of dichotomatized divisions. These, he argued, had come to characterize the disharmonious modern period (as opposed to the harmony of Greek antiquity). The theoretical had become divided from the practical, duty from inclination and desire, form from content, the sensual from the spiritual, and so on. One might say, in schematic summary of Schiller's complex argument, that he seeks a possible bridge to these polarities by advocating aesthetically creative play.

I would like to emphasize one particular aspect of Schiller's *On the Aesthetic Education of Man*: the text clearly establishes the essential importance of sensuality and emotion in the individual's *Bildung*. Schiller argued that modernity's devastating division of the different sides of human subjectivity had led to the distillation and refinement of reason and the neglect of sensuality, emotions and desire. *Bildung*, in this perspective, involves a process of re-integration. Emotions are to be cultivated in the same way as reason; the two sides are to be brought into mutual harmony. In an ideally formed process of *Bildung*, emotion and reason strive together towards the same goal. Humans who undergo this process shall possess the will, inclinations and desires that harmonize with rationality, and, in the final count, with truth itself.

It is important to note that Schiller's argument does not suppose opposition between (supposedly) spontaneous, true emotionality and artificial, corrupted reason. Many histories of the so called Romantic Period—not least in older works— have tended to argue that those who reacted against the Enlightenment sought to delve beneath man's shallow rationality and free his deep, true emotional layers, in other words to allow genuine mystery to win out against false reason. This line of thought was, in fact, deeply foreign to Schiller and his contemporaries (although it had been cultivated by him and a number of other authors in the *Sturm und Drang*-movement of foregoing decades). At this point, however, Schiller's task was consciously to cultivate and form emotions in *harmony* with the work of reason.

What, then, did the concrete cultivation of emotions mean to those thinkers who developed the modern concept of *Bildung* around 1800? There is no doubt about it: the most influential approach called for the awakening and cultivation of love (cf. Beiser 2003, 103ff). The inner essence of *Bildung* was, in short, the nurturing and promotion of every individual's ability to give and receive love. Many who spoke for Romanticism felt that the Enlightenment had robbed love, as an emotion, of its position. The task at hand was to reinstate love in the central position it had held in culture and in human consciousness during the Christian period. Only through the power that lay in love could feelings be brought in harmony with reason; only thus could the individual's true self-realization become a reality. "Only through love and the consciousness of love does man become man", as Friedrich Schlegel expressed it in one of his famous fragments (Schlegel 1967/1800, 263).

The coupling, around 1800, of *Bildung* to love can be easily linked to the increased sensibility that suffused culture during the second half of the 1700s (Giddens 1992; Luhmann 1994). It is part of a growing cluster of ideas which inserted humans' emotional life into the midst of general culture, creating what has been termed a "cultural subsystem" (Faulstich 2002, 103). As the content of older institutions changed, their normative power diminished. Simultaneously, emotions were given a more prominent role in guiding action and promoting social integration. But it is evident that emotions, as they were thematized around 1800, did more than fill the empty space created when traditional institutional structures lost validity. Many thinkers also set them—often with the help of the concept *Bildung*—in concrete relation to the revivification of societal institutions. These institutions were, in short, to be impregnated with emotion. This applied not least to the university.

Bildung, Emotion and Institution in the Past

Some commentaries on those German Romantics active around 1800 assert that the their discussion of *Bildung* was limited to abstract theories concerning the individual learning subject. Hence, it is stated, the generation of Romantics failed to formulate practical, precise ideas on how to reform educational institutions (one example is Beiser 2003, 105). Such an assertion is possibly justified if one limits one's perspective narrowly to the most inner circle of *Frühromantiker* who were active in Jena (on Jena Romanticism, see Behler 1992; Behler and Hörisch 1987). But one does not need to look far beyond to find the architects and leaders who inspired the new university ideals, practices and structures that emerged towards the end of the 1700s and the beginning of 1800s. They often used the concept of *Bildung* when speaking of concrete issues within research and education. Indeed, several of the leading representatives of that generation of German intellectuals, who had focused on and used the concept *Bildung* in order to think about pedagogical and educational questions, were also engaged in the contemporary debate concerning schools and universities (hereto see for instance the discussion in Tenorth 2010). Moreover, they strongly emphasized the emotional aspect of *Bildung* when they formulated their thoughts concerning the reformed educational institutions such as the new university.

One example of such ideas we find in Daniel Ernst Schleiermacher, the theologian that held a leading position within the Romantic generation around 1800. In his oft-cited comprehensive program text of 1808, concerning plans for a Berlin university, one finds the idea that the university and its process of *Bildung* should, ideally, be suffused with emotions, and the institution's residents should show each other mutual affection—an affection which was also to be directed towards toward truth itself (Schleiermacher 1956/1808). Among other things, Schleiermacher described academic everyday practice such as the seminar as taking place in a free, strongly emotionally charged community, cultivated and nourished by fellow researchers and students (see further Karlsohn 2016b). These themes in Schleiermacher's text reappear in the work of Wilhelm von Humboldt (cf. Karlsohn 2014). He was responsible for the realization of Berlin's new seat of learning in 1809–1810—that is, the institution which would later be perceived as the prototype of the modern research university.

There exist additional examples of how *Bildung*, emotions and educational institutions were linked in the decades around 1800. But those cited above suffice for me to make several points. First, it is obvious that conceptualizations of what a university is and should be, as formulated by theoriticians of *Bildung* such as Schiller and Schleiermacher, were, in one perspective, linked to religious thought. When closely examined, the university and its *Bildung* can in fact be interpreted as a sort of *Ersatzreligion*, a replacement religion in an era of increasing secularization (see further Karlsohn 2017). It is no coincidence that so many religious practices and modes of thought would, albeit in new forms, accompany the new research university when it took form. The professors are spoken of as a priesthood, the university's communities are seen as types of congregations, the academic lecture is a sort of sermon, and so on. And the emotion that constitutes the center of this thinking is love—both as it is roused between those who partake in the community, and regarding truth itself. A conscious cultivation and development of love, a thought with clear roots in Christian culture, is, according to those who inspired the modern research university, absolutely essential.

The common description of the period around 1800 as a time of secularization, when the university broke itself free from the church, often found in research on the history of the university, is thus only partially true. Religious impulses survived for a long time both in the area of individual self-perception and in institutional ideals. Indeed, in some ways it is only in the post-war period that secularization seriously influenced the world of the university. This applies to the ideas concerning *Bildung* and emotions on the individual as well as the institutional level. As we remember from the argument above, also on the individual level, the concept was characterized by tones reminiscent of the sphere of theology and the Christian religion.

Thus, it is clear that the theme of *Bildung* and emotions is linked to religion. But how should one describe this link? At first glance, one might get the impression that the Romantic thinkers who discussed the theme saw its transferal from the individual context to supraindividual social institutions as unproblematic. The essence of the university consists, quite simply—in their view—in "internally connecting objective science with subjective education", as the matter is expressed in Humboldt's program text for the Berlin university (Humboldt 2017/1809–1810, 1). Thus, the theme's link to religion would be the same regardless of the level—the individual or the institutional—the connection was made.

But closer reflection shows that the relation between *Bildung*, emotions and religion was more complicated than that. The religious content of the body of thought focused, around 1800, on *Bildung* as a concept, had a particular origin that makes it more applicable on an individual than institutional plane. *Bildung* as a modern concept was greatly influenced by German Protestant countries' pietistic movements (here, see for instance Horlacher 2017, 11ff). Pietism provided a new way of emphasizing the individual's inner spirituality. Further, it celebrated spontaneous communities and the primacy of free studies over traditional, institutionalized Lutheran orthodoxy. Pietism directed attention to the individual task: to strive daily towards sanctification and perfection in life as it is lived. It emphasized the individual's relationship to God and the universal priesthood at the cost of established doctrines and inherited church structures. Thus, pietism encouraged introspection in each and every person, while inspiring meetings between people outside the context of the official practice of religion.

Pietism's critique of the tradition-bound church as institution also engendered palpable ambivalence vis-a-vis established educational institutions. On the one hand, several such institutions grew forth under the movement's aegis, and many of its leading representatives were active within them. On the other hand, pietists criticized the value of institutional knowledge and the science in a way reminiscent of the attacks upon the traditional (Catholic) university and, of course, the cloister as institutions, launched during the first wave of the Reformation.

This tension between the institutional and the anti-institutional is clearly discernible in thinkers of education such as Schiller, Schleiermacher and Humboldt. The university can, of course, be seen as a sort of positive replacement for the church. However, contemporaries also tended, not infrequently, to castigate the institution as a potential obstacle to spontaneous, living, dynamic, free intellectual life.

This ambivalence seems especially prominent when we contemplate how those who thought about the university around 1800 handled the emotional aspect of *Bildung*. On the one hand, as we have seen, a thinker like Schleiermacher was convinced that emotional animation was important to the reform of the institution and to actively guide the practice of scientific reason. This emotional vibrancy was fostered through the controlled, self-conscious cultivation of teachers and students' emotions. The ideal result aimed at was a mutual, cathartic love, both growing between student and teacher and directed to the tasks they undertake together. The institution would, in other words, bring emotions, as an aspect of the experience of *Bildung*, into harmony with reason, and the two would not be set in opposition.

On the other hand, those same turn-of-the-century thinkers often presented the institution as an obstacle to the free play of feelings which characterized the spontaneous intellectual community. Schleiermacher's program text, for instance, describe emotions as growing spontaneously from within the human, not as being awoken by institutional means. When the text evoke the teacher's and students' mutual affection, it treat it as a phenomenon generated from the subject's inner being, not as effected by an exterior structure. Despite their engagement in the reformation of the university and its adaptation to modern times, this attitude shows the thinkers' skepticism towards institutions. I believe that this skepticism derives, in part, from Protestant and not least pietist distrust of the official church and its collectively binding dogmas and rituals. In the final analysis, the Romantic generation seems to nurture, in its modern conceptualization of *Bildung*, a vaguely articulated but highly discernable dream of a free, egalitarian, community of feelings and thought, removed from *all* inherited worldly contexts.

Exit: Absence in the Present

Where does this historical investigation lead us in relation to the problems we face today? I would like to end this chapter by highlighting two aspects of the discussion on education that took place around 1800, and relating them to the present era. The first applies to the link between *Bildung*, emotion and individuals; the second to the link between *Bildung*, emotion and institutions. Both these aspects are overly absent from the present.

One fundamental insight concealed in the modern concept of *Bildung* is the indissoluble relationship between the individual person's use of reason, and his or her emotional life. This insight derives, at bottom, from antiquity, the pre-modern era, and not least the Christian concept of the given role of desire in the individual's acquisition of knowledge. However, this has frequently been ignored by those using the concept in the educational-political discussions of later years. In part, this is probably due to the modern epoch's general tendency to deny, repress or reformulate the relationship between emotion and reason. Emotions are often closely linked to unpredictability, irrationality or even pure mysticism. To be sure, during the two centuries or more that have passed since the modern reconceptualization of *Bildung*, there have also been numerous attempts to think through the cultivation of human emotional life and its role in the acquisition of knowledge—extending to the idea that feelings might constitute a sort of thinking in their own right (cf. for instance Nussbaum 2001). The main inclination, nonetheless, has been towards a clumsy or dismissive treatment of emotional life.

The contemporary discussion of the university would gain a good deal through renewed emphasis on the emotional aspect of *Bildung*. This is especially true of the idea that emotions are integral to human subjectivity in such a way that we all must actively care for and nurture them. According to this line of thinking emotions must be thought of as formed in close relationship to reason and its requirement of rational argumentation and logical stringency.

For one thing, this clarifies what is demanded of us who work in academic institutions. For instance, when we direct attention towards the all-important scientific ideals of balanced objectivity, unprejudiced argumentation, and the reasonable use of evidence, we should also always underscore that these ideals must be supported by emotional engagement and formation. Our inherited scientific ideals will survive in a proper form only if we are capable to wisely relate what we know to what we feel, and not until then will our *passion for science* (to return to my introductory example of recent academic attempts to defend science against populism and anti-intellectualism in the public sphere) regain the anchorage and stability it currently often lacks. Moreover, if we were able to increase our comprehension of our academic emotions we would also be better equiped when it comes to transfering our ideals to students. Such a scenario would in turn increase our ability to advance the cultivation of culture, necessary to counteract the superficiality and brutality that increasingly characterizes today's public sphere.

Thus far my argument on *Bildung*, emotions and individual. The other aspect of the concept I would like to emphasize in conclusion concerns the level of the institution. As argued above, thinkers on the university around 1800 found that the institution introduced a field of tension. On the one hand, they maintained that academic institutions were completely dependent on an emotional charge in order to perform well their basic functions of research and instruction. On the other, their declarations on the modern university were often imbued with vaguely formulated skepticism concerning the institution's ability to generate and consolidate the necessary emotional patterns of reaction, and thereby enrich intellectual endeavor.

This uncertainty on how and whether emotions can be properly cultivated within the modern university is integral to the tradition surrounding *Bildung*. The perception of tension is connected, as we remember, with a modern, essentially Protestant and pietist ambivalence about the role of established institutions in people's emotional life. This ambivalence seems, if anything, to be stronger today. Not seldom, it is transformed into pure antipathy, as social institutions have been destabilized and a general preference is expressed for what has been described as "an anti-institutional mode" (Zijderveld 2000, passim). One perception, shared by many, is that the university is a monolithic, institutional colossus that kills living feelings, limits free creativity and through its enforced conformism stifles true intellectuality. To be sure, such statements do—as most people with insight into the university could confirm—often contain more than a grain of truth. Nonetheless, we are often too ready to follow our instinctively negative attitude in disparaging the university. This induces us to renounce our responsibility for maintaining the symbolic pithiness and depth which must surround and imbue a meaningful, well-functioning university. Further, such negativity obscures the opportunities of emotional engagement that the researcher, teacher or student actually do encounter, opportunities which allow the institution to foment desire and to bring forth the intellectual intensity that makes university work worth-while.

When it comes to the specific relationship between emotion and institution, it seems to me that the tradition apparent in Anglo-Saxon university history—most often referred to as *liberal education*—provides more insights than does the German tradition of *Bildung*. Within the Anglo-Saxon tradition, there is more deep reflection on how the institution managed to give concrete shape to the emotional relations between teacher and student and between colleagues. This affects its appreciation of the importance of the institution in incorporating and forming the individual, both emotionally and individually. I shall not develop this line of argument here, as it is in fact worth a separate investigation. But I would like to note the point that future reflections on the university as a thinking institution, one that aspires to bear real, nourishing fruit, useful to contemporaries, has every reason to search in different directions—German, Anglo-Saxon and other—within the history of educatiuonal ideas.

Finally: he concept of *Bildung*, as I have discussed it in this chapter, has long been subject to criticism (see for instance Nietzsche 1997/1872; Adorno 2006/1959). Nonetheless, for more than two centuries, it has furnished a self-evident reference point in discussions on the university. Today, increasing numbers of commentators seem to perceive the concept as elitist, peculiar, overly idealistic or simply irrelevant. There doubtless exist elements within older traditions surrounding *Bildung* which rightly ought to be discarded as unnecessary or ill-suited to the democratic era of the mass university. But at the same time the concept's rich complexity means that we can find new ways of thinking which are hidden within the its history and thus let the past speak meaningfully to the present. Indeed, it is only through such a relationship to the past that the university can be a thinking institution in a deeper sense.

References

Adorno, T. W. (2006/1959). *Theorie der Halbbildung*. Suhrkamp: Frankfurt am Main.
Beard, C., Clegg, S., & Smith, K. (2007). Acknowledging the Affecive in Higher Education. *British Educational Research Journal, 33*(2).
Behler, E. (1992). *Frühromantik*. Berlin: de Gruyter.
Behler, E., & Hörisch, J. (Eds.). (1987). *Die Aktualität der Frühromantik*. Paderborn: Ferdinand Schöningh.

Beiser, F. C. (2003). *The romantic imperative: The concept of early modern German romanticism.* Cambridge: Harvard University Press.

Bell, E., & Sinclair, A. (2014). Reclaiming eroticism in the academy. *Organization, 21*(2), 268.

Bellas, M. L. (January, 1999). Emotional labor in academia: The case of professors. *The Annals of the American Academy of Political Science, 561*, 96–110.

Bloch, C. (2012). *Passions and Paranoia: Emotions and the culture of emotions in academia.* Farnham: Ashgate.

Bollenbeck, G. (1996). *Bildung und Kultur: Glanz und Elend eines deutschen Deutungsmusters.* Frankfurt am Main: Suhrkamp.

Burch, K. (1999). Eros as the educational principle of democracy. *Studies in Philosophy and Education. Vol., 18.*

Danner, H. (1994). 'Bildung'. A basic term of German education. *Educational Sciences, 9.*

Dear, P. (1992). From truth to disinterestedness in the seventeenth Cenury. *Social Studies of Science, 22*(4), 619.

Di Leo, & Jeffrey, R. (2006). Shame in academe: On the politics of emotion in academic culture. *JAC. Journal of Rhetoric, Culture, & Politics, 26*(1–2), 221–233.

Dohmen, Günter (1978). Was heißt 'Bildung'?. Jürgen-Eckardt Pleines, ed. *Bildungstheorien: Probleme und Positionen.* Freiburg: Herder 1978.

Draper, H. (Ed.). (1965). *Berkeley: The new student revolt.* Alameda: Centre for Socialist History.

Dror, O. E., Hitzer, B., Laukötter, A., & León-Sanz, P. (2016). An introduction to history of science and the emotions. *Osiris, 31*, 1.

Ehn, B., & Löfgren, O. (2007). Emotions in Academia. In H. Wulff (Ed.), *The Emotions: A Cultural Reader.* Berg: Oxford.

Faulstich, W. (2002). *Die bürgerliche Mediengesellschaft (1770–1830).* Göttingen: Vandenhoek & Ruprecht.

Froese, Leonhard (1978). Begriff- und Bedeutungswandel der Bildung. Jürgen-Eckardt Pleines, ed. *Bildungstheorien: Probleme und Positionen.* Freiburg: Herder 1978.

Gadamer, H.-G. (1988). Die Idee einer Universität. In M. Eigen et al. (Eds.), *Die Ide eder Universität: Eine Standortbestimmung.* Berlin: Springer.

Giddens, A. (1992). *The transformation of intimacy: Sexuality, love, and eroticism in modern societies.* Stanford: Stanford University Press.

Gordon, J. (2012). *Plato's erotic world: From cosmic origin to human death.* New York: Cambridge University Press.

Hörisch, J. (2006). *Die Ungeliebte Universität.* München Carl Hanser: *Rettet die Alma Mater.*

Hörisch, J. (2009). Die ungeliebte Universität. Ulrike Haß & Nikolaus Müller-Schöll, ed. *Was ist eine Universität? Schlaglichter auf eine ruinierte Institution.* Bielefeld: Transcript.

Horlacher, R. (2017). *The educated subject and the German concept of Bildung: A coparative cultural history.* London: Routledge.

Hull, K. (2002). Eros and education: The role of desire in teaching and learning. *The NEA Higher Education Journal. Fall,* 19–32.

Humboldt, W. (2017/1809–1810). On the internal and external organization of the higher scientific institutions in Berlin (T. Dunlap Trans.). German History in Documents and Images. Volume 2: From Absolutism to Napoleon, 1648–1815. Available at: http://germanhistorydocs.ghidc.org. Downloaded 2017-07-20.

Jewett, A. (2017). How the march for science misunderstands politics". *The Atlantic.* April 21.

Josephson, P., Karlsohn, T., & Östling, J. (2014). *The Humboldtian Tradition: Origins and Legacies.* Leiden: Brill.

Karlsohn, T. (2014). On Humboldtian and contemporary notions of the academic lecture. In P. Josephson, T. Karlsohn, & J. Östling (Eds.), *The Humboldtian Tradition: Origins and legacies.* Brill: Leiden.

Karlsohn, T. (2016a). On emotions, knowledge and educational institutions: An explorative essay. *Confero, 4*(1), 137.

Karlsohn, T. (2016b). The academic seminar as emotional eommunity. *Nordic Journal of Studies in Educational Policy*. Special Issue: Life in Academia, (2–3).

Karlsohn, T. (2017). The idea of the university and the process of secularization. *PARSE Journal, 4*.

Knouf, N. (2010). Whither the libidinal university? *Canadian Journal of Media Studies, 7*.

Koselleck, R. (1990). *Einleitung: Zur anthropologischen und semantischen Struktur der Bildung. Reinhart Koselleck, ed. Bildungsbürgertum im19. Jahrhundert. Teil II: Bildungsgüter und Bildungswissen*. Stuttgart: Klett-Cotta.

Kroflic, R. (2003). Eros and Education. *School fields, 14*(3–4), 33–52.

Lichtenstein, E. (1971). Bildung. Joachim Ritter, ed. *Historisches Wörterbuch der Philosophie: Band 1*. Darmstadt: Wissenschaftliche Buchgesellschaft.

Luhmann, N. (1994). *Liebe als Passion: Zur Codierung von Intimität*. Frankfurt am Main: Suhrkamp.

Mendelssohn, M. (1784). *Ueber die Frage: was heißt aufklären?* September: Berlinische Monatschrift.

Merton, R. (1973 [1942]). The normative structure of science. *The Sociology of Science: Theoretical and Empirical Investigations*, Chicago: University of Chicago Press.

Nietzsche F. (1997/1872). *Über die Zukunft unserer Bildungs-Anstalten: Sechs, im Auftrag der 'Academischen Gesellschaft' in Basel gehaltene, öffentliche Reden*. Karl Schlechta, (Ed.), Werke (Band 3). Darmstadt: Wissenschaftliche Buchgesellschaft.

Norton, R. E. (1995). *The beautiful soul: Aesthetic morality in the eighteenth century*. Ithaca: Cornell University Press.

Nussbaum, M. C. (2001). *Upheavals of thought: The intelligence of emotion*. Cambridge: Cambridge University Press.

Pleines, J.-E. (1971). *Bildung. Grundlegung und Kritik eines pädagogischen Begriffs*. Heidelberg: Quelle & Meyer.

Rauhut, F. (1965/1953). "Die Herkunft der Worte und Begriffe 'Kultur', 'Civilisation' und 'Bildung'. Wolfgang Klafki, ed. *Beiträge zur Geschichte des Bildungsbegriff*. Weinheim: Julius Beltz.

Readings, B. (1996). *The University in Ruins*. Cambridge: Harvard University Press.

Scharschmidt, I. (1965). Der Bedeutungswandel der Worte 'Bilden' und 'Bildung' in der Literaturepoche von Gottsched bis Herder. Wolfgang Klafki, *Beiträge zur Geschichte des Bildungsbegriff*. Weinheim: Julius Beltz.

Schiller, F. (1963/1795). *Über die ästhetische Erziehung des Menschen in einer Reihe von Briefen. Schillers Werke. Nationalausgabe. Band 20*. Weimar: Hermann Böhlaus Nachfolger.

Schlegel, F. (1967/1800). *"Ideen". Kritische Friedrich Schlegel-Ausgabe. Erste Abteilung. Band 2*. Paderborn: Ferdinand Schöningh.

Schleiermacher, F. D. E. (1956/1808). *Gelegentliche Gedanken Über Universitäten im deutschen Sinn. Nebst einem Anhang über eine neu zu errichtende. Ernst Anrich Die Idee der deutschen Universität: Die fünf Grundschriften aus der Zeit ihrer Neubegründung durch klassischen Idealismus und romantischen Realismus*. Darmstadt: Hermann Gentner.

Scott, P. (2004). The transformation of the idea of a university. In F. Inglis (Ed.), *Education and the Good Society*. Basingstoke: Palgrave Macmillan.

Tenorth, H.-E. (2010). "Was heißt Bildung in der Universität? Oder: Transzendierung der Fachlichkeit als Aufgabe universitärer Studien". *Die Hochschule*. No. 1.

Tushnet, E. (September, 1999). *Eros and education*. The Yale Free Press.

Vierhaus, R. (1972). Bildung. In O. Brunner, W. Conze, & R. Koselleck (Eds.), *Geschichtliche Grundbegriffe: Historisches Lexikon zur politischsozialen Sprache in Deutschland* (Band 1). Stuttgart: Ernst Klett.

Widdowfield, R. (2000). The place of emotions in academic research. *Area, 32*(2), 199–208.

Ylijoki, O.-H. (2005). Academic Nostalgia: A narrative approach to academic work. *Human Relations, 58*(5), 555–576.

Yong, Ed (2017). What exactly are people marching for when they March for science?. *The Atlantic*. March 7.

Zijderveld, A. C. (2000). *The institutional imperative: The interface of institutions and networks*. Amsterdam: University Press.

Ziman, J. (2004 [2000]). *Real science: What it is, and what it means*. Cambridge: Cambridge University Press

Chapter 9
Technicising Thought: English and the Internationalisation of the University

SunInn Yun and Paul Standish

Introduction

We present an argument in ten steps. Thus, we provide: (1) a characterisation of salient features of thinking in the university today; (2) reasons for seeing this as a lack of thinking; (3) an argument for connecting thinking to language; (4) reflection on the plurality of language and its interconnections with belonging and thinking; (5) a contextualising of these matters in relation to internationalisation; (6) a worked example where issues of belonging and propriety come to the fore; (7) an exploration of the wider ramifications of this in terms of English for academic purposes; (8) an acknowledgement of problems relating to the English language itself; (9) a reflection on this in relation to education and social advancement; and (10) some suggestions for improving thinking in the university today.

The University that Thinks

The university today can be said to think as never before. It has all the hallmarks of an intelligent system, with its self-monitoring, quality-control, and feedback loops; its future is projected in five, ten, and sometimes twenty-year plans; and it is undoubtedly data-rich and extensively networked. Students today, in some respects,

S. Yun (✉)
Incheon National University, Incheon, South Korea
e-mail: syun@inu.ac.kr

P. Standish
University College London, London, UK
e-mail: p.standish@ucl.ac.uk

© Springer International Publishing AG, part of Springer Nature 2018   119
S.S.E. Bengtsen, R. Barnett (eds.), *The Thinking University*,
Debating Higher Education: Philosophical Perspectives 1,
https://doi.org/10.1007/978-3-319-77667-5_9

must think as never before, as they decide first which university, which career path, which course, is right for them, as they negotiate their way through arrays of option modules, as they identify the learning outcomes and the criteria by which they will be assessed, and as they manage their learning in order most efficiently to reach their desired ends. University teachers, in some respects, must think today as never before, as they struggle with a burgeoning workload, keep sight of the demands of quality assurance, and plan and set out what they will teach and how it will be assessed. And university researchers too, in some respects, must think today as never before, as they track the available funding opportunities and mould their abilities to compile credible applications. To think in this way brings considerable benefit – whether to the student, the academic, or the administrator: it builds capacity for identifying targets and efficient means to realise them. For all our protagonists, such thinking provides a clear sense of purpose and measures of success in their roles. It brings to the university more or less explicit criteria according to which to measure its performance, as is apparent, for example, in the prevalence of national and world rankings of various kinds. And of course these capacities, of the student, the teacher, and the institution, are mutually reinforcing.

But it is also clear, is it not, that to think thus is to think in a particular way? It is to prioritise instrumental reason and to commodify knowledge. The Marxist connotations of commodification imply that the knowledge in question is somehow severed from contexts of use with the result that there is a kind of alienation or estrangement. Examples of the particular forms that this might take in education are to be found, especially in a culture of credentialism, in the fetish power acquired by 'learning outcomes' and 'criteria', which themselves are steps on the way to letters after the name, titles, and certificates on the wall. Career-minded managers and earnest quality assurance committees will savour the recurrent emphasis on learning outcomes and ponderously reiterate the importance of criteria,[1] with the result that concepts such as these become reified. They become credentials students must have or targets they must hit. Emphasis on these factors is often justified in terms of transparency and accountability, but this in fact only accentuates the tendency towards commodification: what is learned is a clearly identifiable product of the process of learning.

Commodification dove-tails with instrumental reason because the separation of learner and content that is a primary aspect of this alienation means that the intelligence engaged must perforce rely on its own resources. Intelligence will not be drawn by the inherent fascination of what is learned, by the inherent demands that this content places on the learner, because the living dynamism of this will have been neutralised: it will have been stifled of its life, and presented again as if behind glass, framed within a set of expectations. What is left are various modifications of intelligence that emphasise not content but procedure. These are learning skills,

---

[1] Debased notions of criteria have detached the idea from its ordinary context and given it a technical gloss. Human practices are unintelligible unless they are characterised by criteria (of what it is to do something appropriately, better or worse), but the technical usage has displaced this ordinary sense.

skills of information access and time-management, and of course the much vaunted 'critical thinking'; for of course we want our students to be critical thinkers, do we not, so that they can confront the complexity of the world of the twenty-first century and face the challenges that changing patterns of work present? What objection could there possibly be to this?[2]

Thinking and Not Thinking

Yet it is now no news that some have said that, for all this apparent busyness of thought, the idealisation of critical thinking in fact ends up blunting the edge of real critique: it neutralises its object and, as if context-free, fine-tunes its reasoning skills. Thinking becomes a smooth-running machine. But, as Wittgenstein puts this, such thinking, then, lacks contact with the rough ground that would give it traction (Wittgenstein 1958: #107). Too confident of our procedures, we are unable to take a step sideways, to see things under a different aspect (Wittgenstein 1958: 193ff.).

For Heidegger, the truth is that we are still not thinking. One iteration of this thought view specifically concerns the university. Amidst much declamation on the mission of the German people and the 'essence' of the university, Heidegger asserts.

'Only if we resolutely submit to this distant command to regain the greatness of this beginning, only then will science become the innermost necessity of our existence. Otherwise it
will remain an accident into which we fall or the dispassionate contentment of a safe occupation, serving to further a mere progress of information' (Heidegger 1990/1933: 7).

Science in the broadest sense, *Wissenschaft*, the pursuit of knowledge, which should be at the heart of the university, risks becoming a mere amassing, passing on, and utilisation of information. The 'distant command' is, at its best, a call from the content of what is studied, not content as the crude data of experience, but content realised in processes of cultural inheritance. The demands of such content on the enquirer is a call to be what we can be, as human beings, as a people, as members of a nation. Such a call is not to be answered in the stockpiling of knowledge in databanks, nor in the acquisition of skills and competences, nor in the tranquilising ease of 'safe occupation'. The phrasing here is redolent of Nietzsche's 'Last Man', the ultimate nihilism of bourgeois life, against which Heidegger's appeal is towards a kind of nobility that, even as it calls from an ancient past, projects a kind of destiny.

But the provenance, the occasion, of these words of Heidegger means that we can scarcely leave matters like that. Heidegger is here presenting his infamous inaugural address following his appointment to the Rectorship of the University of Freiburg in 1933, the year Hitler had come to power. Heidegger was elected to the Rectorship, a position for which his colleagues had persuaded him to stand, in the vacuum of authority created in the university by the political upheavals of the time

---

[2] For a thought-provoking account of objections, see Emma Williams (2016).

and the sackings of his Jewish colleagues. This speech attempts to exploit ambiguity in its phrasing, between a conservative appeal to the call of *Wissenschaft* and nationalistic endorsement of Hitler as leader. But it fails in this and fails abysmally. Can anything of the higher sentiments intimated here about thinking survive the dreadful errors in Heidegger's political judgement? Certainly there is a need to look elsewhere in his work.

In 1954, in *What is Called Thinking?*, such ideas find one of their richest expressions. Heidegger dwells on the phrase: '*Most thought-provoking is that we are still not thinking* – not even yet, although the state of the world is becoming constantly more thought-provoking' (Heidegger 1968: 4). But who, we might ask, is this 'we'? In the years prior to the Second World War, Heidegger was contemptuous of the two political settlements that were competing most prominently on the international stage – the communism of the Soviet Union and the liberal individualism that was increasingly shaping the English-speaking world. Hence, his appeal is not just to those concerned with the fate and promise of the university: he directs the reader to the deep cultural malaise from which, with disastrous consequences, Germany had struggled to extricate itself. By the time of the 1950s that malaise did not, to Heidegger, seem to have alleviated. No doubt he would have found things worse in many respects today – worse, that is, especially with the advent of performativity and the nihilistic culture of credentialism, with which we started our discussion, but worse also with the pervasive influence of the binary thinking of cybernetics.

But what does this impoverishment of thought consist in? As we saw above, it is a dominance of instrumental reason and procedural thinking; it is the devaluing of content, one articulation of which is 'data'; and it is a kind of *irresponsibilisation*, weakening the learner's engagement with and commitment to the substance of enquiry.[3] The new product of this university is increasingly the person with a portfolio of transferable skills – including interpersonal, communication, entrepreneurial, and ICT skills, as well as the primary requirement of the skill of learning-how-to-learn – whose affective development is understood not as drawn by the substance of enquiry but in terms, on the one hand, of 'motivation' and, on the other, of the 'management' of emotions. Current preoccupations with 'student satisfaction' indicate a further degeneration.

The Turn to Language

In response to this depletion of value, Heidegger turns to language itself, where language is not to be understood as a tool of communication or as something that human beings 'have', and where attempts to study it scientifically – in, say, linguistics – fail to get to its essence. Such approaches fail to think through the fundamental nature of language for human beings, its being the always-already-there

---

[3] On proceduralism, see Standish (2001a). On the contemporary emphasis on 'data', see Standish (2001b, 2016).

element in which thinking takes place, behind which we cannot step. Heidegger sees language as the wellspring of thought. Moreover, he sees the German language as having a special importance – as having resources for thinking of a kind that rivals ancient Greek. Hence, the path to thought involves turning to that language itself and to what it and its best thinkers have produced.

There are good reasons to react against such an idea. It is not uncommon for an individual or a people to imagine that their own language has exceptional status, even an *originary* importance *vis-à-vis* other languages – ludicrously as the original language! Indeed, it seems that the ancient Greeks thought that outside their own linguistic world there were only the barbarian utterances of other peoples. Ironically perhaps, it may be true also to say that for some speakers of English – those in monolingual communities – their own language has exceptional status, as if theirs were the only essential language – a language whose universal status was legiti- mated not in originary but in *teleological* terms. To hold these views one would need to be not only relatively uneducated but also insensitive to others' ways of thinking. But perhaps this claim is too quick. Hilary Putnam records that Rudolph Carnap believed strongly that 'for all x, planned x is better than unplanned x': 'Thus the idea of a socialist world in which everyone spoke Esperanto (except scientists, who, for their technical work, would employ notations from symbolic logic) was one which would have delighted him.' With some dismay Putnam relates this to a remark he had heard from a student to the effect that 'it would not be a bad idea if there were only one language and one literature: "We would get used to it, and it might help to prevent war"' (Putnam 1994: 185).

Language, Belonging, Thinking

In her book *Nostalgia*, an unusual reflection on the themes of home and belonging, language, and what it is to think, Barbara Cassin contrasts three kinds of relation- ship – juxtaposing the archetypal figure of the return home in Odysseus with that of exile and the establishment of the new city in Aeneas. These classic, contrasting examples are then followed by a third chapter in which Hannah Arendt's exile from Germany and eventual settlement in New York is examined. The contrast between Odysseus and Aeneas, which constitutes the most powerful part of her argument, might find a parallel in the respective experience of Arendt and Heidegger himself.[4]

The story of Odysseus' return provides one of the most culturally powerful images of home and belonging. This is accentuated by the symbolism of the mar- riage bed, the heart of the home to which Odysseus returns: the bed is carved from a yew tree that is still rooted in the ground. His return is only possible after a hazardous journey that takes many years. Aeneas too will undergo a protracted and

---

[4] Arendt was a student of Heidegger's, and over the course of many years they had an intimate relationship.

hazardous journey. But Aeneas' escape is *from* his home, from Troy the city that has been sacked, and this is a city to which he will never return. It is his fate that he must escape, leaving his wife and children, and – extraordinarily – carrying his aged father on his back. The place where he will arrive is Latinium, and there eventually he will lay the foundations for the city that is to become Rome. While, after years amongst strange peoples, Odysseus returns home, sustaining his native Greek throughout, Aeneas does not return and adopts instead the language of this new place he has found, Latin, the language of the city he will have founded. His experience of and relation to language is then fundamentally different because there is already another language with which this, his second language, contrasts: both languages (and then others) come to be understood in terms of this contrast. Languages exist plurally, opening possibilities of thinking and an experience of the political to which the monolingual Odysseus has been deaf.

When she settled in the United States, Arendt maintained a kind of nostalgia, not for Germany but for German. Her friend, the poet Randall Jarrell, quipped: 'The country I like best of all is German' (Jarrell, quoted in Cassin 2016: 56). As a mark of this perhaps, she never lost the heavy German intonation in the English she came to speak every day. Pluralism was alive in her experience, as in her politics, in a way that escaped Heidegger. It would be wrong to say that Heidegger showed no interest in other cultures (other than that of Ancient Greece). He paid a kind of homage to East Asian thinking (and borrowed liberally from its ideas). But this was not without a certain exoticisation and mystification, demonstrated especially in his 'A Dialogue on Language' (Heidegger 1971). In this text, the two men in dialogue are identified mysteriously as 'A Japanese' and 'An Inquirer', the latter bearing a remarkable resemblance to Heidegger himself. The Inquirer comments on the mystery and unfathomability of the Japanese way of thinking, and attention is given to the untranslatability of essential ideas, especially concerning language. But the Inquirer fawns before the Japanese, revealing, inadvertently, so it seems, that he at least has understood something. Apparent humility conceals hubris, quite failing to countenance the alterity that would lay the way for a plural politics and philosophy.

We have, then, moved towards a conception of thinking that is outward-turning and other-regarding. Yet this implies neither a sentimental and moralistic altruism nor the outward-facing entrepreneurialism championed in the university of today. So how might this outward-turning thinking be realised? The crucial importance of plurality that comes to light with Aeneas' experience prompts reflection more directly on language and thought in the university today.

Ironically, however, this presents us immediately with a language problem, for the move from Heidegger and the myths of ancient Greece to the scene of the contemporary university involves a shift of register in the literature and language on which we must draw. Uncomfortable though this may be, such a mixing of idiom is necessary if we are to broach such practical, political matters. Let us begin by considering internationalisation as a prominent dimension of the way the university now thinks.

Internationalisation and English

'Internationalisation' is a term with an agenda. Over the past twenty years it has figured prominently in university statements of purpose and in the wider policy discourse of higher education. Not long before the Brexit referendum, the European Union characterised internationalisation as

> 'the intentional process of integrating an international, intercultural or global dimension into the purpose, functions and delivery of post-secondary education, in order to enhance the quality of education and research for all students and staff, and to make a meaningful contribution to society' (de Wit et al. 2015).

In an earlier affirmation, in the 1990s, the development of internationalised higher education was heralded as a key factor in growing harmonisation in Europe. The irony of subsequent 'events' should not deflect the sense of a continuing groundswell of commitment on the part of the universities themselves to internationalisation, and this for a plethora of reasons. The following less rhetorical OECD statement accounts more fully for what was driving this change, and in the process offers more of a diagnosis:

> '[T]he growing global markets are constituted above all by two factors: on one hand, the economic and cultural weight of the United States; on the other hand, the economic/demographic weight of China, India and the rest of South Asia, and Southeast Asia. The United States pulls the world towards it, taking in a growing number of the rising generation . . . for whom an English-language and American education represents an entry to the global labour market' (OECD 2004: 148).

The upbeat tone of internationalisation has been countered, then, by a recognition of problems. Cooperation in internationalisation can mask a kind of colonialism, with the English-speaking countries gaining an advantage over others in terms of both prestige and economic benefit. This is often counterbalanced by the fact that in other countries university education is sometimes better supported by the state and, hence, recognised as a public good. Nevertheless, the picture is clearly one of inequality and asymmetry, in which the role of English is crucial.

Contrary to the mission statements and policy documents, Rebecca Hughes has questioned how far the process has created the promised global citizens – graduates with marketable communication abilities and high levels of inter-cultural understanding. Her criticism balances qualified optimism about possibly rich developments in the use of English itself with pessimism about the ways of thinking in which such possibilities have become stuck

> '[O]n the one hand, this development should, theoretically, foster truly 'international Englishes'. . . On the other, questions of the range, depth, nuance, accuracy and comprehensibility in the highest levels of academic debate may emerge where the language has to be constrained by mutual intelligibility among a range of language proficiencies in the lingua franca. Ability to communicate sophisticated ideas to a range of peers lies at the heart of academic discourse, and the debates about the medium of instruction sometimes mask this, presenting it as a simple matter of basic proficiency on the part of students (and, increasingly, faculty) – something perhaps on a par with information technology skills' (Hughes 2008: 7).

Hughes' criticisms are close to our own. What she says about language being constrained by the need for mutual intelligibility raises questions about translation and about what, in these circumstances, happens to English that are at the heart of our own concerns.

It will clarify matters, therefore, if we proceed in the light of the following broad distinction. Widespread as the term is, internationalisation is typically understood in two different ways: in Anglophone countries and in the rest of the world. In the former, internationalisation is taken to refer substantially to the recruitment of international students; in the latter, to the raising of the profile of the university on the international, predominantly Anglophone stage. To be sure, in both cases there is scope for recognition of intrinsic educational benefits in such practice, benefits that exceed what is conveyed by these somewhat clipped characterisations. But the point of the contrast is to emphasise the imbalance brought about primarily by the global dominance of English, which of course has become the lingua franca of international academic exchange. In both ways of understanding internationalisation, there is a privileging of Anglophone cultural practices, including conceptions of the university dominant in English-speaking countries, of research, of teaching and learning, and of thinking itself.

For present purposes, two factors about this are especially worthy of consideration. First, there is the fact that much academic communication and publication will require authors to use a language other than their mother-tongue. They may be very fluent in this acquired language, but the language that has now become their academic *modus operandi* is severed from the one that they grew up with. This needs to be carefully weighed, When language is cut off from the everyday, the familiar, and the colloquial, how far does this matter? It may well be that in some subjects, technical ones especially, it does not greatly matter. In the humanities, however, this is far from the case. When the subject of study is the human being, what is studied is not separable from the self-understandings that substantially constitute the human being. It is not surprising, then, that those working in the humanities typically attach great importance to the language of the texts they study *and* to their own language. This is not a matter of detached analysis of that language, in the manner characteristic of linguistics, but rather an engagement. In the social sciences, the scientific orientation can obscure the very nature of what is studied. As Peter Winch has pressed the point (Winch 1958), what is studied are self-interpreting beings, in consequence of which the researcher is confronted by two vocabularies – that of their particular science (psychology, sociology, etc.) and that of the human beings under study. In this the researcher is in a different position from, say, the geologist, because rocks do not have any vocabulary of their own. It is sometimes the case, furthermore, that the demands of a methodology so frame the way in which the object of study is understood that research and enquiry become reductive and scientistic. When this is coupled with the dominance of a *lingua franca* that is not one's native tongue, the propensity towards a more technical language is accentuated. This is an evasion of thought.

Second, there are questions about English itself. Are there particular features of English, especially when adopted as a second or third language, that may themselves have a distorting or limiting effect on thought? These factors disadvantage not only non-Anglophone universities: the presence of non-Anglophone students and researchers within Anglophone universities can provoke a defensiveness on the part of those universities about English, which may arrest the language of the classroom and obstruct teaching and learning. It will arrest it where students feel impelled to adopt not only the vocabulary but the structures of thinking and semantic fields that the required language opens, to the suppression of other ways of thinking their native language makes possible. The practical and political stakes here are high: it will usually be the case that submission to the dominant language will be the means to academic credibility and entry into professional life. In some ways it is difficult to see how things could be otherwise, but realism about this should not blind us to the dangers. We see here possibilities of both the technicisation of language and the ossification of thought.

These practical and political stakes bring into focus some key lexical sites around which further enquiry should indeed take place. There are questions of *property* (ownership) and *propriety* (correctness), and of belonging and identity, that are important not only in terms of justice and equality but in relation to thought itself. Let us turn to these by way of an example.

'This Is Not your Word'

In October 2016, in the United States, the blog post of a student went viral. That the student was not in fact an international student extends the reach of our concerns, showing the mixing of questions of language, race, and class in relation to questions of propriety and power. The student, Tiffany Martínez, was a first generation American citizen, at the time an undergraduate but with aspirations to pursue a PhD. She described how she had been accused of plagiarism. Grading an essay she had submitted, her professor had highlighted a particular word – the word 'hence' – and had commented 'This is not your word', with 'not' underscored with two lines. Martínez complained that the words were indeed her own. Her blog described her sense of despair at language stereotypes: in spite of the ostensible concern to 'fix the lack of diversity and understanding of marginalised communities,' the professor had evidently taken her to be a Latino student, with the baggage of assumptions regarding social class and language register that this brought with it. Scott Jaschik reports how the case set off 'a nationwide online discussion over the assumptions faculty members may bring to interactions with minority students' (Jaschik 2016).

A thorough assessment of what happened would require access to the student's full paper and much else. But what is most striking is the baldness of the assertion, 'This is not your word.' The force of the expression goes beyond allegations of plagiarism, for the implication is that a student like that would not have written a sentence like this. Was the problem:

- [implausibly] that such a student would not have encountered this word before? [Yet she is using it correctly, so why discourage her here?]
- [more likely] that such a student would have the word only in her 'passive vocabulary'? [But then why not encourage her to acquire its active use?]
- [more likely still] that such a word would not be in her accustomed registers and genres of speech? [But then why not encourage her in her attempts to expand these?]
- or [surely the case] that the word has a certain role and status in academic argument? [But then why not welcome her fledgling experimentation with this (if that is what it is)?]

Are the resistances here to be explained in terms of the professor's lack of 'interaction with minority students' as the news article suggests and so as grounds for better diversity-awareness training? Certainly there is good reason to raise awareness of the variety of students' backgrounds and so to enhance sensitivity to the polychromatic intersections of ethnicity, gender, and social class: these are intersections against which, in certain national contexts at least, the clarity of 'international student' begins to blur.

But our focus is somewhat different. The charge against the student is that this is not her word. But whose word is it? Certainly one's relation to a language can connect with a sense of belonging and, hence, with a politics of identity. But it is also the case that to think thus is to harbour a number of fallacies, as our earlier discussion of Odysseus and Aeneas – and, by extension, of Heidegger and Arendt – began to indicate. Such fallacies include the idea that any language is original and self-sufficient. There is an insidious power to notions of property and propriety, which impart at the same time ideas of the pure and the impure, and of the clean and the unclean, that are more or less hidden in English usage but that the French *propre* (clean, neat, own, appropriate, decent . . .) more readily calls to mind.

Heidegger is right in his apparently outrageous claim that it is not so much that human beings speak language: rather it is language that speaks the human being (Heidegger 1950). The fallacy he exposes is the assumption that language is a tool that human beings use – as if, as Aristotle thought and contemporary communications textbooks often maintain, our thoughts were there already and the task was to code them into speech or writing. The fallacy involves the assumption that our thoughts are there prior to our language, when a moment's self-examination should reveal the fact that the stream of thoughts that runs constantly in our waking minds is already overwhelmingly a stream of words. In fact, it will be insufficient to say that these thoughts are 'in language', for in a sense there is no language: there are languages. Languages exist plurally, and so our thoughts are always in a particular language, not language in the abstract. It follows also, as we saw earlier, that a science of linguistics, valuable though this undoubtedly is, will not get to these problems – at least, will not insofar as it takes language to be an object in the world, to be researched like any other. For language is already there, it inhabits us, always prior to our enquiry – not just prior in the sense that rocks are there before the geologist, but prior in the sense that we cannot step behind language: it is the pre-condition of our world.

Heidegger's insights here opened the way for so much in poststructuralist thought, as thinkers such as Michel Foucault and Jacques Derrida have been ready to acknowledge. And Derrida is right when he takes these thoughts further, taking them well beyond Heidegger's propensity to see language as a kind of rootedness in the way we saw above. In *Monolingualism of the Other, or, The Prosthesis of Origin*, Derrida begins with the enigmatic claim: 'I only have one language; it is not mine' (1998: 1). What can it mean for him to say that he speaks only one language, when it is clear that he speaks not just French, but English, German, other languages, and the street Arabic he grew up with. The enigma is dispelled with the thought that there is no tidy boundary that safeguards a language, no clear limit that can be drawn, and hence no pure 'inside'. And the point gains further weight when it is remembered that, for many people, thought slides mostly smoothly from (what we think of as) one language into another.

Yet we must confront the apparently contradictory thought that the language that I speak is *not* my own! But how not my own? Surely this language I habitually speak is mine, is it not? It is not my own, first, as we saw, because it is not that I wilfully take it up and use it: rather it is already there in my taking-up-and-using, always prior to what I do and say and think. Second, it is not mine because it is not something that is self-contained, not something I could pick up and grasp, any more than I could grasp the air I breathe. And third, in not being self-contained, it is always porous and permeable, open to influx from outside, without which it could scarcely *be* language. Languages exist in their plurality, and it would be a fantasy not to recognise thinking's dependence on this. Hence, the insistence on this apparent paradox: I speak only one language, and it is not my own. The assertion helps to dispel complacent assumptions of property and propriety, and so challenges the pernicious operations of these as manifested in the professor's response to Tiffany Martínez. How is the university implicated in this?

English for Academic Purposes and the Templates of Thought

When Martínez correctly uses the term 'hence', she is demonstrating competence in the use of academic English. 'English for academic purposes' is a phrase now widely used to name language courses of various kinds. Such courses answer to a need, and they surely enable students to cope better with the expectations of their courses. They develop in students notions of correct usage and of proprieties of style and approach. How else could they proceed? Such measures extend to more widely encouraged practices where the target audience is not just overseas students but those who are inexperienced in academic writing. Thus, there are writing templates that assist in the structuring of essays, and research methods courses that install models of good practice, including questions of style and presentation. Certainly such measures can help students to gain confidence in what they are doing and to feel that, as they master these techniques, they are coming into the practices of the discipline in question, with the sense of belonging, ownership, and identity that this confers. What objection could there be to this?

If the university is to think, it should not rest comfortably with practices of this kind. Writing templates or rubrics of standard research procedure can become constraints on disciplined thought itself. For disciplined exploration of the territory of enquiry often requires not railway tracks of procedure but trekking back and forth across an open, less well-charted landscape, gradually revealing the lie of the land. Even in technical subjects there is a need not simply to rely on standard techniques and procedures but to be ready to approach the problem from a different point of view. A readiness for this and the exercise of imagination constitute a more rigorous disciplining of thought.

The personification of 'the university that thinks' is less artificial than might otherwise be the case in view of the growing standardisation of the procedures by which universities operate – in teaching and assessment, in the organisation of curricula, and in the ways that research is conceived and undertaken. Such procedures are in part driven by practices of quality control, by international co-operation, comparison, and competition, and by funding regimes that operate on an increasingly international basis. These provide the vocabulary within which universities understand themselves. They are not so much instruments of evaluation and communication as a new channelling of its self-conception. There is no escape from the ways in which we are constructed by discourse, but our becoming aware that we are so constructed can provide at least some distance and means of critique: this is an opening of thought that the university needs.

Problems with English

In the face of these problems, something can be done, and shortly we shall conclude by offering four suggestions. Before this, however, it is important to probe a little further what it is we have become aware of. The asymmetries and inequalities that come with the dominance of English must not be denied. But there is, we have tried to indicate, something more problematic still, because closer to the very nature of thought, in the English that becomes the global language.

That language is not English *tout court*: it is English-as-a-second-language. Now it may be objected that there is no 'language *tout court*': on our own account, language is porous and impure, and so it exists in complex plural patterns of interaction; and surely English has for centuries existed in unequal and sometimes uneasy relationships alongside other languages, just as other dominant languages do and have done before. So what is new? The dominance of the British and then, especially, the American empires has coincided with extraordinary advances in communication and knowledge technologies. Over the past century these factors have not only contributed to the modern incarnation of the university but have shaped the form of English that has become current internationally. In consequence of what are often largely functional exchanges between scientists and engineers, and with the standardisation of performance measures alongside protocols of good practice in the language itself (English for academic purposes, research methods training, writing frames, etc.), English has become technicised in significant ways.

We want to supplement this thought with the conjecture that there may be within English itself a propensity towards a structuring of thought that is amenable to technical orientations. Utilitarianism was born and flourished in response to pressing social hardship, but is it perhaps significant that this was in an English-speaking country? Sentence construction in English is more simply functional than in, say, German. Its verbs lack the middle-voiced forms of Greek. Its manners of address and reception are less fine-grained than in Japanese. Moreover, its vocabulary is divided between (north European) everyday terms and technical or scholarly words (drawn from Greek and Latin), giving it a kind of dividedness not available to contemporary speakers of Italian or Greek – a fault-line extending through social class distinctions and into proprieties of speech that are jealously guarded ('This is not your word.').

Education and Social Advancement

Bernard Shaw's *Pygmalion* comically illustrates the promise of transformation that the adoption of a vocabulary and manner of speech can bring. This is a transformation easily confused with education. In fact, the popular Michael Caine film, *Educating Rita*, based on Willie Russell's play of the same name, follows a similar pattern of transformation, of a working-class mature student through higher education. It shows the ways in which Rita is both drawn towards education with some real intuition of what this might mean and confused by its proximity to such insignia of success as knowing which wine to choose, what accent to cultivate, and how to beat someone in an argument. The film deftly depicts Rita's eventual education as she comes to see the emptiness behind the allure of the latter.

Educating Rita is located in an English social milieu, but it is clear that it has broader resonance. It provides an analogy for power-relationships that are played out on a wider stage within education. The prestige and power associated with command of English (sometimes flaunted in the reiteration of English terms) can superimpose layers of meaning on more authentic, local ways of understanding, as is evident in aspects of policy-borrowing. Consider, for example, the emotive but politically important term 'social justice'. It is not just that this term will be used in international contexts where English is the *lingua franca*: it is rather that the term is sometimes imported in some way into the native language of those engaged in research or policy-development. A parallel would seem to be the situation where, in native English-speaking contexts, a researcher makes reference to *Bildung*, using the German word. But here this may be taken to reflect a breadth of outlook on the part of the speaker, even a largesse in welcoming a concept apparently outside the compass of English; for non-native speakers, by contrast, the inclusion of key

English terms may be required to show that they are not *ingénus* of the international research scene. Such (academic class) distinctions are sometimes played out with finesse. In Japanese 'social justice' is commonly translated with the katakana phrase *sosharu jasutisu* ('katakana' being the term for foreign words imported and duly adapted into Japanese), notwithstanding the fact that, in *shakai seigi,* a more authentic Japanese term is available. Naturally the latter term opens up semantic fields somewhat different from the anglo-connections of *sosharu jasutisu,* yet it is the imported term that tends to be favoured. This is, in some ways, a more surreptitious colonisation not only of language but of thought itself. It colludes with technicisation, the severance from the language of everyday (see Standish 2011a).

Privilege accrues to native English-speakers in the contemporary context of higher education, but it is important to acknowledge also the impoverishment of thought that can accompany this. Here the experience of translation is key.[5] In international environments, non-native speakers of English are confronted on a daily basis with this experience, whether over explicit words or problematic phrases upon which their attention is focused, or as a running undercurrent to more fluent language use. This is an awareness in some degree of what was described in the previous paragraph as the different semantic fields that are opened up by different languages, and of what was identified before that as differences in structure, verb form, and manners of address. This can be understood at an intellectual level, as it is here; to experience it will be something different. In translation, there is the experience of an incommensurability. The point is not that this is incapacitating: after all, people do translate! The point is rather that translation involves the exercise of judgement. Given the proximity of this to other occasions for judgement where, again, one is confronted by incommensurable sets of values and ways of thinking that are disparate, the experience of translation involves a kind of thinking that has wider practical (and, that is, moral) importance. It means that the monolingual person may in some degree remain morally blind (see Standish 2011a, b).

What Is to Be Done?

We conclude, then, by advancing four practical principles to enable better thinking in the university today.

First, the *intellectual* lesson needs to be learned. To acknowledge that languages open up the world, and the fact that they open it differently makes it possible to think differently, will be an advancement in learning and an improvement of thought.

Second, the *experience* of particular examples of the above can also be constructed and encouraged. The discussion of *Bildung* provided one reasonably familiar example of what is possible here. Similarly, comparison of the English term

---

[5] See Suzy Harris's *The University in Translation: Internationalizing Higher Education* (2011) for a thorough discussion. For further consideration of translation and thought, see Standish and Saito 2017.

'teacher' with the somewhat richer French *maître* and the still richer and grammatically slightly different Japanese *sensei* would be instructive – all to be tested, of course, against contemporary notions of the 'facilitator'. The point is that differences of this kind can be sought out and examined such that those whose first language is not English should not seek merely to emulate the native speaker but should also exploit their experience of translation.

Third, there is every reason to encourage the learning of at least one foreign language to a level of competence sufficient to enable the experience emphasised above. That this is stubbornly difficult to achieve in Anglophone countries is both understandable and a *symptom* of the very problem.

Finally, the humanities must be supported. The human being is self-interpreting, and so its ways of interpreting, its languages, are of the essence. This is not a rejection of science – quite the reverse – but an endorsement of the overarching meaning-making within which the sciences and all forms of enquiry have their place. It requires an engagement in judgement for which the technicisation of thought can never substitute. The point is that the humanities deserve a place in the university alongside the sciences, for in a sense they have prior importance. Attention to forms of language within which human beings make sense is an attention to thought itself, to thought's refinement; and this is to the benefit of the range of disciplines themselves.

No natural language exists in a pure definitive form, and our discussion has acknowledged the distinctive contemporary varieties of English, including the phenomenon of English-as-a-second-language. The university must not hide this diversity: it must neither rely on standardised forms of expression nor shelter behind the idea that translation is a purely technical matter – the substituting of one code for another, where each unlocks the same ideas. The difficulties here are diverse and real, traversing historically charged tensions of ethnicity, gender, and social class, in which disparities of power are not easily overcome. But this is not a counsel for despair. We have indicated steps to be taken – modest and piecemeal perhaps, but a development of thinking in the university.[6]

References

Cassin, B. (2016). *Nostalgia: When Are We Ever At Home?* (trans: Pascale-Anne Brault). New York: Fordham University Press.

de Wit, H., Hunter, F., Howard, L., & Egron-Polak, E. (2015). Internationalisation of higher education. In *Policy department B: Structural and cohesion policies culture and education*. European Union.

Derrida, J. (1998). *Monolingualism of the Other, or, The Prosthesis of Origin* (trans: Patrick Mensah). Stanford: Stanford University Press.

Harris, S. (2011). *The University in Translation: Internationalizing higher education*. London: Bloomsbury.

---

[6] Suzy Harris is thanked for comments on this paper.

Heidegger, M. (1950). Language (*Die Sprache*). *Poetry, Language, Thought* (1971) (trans: Albert Hofstadter). New York: HarperCollins.

Heidegger, M. (1968). *What is Called Thinking?* (trans: Fred.D. Wieck and J. Glenn Gray). New York: Harper and Row.

Heidegger, M. (1971). A dialogue on language, between a Japanese and an inquirer. *On the Way to Language* (tans: Peter D. Hertz). New York: Harper One.

Heidegger, M. (1990/1933). The self-assertion of the German university. In G. Neske & E. Kettering (Eds.), *Martin Heidegger and National Socialism*. New York: Paragon House.

Hughes, R. (2008). Internationalisation of higher education and language policy: Questions of quality and equity. *Higher Education Management and Policy, 20*(1), 1–18.

Jaschik, S. (2016, October 31). When Latina student wrote 'Hence,' Her Professor Assumed Plagiarism. Inside Higher Ed, Retrieved 5 May, 2017, from https://www.insidehighered.com/news/2016/10/31/latina-students-story-about-how-professor-reacted-word-hence-sets-debate-stereotypes

OECD. (2004). *Internationalisation and trade in higher education: Opportunities and challenges*. Paris: OECD.

Putnam, H. (1994). Pragmatism and relativism: Universal values and traditional ways of life. In J. Conant (Ed.), *Words and Life*. Cambridge, MA: Harvard University Press.

Standish, P. (2001a). Disciplining the profession: Subjects subject to procedure. *Educational Philosophy and Theory, 34*(1), 5–23.

Standish, P. (2001b). Data return: The sense of the given in educational research. *Journal of Philosophy of Education, 35*(3), 497–518.

Standish, P. (2011a). Social justice in translation: Subjectivity, identity, and Occidentalism. *Educational Studies in Japan: International Yearbook, 6*(Dec.), 69–79.

Standish, P. (2011b). One language, one world: The common measure of education. In G. Biesta (Ed.), *Philosophy of Education 2010*. Urbana: Philosophy of Education Society.

Standish, P. (2016). Making sense of data: Objectivity and subjectivity, fact and value. *Pedagogika, 66*(6), 622–637.

Standish, P., & Saito, N. (2017). *Stanley Cavell and philosophy as translation: The truth is translated*. London: Rowman & Littlefield.

Williams, E. (2016). *The ways we think: From the straits of reason to the possibilities of thought*. Oxford: Wiley-Blackwell.

Winch, P. (1958). *The idea of a social science and its relation to philosophy*. London: Routledge and Kegan Paul.

Wittgenstein, L. (1958). *Philosophical Investigations* (trans: G. Elizabeth M. Anscombe). Oxford: Blackwell.

Part III
The Thinking University: Making Connections

Chapter 10
A Complexity Thinking Take on Thinking in the University

David Beckett and Paul Hager

Introduction

Universities are explicitly sites of thinking: they present myriad ways to think – and to provoke thinking. Heidegger, in his famous work '*What is Called Thinking?*' (1954) marks out the relational quality of thinking, thus: 'thinking is thinking when it answers to what is most thought-provoking' (p28); and 'we learn to think by giving our mind to <u>what there is</u> to think about' (p4). Both 'answering' and 'giving' are examples of thinking *relationally*, that is, by doing it under provocation – it is in the doing of thinking that our learning emerges. In this chapter, we develop the significance of this 'learning thinking by doing thinking' to which Heidegger draws attention, and we do so by setting out a contemporary account of complexity. First, we provide a theorisation of complexity, which comes across from the natural sciences to the social sciences, though in a somewhat different form. Secondly, we put this theorisation to work, in raising some challenges and opportunities for re-thinking thinking for universities, by tackling some of the big issues facing learning in universities. These include excessive individualism, narrow cognitivism and an emaciated notion of learners' agency, all of which under-acknowledge the formative power of groups, especially for shaping subsequent professional practice broadly conceived. We close with some practical implications for universities' core work of this complexity thinking 'take' on thinking.

D. Beckett (✉)
The University of Melbourne, Victoria, Australia
e-mail: d.beckett@unimelb.edu.au

P. Hager
University of Technology Sydney, New South Wales, Australia
e-mail: Paul.Hager@uts.edu.au

© Springer International Publishing AG, part of Springer Nature 2018   137
S.S.E. Bengtsen, R. Barnett (eds.), *The Thinking University*,
Debating Higher Education: Philosophical Perspectives 1,
https://doi.org/10.1007/978-3-319-77667-5_10

Why Complexity Thinking Has Come to the Fore

Complexity thinking begins with the observation that humans inhabit a world that is infinitely complex. As Richardson and Cilliers (2001) note, complexity is *ubiquitous*. Humans employ complexity reduction in order to cope with this overwhelming complexity of the world. We make sense of it by focusing on some features and ignoring others. Much complexity reduction is done for us thanks to biological evolution. Humans are equipped with complexity-reducing sensory structures. Nevertheless, as this chapter will argue, particularly in the domain of the social, humans also have significant freedom to choose the degree of reduction that will be serve their given purposes.

Since complexity has all along been a feature of our world, one might well ask why it is only comparatively recently that it has begun to receive serious attention. Morin (2007) credits the advent of the second law of thermodynamics and concepts such as disorder and chaos with science's increasing acceptance of complexity. As the concept of complexity gradually proved its value to the natural sciences and mathematics, it became influential in the fields of philosophy and the social sciences. The term 'complexity' has also come to be understood somewhat differently between disciplines, and even within the same discipline (Byrne and Callaghan 2014). Thus, there has been growing debate about the essential features of complexity, with distinctions emerging between different kinds of complexity.

This diversity of theories lies behind our preference (following Richardson and Cilliers 2001) for the term 'complexity thinking' rather than 'complexity theory', *complexity thinking* being a useful tool for reflection about our *ontologically* complex world and our interactions with it.

An Overview of Complexity Thinking

Firstly, complexity is a property of *systems*. Very familiar are *simple* systems. Their states can be specified readily and their operations can be described in linear terms using Newton's Laws. Though simple systems can be intricate, their states and operations still can be specified and accurately described. Such simple systems are better described as complicated, rather than as complex. A state of the art submarine or a Boeing 747 are examples of complicated yet simple systems. Genuinely complex systems are something very different. They elude understanding and description via linear mathematics and Newton's Laws. In a complex system, "the causal categories become intertwined in such a way that no dualistic language of state plus dynamic laws can completely describe it." (Rosen 1987: 324). Put more simply, a complex system is "a set of inter-related elements ....in which ...the whole is greater than the sum of its parts." (Byrne and Callaghan 2014: 4) (Although, as will become clear, this formulation needs careful interpretation.).

Secondly, complexity arises from the *relations* between entities, rather than from the entities themselves. Extending the first point, complex systems are characterised by multiple non-linear relations between the entities within the system. It is the interaction of these non-linear relations that can give rise to new structures or qualities which, though constrained by the original relations of the system, are not wholly predictable from them, nor reducible to them. This phenomenon, known as *emergence*, is a characteristic feature of complex systems. Any understanding of complexity must include a careful investigation of the *relations (interrelationships) between entities*, rather than the traditional focus on the entities themselves, i.e. on the relata.

The focus on relations challenges more familiar modes of thinking. Some philosophical views seek to subsume relations into the particulars (relata) between which the relations hold. This approach, which effectively reduces relations to properties of their *relata*, might be called the 'Lego view' of relations – mere collections of suitably shaped particulars. Scepticism about the ontological reality of relations has been fuelled further by the apparent *reification* of relations by some relational realists, that is, in making reference to relations, they seemingly treat them as things (particulars, substances) on a par with non-relational things or entities. This practice is mistaken.We are also sceptical of representational assumptions: where what there is is already 'out there', pictured for us in language, or perception as a 'given'. For us, by contrast, the activities of life shape experiences, including experiences of *relatedness*, as well as of the complexity of the relational reality within which *relata and their relations* persist.

In order to illustrate the dominance within Western thought of a substantialist perspective, Emirbayer (1997) points to the statement that 'the wind is blowing'. Here the implication is that a discrete particular, the wind, is engaging in the activity of blowing. In truth a more accurate description of the wind blowing would consider relational differences across various parts of the earth's atmosphere.

Similarly, the Western world is shaped by natural languages where nouns-and-verbs represent experience atomistically: we 'see' these first when we describe the world. By contrast, for those from some indigenous experiences, what is 'seen', for example, is not a 'canoe-on-a-beach' (that is, atomistically, a canoe and a beach in a relationship), but 'canoe-on-ness' (a relationship, within which *relata* make sense) (Watson-Verran 1989 p14). In subsequent work on indigenous relationality, Watson-Verran draws on the later Wittgenstein to claim that how we act in the world is bound up with how we see and communicate: '…particular predicating-designating…originates in language-users' embodied certainty of relationality in acts' (Verran 2001, p224).

Overall, and for various reasons, relations have been viewed widely as being ontologically suspect and theoretically superfluous. It is clear then that a complexity perspective, insisting that complex systems are constituted by the relations between entities, rather by the entities alone, poses a direct challenge to much established thought, and to traditional 'thinking'.

Thirdly, the term 'reduction' has occurred severally in this chapter. Reduction of complexity - some of it biologically programmed, some consciously chosen - has been proposed as a major mechanism for human coping with a complex world. Reduction has also been presented as one of the fundamental explanatory principles of science. There it can be a knowledge claim: an understanding of the basic constitutive elements of a composite is sufficient for knowledge of the composite. Or it can be an ontological principle: composites are nothing more than the sum of their basic constitutive elements.

What is common to each of these citings of reduction is that either the relations within the whole (or composite) are ignored or a minimalist understanding of the relations is adopted. Such reductions are undertaken for a variety of purposes. For example, musical works written for large scale forces, such as singers and orchestra, are reduced to a piano version to facilitate the early stages of rehearsals when the orchestra is not yet available. Likewise, simplified arrangements of famous, yet advanced, piano pieces are developed to enable beginning pianists to have some experience of this music. In such instances, the purpose is often a pragmatic reduction to make the best of particular circumstances. In addition, these examples suggest that reduction is commonly a matter of degree. For instance, arranging a symphony for solo piano would be more reductive than an arrangement for a chamber orchestra.

In the sciences, somewhat different purposes of reduction become evident. In some cases, there is acceptance that the complexity of the world cannot be taken into account all at once. The mathematics would be far too complicated for an initial 'all or nothing' approach. Thus, theories and models are constructed that deliberately simplify. These are then tested, refined and developed further till their predictive power approximates reality. Models are reductive conceptual tools that are refined empirically to take account of limited, but key, aspects of natural or controlled systems. As such, they ignore the roles of certain relations and interactions, for example, 'ideal' gases are assumed to have negligible interactions between the gas molecules. Statistical modelling is a related reductive strategy that provides quantitative data on many phenomena. In the modern era, statistical tools such as surveys, budgets, maps, and accounts, have become essential underpinnings of bureaucratic administration within nation states. Social life in general is an instance of complexity reduction. Social norms that shape human interaction and communication bring order and even routine to situations that otherwise would be complex in the extreme. Similar considerations apply to human behaviour within particular organisations, institutions, and communities. Each has evolved its own distinctive form of complexity reduction, its ethos, identity, and particular ways of doing things ('organisational culture' is often defined as 'how we do things around here').

There are, therefore, many reasons for complexity reduction, and multiple ways of doing so. They are often unnoticed and unacknowledged. Common to all is the downplaying or ignoring of specific relations. Thus, complexity reduction strategies offer tacit support to scepticism about relations in the overall furniture of the world. Another drawback is that by treating relations reductively while focusing on particulars, it leaves our dominant conceptual frameworks less open to the more process-oriented, generative aspects of human functioning, aspects characterised by their relationality.

Take the theorisation of meaning. The dominant focus on particulars has seen many attempts to understand meaning as fixed or precise, though none has gained lasting acceptance. We endorse Malpas (2002), who has argued that meaning is inescapably relational, being always context dependent. On this view, meaning can never be fully determinate since it is always 'in the making'. Thus, complexity thinking strongly suggests that the presuppositions that structure our conceptual frameworks themselves need to be the subject of searching inquiry. In addition, as Cilliers (2001, 2013) stresses, complexity thinking points to the necessary incompleteness of all theorising. It follows that complexity thinking is necessarily incomplete, and so it is not so much a replacement for other theories as a useful adjunct.

Crucially, for complexity thinking, the relations between entities have ontological salience. But this should not be understood as implying that entities (or particulars) are irrelevant. According to complexity thinking it is *the processes of the relations between entities* that are central. From a complexity perspective, structure is not a mere assemblage of entities but is emergent from these processes of the relations.

The next section of this chapter centres on how certain types of group processes favour emergent thinking within universities. For emergence to occur, we need groups that are complex systems, not just simple, or even complicated, systems. The difference is that for complex systems, which are, of course, nonlinear, changes can be "disproportionate to the changes in the causal element(s)" (Byrne and Callaghan 2014: 18). As Nicolis puts it:

> In a linear system the ultimate affect of the combined action of two different causes is merely the superposition of the effects of each cause taken individually. But in a nonlinear system adding two elementary actions to one another can induce dramatic new effects reflecting the onset of cooperativity between the constituent elements. This can give rise to unexpected structures and events whose properties can be quite different from those of underlying elementary laws.... Nonlinear science is, therefore, the science of evolution and complexity. (1995: 1–2)

Thus the strong connection between the nonlinearity of complex systems and the phenomenon of emergence is crucial. This has both ontological and epistemological implications. The ontological point is that our account of 'what there is' needs to include the emergent properties that characterise complex systems. Emergent properties are irreducible to the properties of the individual components of the complex system. The epistemological point is that, without an account of these emergent properties, any understanding of reality will be defective.

Complex systems are also *open systems*, in that they can exchange material and/ or information with their environment. They feature internally generated processes, i.e. *self-organization*. However, and importantly, there are also different types of complex systems, as marked by Morin's (2007) influential distinction, between "restricted complexity" and "general complexity" (see also Byrne 2005; Lancaster 2012).

Restricted Complexity

Restricted complexity is "the emergent product of interaction amongst simple agents", i.e. the complexity that "emerges from rule-based interactions among simple elements" (Byrne and Callaghan 2014: 5). As Morin points out, though it has led to "important advances in formalization, in the possibilities of modelling", it is "firmly anchored in the epistemology of classical science" (Morin 2007: 10). That is, it adheres to explanatory principles of classical science, principles that Morin argues have served to mask the significance of complexity. Specifically, as its focus on rule-based interactions among simple elements suggests, *restricted complexity adheres to the principle of reduction*. It is characteristic of restricted complexity that the micro-level of the system is at the physical level, thereby preserving key features of the Newtonian science framework. At the same time, it is accepted that restricted complexity arises from non-linear relational interactions. However, the emergents from the processes of these non-linear relational interactions are patterns or networks, which can be subject to algorithmic formulation and computation. The general idea is that for restricted complexity, if only we have sufficient information we can, in principle, 'explain' any emergent:

An oft-quoted instance of 'simple components interacting simply' is the formation of sand dunes. Simple relations between multiple grains of sand, powered by various environmental forces over time, produce a sand dune. Further applications of restricted complexity to understand complex phenomena include bird flocking, traffic flows, voting behaviour, and patterns of disease. It is notable that in each of these instances the individual birds or humans are treated reductively as statistical variables, similar to grains of sand. These successful uses of restricted complexity represent its extension from mathematics and the natural sciences, into the social and human sciences. However, it soon became apparent that this reductive form of complexity has limited applicability in the social and human sciences. It breaks down where humans need to be treated as distinct individuals and the specific interpersonal relations between individuals are relevant to the particular focus of the inquiry. In such cases, it is uninformative to view individual persons reductively as statistical variables. At best, restricted complexity provides broad-brush understandings of organisational, institutional or population-based aspects of social functioning. To appreciate the wider possibilities for applying complexity thinking to the social and human sciences we need to consider another kind of complexity – general complexity.

General Complexity

Morin introduces general complexity by contrasting the respective "paradigms" of classical science and of complexity thinking. He views the knowledge paradigm of classical science as one of simplification regulated by "a principle of reduction and a principle of disjunction". In contrast, the knowledge paradigm of general complexity features "a principle of distinction and a principle of conjunction" (2007: 10). Morin characterizes general complexity as follows:

> *In opposition to reduction, [generalized] complexity requires that one tries to comprehend the relations between the whole and the parts. The knowledge of the parts is not enough, the knowledge of the whole as a whole is not enough, if one ignores its parts; one is thus brought to make a come and go in a loop to gather the knowledge of the whole and its parts. Thus, the principle of reduction is substituted by a principle that conceives the relation of whole-part mutual implication. (10)*

Whereas restricted complexity remains as faithful as possible to *three fundamental explanatory principles of classical science*, Morin characterises general complexity as substituting three contrasting principles. As the above quotation suggests, the principle of *reduction* is replaced by a principle of whole-part mutual implication. Likewise the principle of *disjunction* is replaced by a principle of conjunction. That is, while recognising the distinctions between things, we also need to take proper account of the relations between them (Morin 2007: 11). Finally, for the principle of *determinism,* Morin (2007: 11) substitutes a "principle that conceives a relation between order, disorder and organization". Morin's elaboration of this principle centres on the key terms - system, emergence and organization - and the relationships between them. Byrne and Callaghan (2014) strongly support the importance of Morin's general complexity for the social and human sciences:

> *....any general complexity social science has to get beyond micro-determined emergence. It has to allow for structures with causal powers and it has to address human agency as capable of transcending narrow rules for behavior. (2014: 56)*

Vital to general complexity is that individual humans are themselves complex systems (Byrne and Callaghan (2014: 41). This makes them more complex in many ways than the rule-following agents in the agent-based simulations that exemplify restricted complexity. In general complexity, humans have the power of agency both individually and collectively. In positing collective agency, Byrne and Callaghan maintain that "collectivities have a reality beyond the individuals who constitute them" (2014: 41). This idea opens up the important concept of

> *....the ontological reality of nested and interpenetrating complex social systems beyond individuals, although of course with individuals as elements in those systems... (2014: 41)*

Byrne and Callaghan view social systems and entities as both nested and interpenetrating with causal powers running in all directions (2014: 45). They summarise this idea as follows:

> *.....there is a 'social' at whatever level from the smallest collective assemblage of human beings to the level of the world system as a whole. The social we see as emergent but not simply as emergent from individual interactions. There is a reality within which all the entities operate, interpenetrate, and mutually and reflexively express causal powers. (2014: 45)*

Putting Complexity Thinking to Work in Universities

Universities are sites of human thinking, where provocations are, as it were, built in to the mission. Emergence of knowledge, filtered through rigorous critical scrutiny, is at the heart of scholastic and of research activities. Learning-to-learn involves coming to understand oneself as part of communities and cultures which already relate to the wider world as well as to various parts of the university, such as through (traditionally) disciplines, or (currently) 'wicked problems'. Evidence of achievements in scholarship and research, and therefore in teaching, is typically taken to signify 'truth': all these arise from powerful thinking which is relational and organic – always on the move and yet embedded in traditions of thinking which construct identities. As Heidegger (1954) asks, 'what is it that calls on us to think?', and, 'by thinking, be who we are?' (p121). He asks, what is our food for thought? In universities, we *become* thinkers (that is, assume the identity of a thinker) because we are appropriated, that is, joined, to thought.

Traditionally, and by contrast to the Heideggerian view, universities have engaged our thinking by joining us to thoughts – in the sense of accessing items, or imbibing atoms of 'food', to think about (also known as propositional knowledge). This has traditionally occurred through three assumptions about, or 'appropriations' of, experience:

- Universities readily *atomize* human performance into component parts. Traditionally, lectures give theories, and the tutorials or laboratories give applications of these. The sum of these experiences is then assumed to be equivalent to the original whole. Complexity thinking suggests this is unhelpfully reductive of human experience.
- Universities focus on the more overtly *cognitive* aspects of human performances. Traditionally, the learning that is privileged is the ordering (in a lecture and a library) and re-ordering (in a tutorial or examination paper) of propositions (or 'knowing that x'). This generates 'thin' understandings that overlook other crucial aspects of experiences, such as affect, know how, judgement, and the various influences of context.
- Universities traditionally assume that the *individual* agent is the appropriate unit of analysis for understanding human performances. If 'I' get it right, I will do well. Yet the atomised 'me' typically has a thoroughly social campus experience, in groups most of the time, at least formally. This assumption fails to acknowledge the sociality of university learning.

Complexity-inspired understanding of what a university is, or (in Heideggerian terms), how such an understanding 'calls forth' or provokes thinking, challenges these three traditional appropriations of experience, in particular by:

- Insisting upon *holistically relational* understandings of the interactions within human performances.
- Recognising the roles of the *affect* and other non-cognitive attributes in the judgments involved in human performances.

- Taking *groups* as the focus of analyses, within which the roles of the group can be synthesised in judgments.

Why this emphasis on groups? Small groups of people (say, between two and a dozen) working cooperatively to achieve common goals are major ubiquitous features of the human world, and are very prominent though under-recognised, in the ways universities are structured and function. Complexity thinking brings these features to prominence, and indeed advocates small groups as a logical extension of this prominence, in the particular case of universities as sites of thinking.

Universities require myriads of small groups to function under a wide variety of names according to particular circumstances: executives and committees, research centres and hubs, teaching teams and programs, departments and offices and so on. Even when research papers require hundreds of co-authors' names, this frequently reflects a federation of smaller groups working in labs in various locations, all contributing to the final effort. At the other extreme, a single-authored humanities book will often be underpinned by a team of research assistants. Overall we can see that university research infrastructures, and their purpose and functions, are well-explained by complexity thinking.

The provocation of thinking, which is the mission of a university, to which all these structural small groups are intended to contribute, also requires small pedagogical groups: tutorials, laboratories, study and writing groups, workshops, seminars and excursions, and work-integrated learning (which implants learners away from the university into other organisations' small groups). Similarly, these sites of 'thinking-provocation' mirror the wider world, such as family life, book clubs, community choirs, surgical teams, legal teams, swimming squads, and so on. All these provoke thinking, but for universities, it is their main pedagogical mission to do so, not as a consequence of other activities.

Small groups have a shared purpose and a shared commitment to achieving that purpose, albeit for the good of the individuals within the groups, as well as for the groups. That is why complexity thinking as we set it out here is *less* reductive, not *non*-reductive. There is a legitimate expectation shared by members of a small group, namely, that each individual will benefit from her or his membership of it (cf. Simpson and Beckett 2014). So our account of complexity is 'general' in the sense that it minimises reduction to the atomistic, whilst acknowledging the legitimacy of particular expectations held by individuals. But our ontological priority is general relationality: how groups as sites of practice (and therefore of identity) generate, *through their relationships*, these practices and identities. Within this ontology, the particular *relations* of individuals to each other and to the group (which altogether give the group's activities its purposes – its *telos*), are what give the group an identity *as a group*.

Our emphasis on complexity *theory*, defined earlier as the general or overarching relations of the parts (the individuals and their *relations*) to the whole (the group), flows logically through to our claim that universities are sites of complexity *thinking*. Small groups are ubiquitous in universities, as we showed earlier. Now we refine the notion of small groups.

What do university-based instances of small groups at work have in common? Most obviously, and most generally, these groups focus on a shared process towards a shared goal. In replacing the lone university student as the archetypical 'thinker', we propose the notion of the 'co-present group', a type of complex system defined by and constituted in:

- an ontological prioritisation to the *relationships of the group* – which contain 'thought-ful' experiences amongst the individuals who are members of it, both to each other, but also to the group as a whole;
- a holistic appreciation of *affective* group experience, not merely of the cognitive (traditional thinking or ratiocination); and, arising from those two characteristics, this leads to:
- an assumption that these relationships and experiences are constitutively *social* – that is, they give the group its identity as a group, as knowledge emerges from shared understandings (note that these understanding do not assume 'agreement': it is common to agree to differ).

'Co-present groups' (Lancaster 2012, 2013) are ways of addressing shared purposes; these particularities consist in acknowledging the 'provocative' potential of the *relational processes of such groups*. Complexity thinking thus directs attention to the *generative* significance of 'thought-ful' experiences within groups – including cognitive, affective and social phenomena. These experiences are inevitably (since they arise amongst humans) messy! Recall that our account of general complexity in the previous section drew attention to the significance of *emergence*, where what emerged was unpredictable and not reducible to the relations from which it arose. For a much fuller discussion of general complexity, emergence and their exemplification in co-present groups, see Hager and Beckett (forthcoming).

University tutorials and laboratories, as examples of working in co-present groups, are generative of thinking, but cannot predict, nor can they retrospectively explain, their outcomes. Complexity thinking, as manifest in co-present groups in universities, provokes the emergence of better thinking, but does not go the next step: setting up the 'best' outcome.

We Now Take this a Little Further

The 'co-presentness' of a group is constituted by the willingness of the members to own its relational, holistic and social significance. A co-present group is engaged in a shared endeavour: the makings of meanings (that is, sense-making) of some aspects of the world in which the group operates. This is fundamental to the mission of a university, but a co-present endeavour does not insist on shared agreement as an outcome of the group's functions. A co-present group, such as a tutorial, workshop or laboratory, therefore has an onto-epistemological significance: it exists to seek understandings of, and to progress, some significant experiences towards these becoming knowledge in and of the world. Thinking is 'called forth', or generated, by the co-present group. Diverse makings of meanings are expected to emerge from the complexity thinking inherent in such groups.

But how can this occur? Not surprisingly, *affective relations* between co-group members are vital to seeking and progressing these significant experiences. Similarly vital are *tacit* (inarticulable, and typically embodied) experiences. 'We know more than we can tell', famously stated Polanyi (1966; p4).

Because we are defining the co-present group as constituted by its relationality, its holism and its sociality, we believe the ideal size of such groups is between two and about twelve members, and they do not have to be physically present. A virtual or semi-virtual co-present group may exist across the globe, and may include some members in the same room at the same time. Moving further into double figures increases the relationships exponentially and unrealistically complicates expectations of shared experiences from which shared understandings and new knowledge can readily emerge. The affective and the tacit would be two early casualties of a larger group trying to act 'co-presently'.

Instead of formal management, we believe co-present groups are structured through sensitivities to the *performative* nature of their relations. Hence the inherent messiness of co-present groups, as we noted earlier. Performances can range from the tightly scripted to the completely improvised. Members of groups are changed by their own, and others', diversely performative participation in them. This is 'transactional' activity (cf. Dewey and Bentley 1949), because both *relations* and the entities (relata) related by them, are altered by participation in them. In the tutorial or workshop, participation changes relationships *and* those who are in the room.

So, for us, co-present groups are constituted in transactionally-relational activities. In particular, the onto-epistemological significance of a co-present group is apparent in how it makes experiences meaningful: this is found through undergoing performative activities where affective relations, and the tacit, are shared. In universities (both in their research and also in their pedagogical functions), learning, and thinking, *emerge by doing* these activities. 'Sharing' and 'undergoing' are *relations*. This is the heart of a retrieval of a thinking university, but one that is informed by complexity thinking.

Heidegger (1954) reminds us of our legacy: '[O]ur own manner of thinking still feeds on the traditional nature of thinking, the forming of representational ideas' (p45), shaped, in the West, by *logos* (p163). Under complexity-informed thinking, we move beyond the traditional 'representational' account of thinking and the cognitivism that it assumes – where ideas are transmitted as propositions from libraries, their books, and from the memories of academics, into the heads of learners. Instead, following this insight, we propose co-present groups as sites of provocations (or 'callings forth') to thinking, where provocations are a form of *doing ideas*, not of transmitting ideas. In universities, co-present groups 'share', and learners 'undergo', what is generative – namely, thinking, out aloud (that is, with each other).

Of course, in these 'doings' (both the sharing and the undergoing), propositional knowledge is essential, and the significance of teaching from 'representational ideas' is profound. Thinking aloud (in language) would be Babel without direction and leadership in what to think about – provocations as mere provocations can be mindless and trivial. Heidegger notes that: 'We are capable of thinking only insofar as we are endowed with what is most thought-provoking' (p126). We are called, through the shared experience of conversations, that is, in language, into acts of more-or-less 'sense-giving' (p129). Sense-making, or meaning–making, is the pedagogical challenge, no less so under complexity thinking. Sound university teaching directs learners to start with what we know or make sense of (commonly), and work out the 'well-springs' (that which is the most generative) which are 'dug up in the telling' (p130). And for us, co-present groups require leadership, in the direction of 'what there is to-be-thought', where the food, or well-springs, are most likely to nourish thought. Co-present groups need leadership – there needs to be a director of the research, and a lecturer/tutor of the class. This is fundamental to co-present groups in a university. Knowledge which emerges from co-present groups needs to be shared authoritatively – by which we mean underpinned by norms of rigor, which experts have as part of their expertise in the field of research or pedagogy. Astronomy cannot be allowed to drift into astrology!

The other significant *relation* in 'doing' thinking is 'undergoing'. A co-present group has an immediacy born of the generative activities which are shared. The group has to stay with the telos, with what is the focus: 'Present and presence means what is with us. And that means: to endure in the encounter', states Heidegger (p234). Staying with the activities, and knowing that is important, brings with it sustained exposure to thinking. Thinking in learning situations through co-present groups (in contrast to the traditional atomistic and cognitivist account) exposes individuals to learning about each other and about themselves, through what is relationally undergone.

On the way through to an outcome (whether agreed or not) – say, a judgement that this is indeed valuable learning, or new knowledge, or worth thinking about – the group's affective and social functioning intertwine over time. Time and being are thus co-implicated in the existence of the co-present group. Following Heidegger (1954 *Lecture X* passim), time is both always experientially present, and also is always 'the present', even when the past and the future are engaged in teaching, in propositions, through memories of earlier research, or in plans for proposed future work. So, co-present groups in universities are marked by persistence over time, and are 'in' time, where the time is the present, as a feature of their 'doing thinking'.

We want to take this retrieval of thinking into the equally-significant vocational mission of a university. Co-present groups in universities are heavily involved in the educational formation of future workers in the wider world, mainly, professionals. And in, and for, this wider world, vocational success is frequently attributed to teams, projects and inter-disciplinary practices all of which instantiate our three complexity-driven features: *holistic relationality*, *affective functioning* and the *sociality of the workplace*. Co-present groups can also exhibit *agency* (cf List and Pettit 2011). Such a group can *in itself* (without reduction to the actions of individuals in it) make a difference in the world and be accountable for it. The power of 'thinking' in and beyond university experiences via co-present groups is profound, as Carol Rovane explains, in entering the debate over groups and agency:

When philosophers are open-minded about the possibility of group agency, they accept...
that a group of human beings can realise, or at least approximate, at the level of the whole
group the same kind of rationality that is characteristically realised by normal adult human
beings (Rovane 2014, p1663).

Since 'co-present groups' are co-constitutive of thinking and doing, it comes as
no surprise to read that expertise (and skills, and competence) emerge from relations, where affective functioning and the sociality of work are paramount. In setting out an account of such vocational formation, Anne Edwards (2010) draws
attention to:

...the relational turn in expertise as professionals work in and between work settings and
interact with other practitioners and clients to negotiate interpretations of tasks and ways
of accomplishing them. **The central argument is that the resources that others bring to**
problems can enhance understandings and can enrich responses. *However, working in*
this way makes demands on practitioners. At the very least, it calls ... the capacity to rec-
ognise and respond to what others might offer. (p13 emphasis added)

We think better amongst others! Confident engagement and a capacity to recognise and respond to what others might offer are features of working together in a
team environment – on a project, such as a surgical operation (e.g. Bleakley 2006),
a lawsuit, an art exhibition or performance, the construction of a building and so
on – through the many associated generic *capacities* such as: communicability,
problem-solving, conflict resolution, literacy, numeracy and so on.

These 'thinkings-and-doings' should be explicitly apparent in most learning
activities, such as simulations, role plays, skills training, job rotations, formal studies and so on (Beckett 2012a, 2012b). Outside universities, an entire vocational
education and training sector exists, from which much can be learned about the
power of co-present groups in professional and other labour-market configurations
(such as trades, casual work, franchise operations).

What is required is an account of the agency of the co-present group in generating the emergence of expertise of the kind Edwards calls for, that is, which is *relational*. By this, she means that, in the workplace, responses and solutions to
particular situations that arise there emerge from the *relational processes* – the
myriad, messy but purposeful decisionality that a group generates as it grapples
with routine, non-routine and sheer unintended circumstances: the happenstance of
life at work. Informal learning frequently and powerfully arises from this messiness,
(Hager and Halliday 2006, pp235–238).

So, our co-present groups possess an agentive capacity, and their expertise is
found in their *affective functioning*, as much as in their *social* characteristics. The
co-present group's decisionality emerges from its socio-affective activity. Its outcomes are the group's outcomes; its processes are equally integral to the group.

A co-present group has agency constituted in human experiences that are holistic, and are significantly affective: we want and desire various 'goods'. Life is normative, and the particularity of this – locations of practice – no less so. The ethos of
nursing, for example shapes the practical judgements and decisions of nurses: what
counts as an improvement in wellness for the patient in Bed Three is driven as much
by normativity as reasoning: both are involved in a clinical judgement made by

nurses in the Post-Operative Ward. Indeed these are intertwined. What counts (to peers) as a 'good' reason is, by definition, normative. Its 'goodness' is found in its normative fitness, according to the ethos of the practice.

So our co-present groups – both in universities and beyond them in the vocational world that normally follows – advance practical purposes and are thus *constituted* in the quest to achieve them, through the decisions (or judgements) made *by the group*. Aristotle argues that judgements that are practically wise are about '… what is to be done. For the originating causes of the things that are done consist in the end at which they are aimed' (*Nichomachean Ethics*, Bk 4, Ch5). So, we see how, in co-present groups, normativity *constitutes* practical judgements: the reasoning and the justifications for actions which peers and individuals have and can give one another are enfolded within *what it is to be*, not just a human-with-agency, but more particularly a group of (nascent) practitioners-within-a-practice. This embedded, constitutive agentive capacity is part of who we are, at and through our work. It gets us moving. Moreover, there is a larger claim. Our group-based agency helps to make us ontologically distinctive – how (and how well), and with whom, we do our work, makes us who we are, and so identity is an emergent property, spinning off from deep within our evolving purposes – what Aristotle calls 'good actions'. As Edwards (2010) sets out:

> …identity is not a stable characteristic, but is dialogical, negotiated and accomplished within activities…which are in turn located in practices. … One's identity is also an organising principle for action: we approach and tackle what we think we are able to change and make changes in line with what matters to us: our interests. These interests are culturally mediated, but nonetheless experienced personally in terms of our commitments, standpoints and the resources available to us. (p10)

In a world increasingly sensitive to the 'relational turn', our agency is itself in the relational mix. Practitioners, including researchers and pedagogues in universities, act amongst the fluidity of daily work, so our experience of our agentive selves is itself a component in the construction of our identity. 'Academic freedom' is an aspect of the identity of the university practitioner, prized and defended at least in the West, and it has emerged from the ideal of the autonomous pursuit of truth. This normativity assumes agency. In universities, we typically 'see' ourselves as more or less agentive, depending on the practical exercise of that 'relational agency'. To reiterate, most of our daily university work revolves around and amongst small groups and the thinking which they generate. But can our very sense of agency *emerge from* complexity thinking in co-present groups, as such?

Deborah Perron Tollefsen (2015) has recently set out an account of joint intentionality and collective responsibility. She argues that this depends on making sense of others, by attributing to others 'a unified perspective - a rational point of view - and that [the group] shares our norms of rationality… [thus] we attribute beliefs, intentions and desires [to groups] in the same way we do to individuals' (p104). Tollefsen claims our practice of interpreting the actions of groups is 'just an extension of our practice of making sense of individuals' (ibid.). Thus her claim fits with the model of complexity theory we have developed in this chapter, namely, as we stated earlier, to give onto-epistemological prominence to the 'general or over-arching relations of the parts (the individuals and their *relations*) to the whole (the group)'. We claim that thinking is a prominent manifestation of this 'group agency', particularly through the myriad co-present groups experienced in universities.

Co-present groups in and beyond universities, therefore, are central to the formation of vocational identities (including the identities of academics), and, indeed to the formation of adults-as-citizens who are confident participants in society. This latter outcome is the traditional virtue of a university experience, now, re-vitalised through complexity thinking, especially through the notion of co-present groups wherein agency is embedded.

Conclusion – Thinking Relationally

Universities are sites of human intellectual endeavour where all learners expect to be changed for the better, and, within this, some major institutional and national structures and systems are dedicated to professionals' formation and development. Both traditional and current frameworks of the 'vocational' are simultaneously apparent in how universities are structured and operate – stridently 'vocal', as institutional identities compete across the globe. Thinking is called for, and claimed, everywhere.

Our 'take' on thinking started with Heidegger's 'calling forth' of thinking by which he meant the vocalisation of thinking as a manifestation of our very being. Discourses, conversations and the doing of learning are symbiotically related as the very stuff of a university. We have set out how complexity thinking challenges traditional onto-epistemological assumptions about the learner ('student'), her state of knowledge, her capacity to change, her teacher ('lecturer') and her capacity to transmit knowledge – and all the relations implicit herein. We have called here for a reversal of the implicit assumption that *relations* are residual phenomena of university experience.

By contrast, general complexity thinking requires persistence with university structures and practices which start with relationality: how *relations* stand up to, shape and encompass entities such as learners, teachers, knowledge and professional formation. Expertise, and skilled performances, in all these respects, are better regarded as emergent phenomena where co-present groups are fundamental in university life. We advocate what we call 'thinking relationally', as the constitutive characteristic of the Thinking University, and we see this as a provocation in the Heideggerian sense – it is 'food for thought', which should be a gastronomic metaphor informing every faculty, department, research centre, chat-room and quadrangle as pedagogies, assessments, qualifications, and registrations, and, yes, even as alumni events are re-shaped. Thinking relationally is mission-critical for a university worthy of the name.

References

Beckett, D. (2012a). Ontological distinctiveness and the emergence of purposes. In P. Gibbs (Ed.), *Learning, work and practice: New understandings* (pp. 69–84). Dordrecht: Springer.

Beckett, D. (2012b). Of maestros and muscles: Expertise and practices at work. (In D. Aspin and J. Chapman (Eds.), *Second international handbook of lifelong learning.* (Part One, pp. 123–127) Dordrecht: Springer.

Bleakley, A. (2006). A common body of care: The ethics and politics of teamwork in the operating theater are inseparable. *Journal of Medicine and Philosophy, 31*, 305–322.

Byrne, D. (2005). Complexity, configuration and cases. *Theory, Culture and Society, 22*(5), 95–111.

Byrne, D., & Callaghan, G. (2014). *Complexity theory and the social sciences: The state of the art.* London/New York: Routledge.

Cilliers, P. (2001). Boundaries, hierarchies and networks in complex systems. *International Journal of Innovation Management, 5*(2), 135–147.

Cilliers, P. (2013). A crisis of knowledge: Complexity, understanding and the problem of responsible action. In P. Derkx & H. Kunneman (Eds.), *Genomics and democracy: towards a 'lingua democratica' for the public debate on genomics* (pp. 37–59). New York: Rodopi.

Dewey, J. & Bentley, A. (orig 1949; 1989) Knowing and the Known. (In J.A. Boydston (Ed.) *John Dewey: The later works 1949–1952*, (Vol 16, Ch 4, pp. 2–294) Carbondale: Southern Illinois Press.)

Edwards, A. (2010). *Being an expert professional practitioner: The relational turn in expertise.* Dordrecht: Springer.

Emirbayer, M. (1997). Manifesto for a relational sociology. *American Journal of Sociology, 103*(2), 281–317.

Hager, P., & Beckett, D. (forthcoming). *The Emergence of Social Complexity: Practice and Learning Reconceptualised.* Dordrecht: Springer.

Hager, P., & Halliday, J. (2006). *Recovering informal learning: Wisdom, judgement and community.* Dordrecht: Springer.

Heidegger, M. (orig. 1954; 1972). *What is called thinking?* (trans: J. Glenn Gray & F. Wieckwith). New York: Harper and Row

Lancaster, J. (2012). The complex systems of practice. In P. Hager, A. Lee, & A. Reich (Eds.), *Practice, learning and change: Practice theory perspectives on professional learning* (pp. 119–131). Dordrecht: Springer.

Lancaster, J. (2013). Complexity and relations. *Educational Philosophy and Theory, 45*(12), 1264–1275.

List, C., & Pettit, P. (2011). *Group agency: The possibility, design and status of corporate agents.* New York: Oxford University Press.

Malpas, J. (2002). The weave of meaning: Holism and contextuality. *Language and Communication, 22*, 403–419.

Morin, E. (2007). Restricted complexity, general complexity. In D. Aerts, C. Gershenson, & B. Edmonds (Eds.), *Worldviews, science and us: Philosophy and complexity* (pp. 5–29). Singapore: World Scientific Publishing.

Nicolis, G. (1995). *Introduction to nonlinear science.* Cambridge: Cambridge University Press.

Polanyi, M. (1966). *The tacit dimension.* New York: Doubleday & Co. Ch.1.

Richardson, K., & Cilliers, P. (2001). What is complexity science? A view from different directions. *Emergence, 3*(1), 5–23.

Rosen, R. (1987). Some epistemological issues in physics and biology. In B. J. Hiley & F. D. Peat (Eds.), *Quantum implications: Essays in honour of David Bohm* (pp. 314–327). London: Routledge.

Rovane, C. (2014). Group agency and individualism. *Erkenntnis,* (Supplement 9: Group agency and collective intentionality), *79,* 1663–1684.

Simpson, D. & Beckett, D. (Eds) (2014). Special issue: Expertise, pedagogy and practice. *Educational Philosophy and Theory, 46* (6)

Tollefsen, D. P. (2015). *Groups as agents*. Cambridge UK: Polity Press.
Verran, H. (2001). *Science and an African logic*. Chicago: University of Chicago Press.
Watson-Verran, H., with the Yolngu community at Yirrkala and David Wade Chambers. (1989). *Singing the land, signing the land*. Geelong, Vic.: Deakin University Press.

Chapter 11
When Thought Gets Left Alone: Thinking, Recognition and Social Justice

Jan McArthur

Introduction

Thought is at the centre of what universities do, while at the centre of thought is a series of complex social relationships. Jerome Bruner highlighted this when he referred to 'our astonishingly well developed talent for 'intersubjectivity' – the human ability to understand the minds of others' (Bruner 1996, p. 20). It is this astonishing capacity that I want to explore further, and particularly emphasise its relationship to social justice. For it is not enough to simply think, or to understand others: these are acts that must be undertaken in just ways, and towards just ends.

I will use the work of third generation critical theorist, Axel Honneth (1996, 2003, 2004, 2014), to explore the intimate interconnection between thought and social justice. The isolation and rarefication of thought is, I suggest, a social justice matter because it impinges on the relationships we can forge and sustain, it distorts the knowledge with which we aim to engage and it fosters a cold instrumentality within society. Based on a commitment to greater social justice within and through higher education I have argued previously 'that higher education could, and should, be a place in which thinking finds a special home' (McArthur 2013, p. 1). But we must always be clear to focus on both the act of thinking, and the object of that thought. The purposes of higher education are defined by both the knowledge we engage with and the nature of that engagement. The importance of higher education rests on engagement with dynamic, contested and complex knowledge. That engagement itself should be similarly active, critical and transformative.

I develop my argument over the next four sections. Following this introduction I consider in general terms the problems involved when thought becomes isolated and

J. McArthur (✉)
Lancaster University, Lancaster, United Kingdom
e-mail: j.mcarthur@lancaster.ac.uk

© Springer International Publishing AG, part of Springer Nature 2018   155
S.S.E. Bengtsen, R. Barnett (eds.), *The Thinking University*,
Debating Higher Education: Philosophical Perspectives 1,
https://doi.org/10.1007/978-3-319-77667-5_11

individualised. I then outline the nature of Honneth's approach to social justice, with particular emphasis on the notions of recognition, mutuality and intersubjectivity. Next I consider, in broad terms, the nature of disciplinary thought within the university through the lens of Honneth's critical theory. In the final main section I look at the example of economics and particularly the drift over the past 30 years to a focus primarily on one school of economic thought. I discuss the implications of this for university thinking and for social justice. Here I make particular use of the insightful critiques offered by some contemporary students in this discipline. In this way I explore thought, recognition and social justice within *the thinking university*.

The Individualisation and Isolation of Thought

Thinking within the university, from a social justice perspective, should reflect the university's place as a site for challenging, diverse and caring thought. But what happens when thought becomes isolated and individualised? What happens when neither the object of thought nor the approach is connected to the social? Such a situation leads, in critical theory terms, to pathologies which distort our relationships with knowledge and with each other, fostering injustice. Issues of power that lie hidden cannot be addressed, and relationships can founder on partial knowledge and misunderstandings. This is particularly important for Honneth, who sees the role of the social philosophical tradition to diagnose 'those developmental processes of society that can be conceived as processes of decline, distortion, or even as "social pathologies"' (Honneth 1999, p. 370). Such social pathologies stand in the way of the living of a *good life* – the essential aim of critical theory.

In the context of the thinking university, one such social pathology occurs if we allow thought to *get left alone*. There are two meanings here. Firstly, when we fail to sufficiently value, nurture and steward knowledge: when we take it for granted, fail to appreciate its complexity and splendour. This is to neglect thinking as a critical and creative set of processes. Here we can focus on the simplification of disciplinary knowledge, the reduction to simple forms to fit standardised assessment tasks. But more than this, it is the neglect of allowing thinking to do its job: to challenge, complicate, explore, surprise. Secondly, and perhaps more concretely, it occurs when approaches to disciplinary knowledge are disarticulated from the social realm in which they are grounded. Separated in this way, knowledge is orphaned from that which gives it life. This is the treatment of knowledge as discrete bits and pieces of factual information, presumed able to exist without reference to social context or social usefulness. Here the distinction Brown and Duguid (2000) make between information and knowledge is useful. Information, they argue, is disembodied, while knowledge 'turns attention towards knowers' (121). But our world, they argue, is increasingly impersonalised, and in this context knowledge is even more important:

> So, while the modern world often appears increasingly impersonal, in those areas where knowledge really counts, people count more than ever (121).

The problem for our thinking university thus occurs if we privilege information over knowledge: the impersonal over the embodied. The social nature of knowledge is thus two way. In some way knowledge always has a social dimension, while our engagement with knowledge is a social act. The wider social realm is what breathes life and purpose into our disciplinary knowledge: this is why we must resist any tendency to isolate or limit thinking and our engagement with knowledge.

I am going to use the discipline of economics to demonstrate my argument for a number of reasons which I will go on to outline, however, I do not want to suggest that this isolation of thinking from the social is a complaint unique to this discipline. We can find examples in many places. In education studies it is the difference between learning understood as a purely individual, cognitive process, or understood as a complex social interaction. In medicine it is the difference between seeing the role of a doctor as one who can list lots of anatomical details or possible diseases, and one who cares for the whole person – a social being. In suggesting that economics, in its current form within many institutions, allows thought to become individualised and isolated, I mean that both the subject of economics has become focused on the individual, free of social connections and obligations, and that the way of engaging with this subject has similarly lost its social framework. In an academic discipline so profoundly related to social wellbeing, it is a matter of social justice if these notions are largely cleansed from the modern curriculum.

Social Justice as Mutual Recognition

Axel Honneth represents a third generation of critical theory, emerging from the original work of the Frankfurt School and the early critical theorists such as Adorno and Horkheimer, and second-generation thinker Jürgen Habermas. All these theorists have influenced Honneth and we can see the antecedence of his work in this critical theory tradition, though this is sometimes more evident in his critique of these earlier thinkers rather than his simple adherence to their work. Indeed, without denying his intellectual origins, Honneth is clearly also keen to assert the distinctiveness of his approach to critical theory. Fundamental to this is his primary emphasis on recognition and its role in human fulfilment, and in distortions and pathologies.

Honneth's conceptualisation of social justice as mutual recognition stresses the intersubjective nature of justice, and indeed of human activity. He argues that before we begin to consider the many other important facets of social justice, such as issues of redistribution, we must appreciate the basic human need to be recognised as a person of innate worth, and similarly for us to give this recognition to others. In the realm of what Honneth describes as 'esteem' recognition, people need to be recognised as having traits and abilities that contribute positively to a common good. Our capacity for thought underpins all such traits and abilities. The challenge we have to ask ourselves within our universities is, what forms of engagement with knowledge would equip our students to be in the position to see themselves, and be seen by others, as full and active members in the social whole? For university graduates an important aspect of such esteem recognition lies in their actions within the world of work. The fundamental link between one's labour and one's innate, human worth is a defining aspect of Honneth's work and critical theory more broadly.

Like Bruner's observation about human thought, Honneth's theory of social justice rests on intersubjectivity. Underpinning Honneth's work is the notion of mutuality and there are two important, and inter-related ways in which he stresses mutuality in the context of social justice. Firstly, recognition itself must be mutual: it is the giving *and* the receiving of recognition that underpins social justice. Secondly, individual self-realisation and social inclusion go hand in hand. Thus there is a dialectic here we must always work between, from the autonomous individual to the social sphere in which such autonomy is realised. Honneth's approach is thus resonate with the German notion of *Bildung*, which also stresses the interconnection between self and social:

> In the world of *Bildung* the self is never a lonely self and world is not a contingent one but expresses a necessary relation. In other words, *Bildung* starts with the individual embedded in a world that is at the same time that of the differentiated other (Løvlie and Standish 2003, p. 3).

In keeping with critical theory, Honneth's approach to social justice is one that is about both critique and transformation: understanding the injustices and distortions in the existing social world, and arguing for a better one beyond it. As with other critical theorists, Honneth is acutely aware of the hidden distortions or pathologies that stand in the way of people achieving genuine freedom and the capacity for a 'good' life. What distinguishes Honneth's approach to social justice is his insistence on recognition as the first order area of concern. Honneth's concern is that approaches to social justice that are based upon redistribution remain:

> blind to forms of disadvantage and harm that are not directly linked to the socio-economic class position or to the reality of working class life. For these types of deprivation only come into view, once the criterion for social justice is not defined as equal opportunity in the narrow sense, but as the integrity of the social life form as a whole (Honneth 2010, p. 14).

Thus Honneth focuses our gaze on a very different point than either other critical theorists or other social justice theorists. Honneth's position is that we must take our analysis of social justice back to the primary realm of individual self-realisation, because to do anything else risks privileging the groups or issues that are most easily seen. The social world runs far deeper than its more obvious veneer. Honneth suggests that we know what is just by:

> that which allows the individual member of our society to realize his or her own life's objectives, in cooperation with others, and with the greatest possible autonomy (Honneth 2010, p. 13).

So we can see from this extract that although the focus is on individual self-realisation this always occurs in a social context: it is dependent upon *cooperation with others*. Indeed, in suggesting that social justice rests upon mutual recognition – the giving *and* receiving of recognition of being a person of innate worth – Honneth ties his conception of social justice to the intersubjective realm. Indeed, societies organise 'around certain patterns of recognition' and 'human beings depend on social forms of recognition in order to develop an identity and to gain a certain understanding and sufficient form of self-relation (Honneth in Marcelo 2013, p. 210).

Honneth (2004) puts forward three dimensions in his conceptualisation of social justice, each of equal importance. These relate to three different forms of mutual recognition essential for just social relationships: emotional, rights-based and social esteem. The first focuses on the realm of individual, personal relationships such as love or friendship. Here there is a high degree of particularity; that is, it is about the mutual recognition between a particular father and his daughter, or between a particular woman and her partner. Such recognition is fundamental to our sense of self-worth and self-confidence: to having recognised the legitimacy of being who we are. The second dimension relates to rights and fosters our sense of self-respect: the extent to which we are recognised as moral agents able to participate in the social sphere. Importantly, the focus is not simply on having certain legal rights, but on understanding and exercising these rights. This dimension is universal, rather than particular, with such rights relating equally to all within their domain. The final dimension is recognition of one's useful contribution to society – this is the esteem recognition I've already mentioned. There is a notion of solidarity here – of society made up by the collective actions of its members, recognised as such by those members. But there is also a complementary individual element to this – it refers to the attributes, abilities and accomplishments of particular individuals, and the contributions they make to society.

In this chapter I want to focus particularly on Honneth's realm of esteem recognition. This is mutual recognition of an individual's social contribution – their skills and attributes which contribute to a common good. I will argue that social justice requires that students at our universities should be able to engage with knowledge that they can use to contribute positively to the social sphere and thus earn this esteem recognition for their contribution. Similarly, their engagement must enable them to appreciate and be able to recognise the contributions of others, even when rather different from their own. Indeed, it is a necessary corollary of the emphasis on mutuality that one also appreciates the necessary virtue of dissent and disagreement.

An Intersubjective Approach to Disciplinary Thought

There are several implications that arise from looking at the ways in which we think and engage with disciplinary knowledge through the lens of Honneth's critical theory. The notion of intersubjectivity, in particular, plays out on several levels. At its heart, Honneth's conception of social justice tells us that what is absolutely crucial are the ways we think about others and ourselves. Let us now cast this net further to see how it impacts on our engagement with the complex knowledge at the heart of the thinking university. To begin with, thinking has implications for who we are and who we may become, and thus also for how others see and interact with us. Thinking, therefore, cannot exist in a vacuum, or only in the neat spatial and temporal box of a particular course, subject or discipline. Thinking affects things and people – and distortions occur if we try to keep thinking isolated (hence also misrecognition). Moreover, the topic of thought is always in some way about other people – for knowledge itself is embodied and representative of the minds of others at work. Knowledge is understood as social and intersubjective, and this is reflected in its complex, dynamic and contested character. Simple forms of easily exchanged information do not sufficiently enable the full potential of the complex meeting of minds evoked by Bruner. Nor do they sufficiently represent the complex realities of the social world they claim to represent. Brown and Duguid (2000) refer to the 'sticky' nature of knowledge as a way to describe the bonded relationship between knowledge and the knower. Therefore the mode of engagement with this knowledge must be similarly complex and dynamic. To achieve its social justice role the university needs to enable complex thinking about contested forms of knowledge.

What we think about in universities, and how we undertake that thought, relates to nothing less than our underlying conception of reason among human beings. Is this an instrumental reason shackled to an isolationist and over-simplified version of reality? Or is it an emancipatory form of reason, located in trying to ensure relations between people free of domination and distortion? Instrumental reason eschews the social, while emancipatory reason emerges from the connections between human beings and in turn nurtures and fosters these. Instrumental reason sees no necessary distinction between social beings and other objects: workers become 'human resources' alongside other inputs such as concrete or cotton. As Honneth explains, instrumental reason is 'a pathology of reason because a certain structure of our society privileges only one dimension of our rationality' (Honneth in Marcelo 2013, p. 219). Emancipatory reason, in contrast, demands struggle and contestation; it insists on diverse perspectives freely exchanged and giving rise to the social whole. There is conscious recognition here of the struggle involved in negotiating knowledge.

Honneth's critical theory gives strength to the importance of diverse and contested knowledge, and engagement with it that embraces struggle and dissent. We can draw upon an analogy from the natural world here to understand the dangers if disciplinary thought becomes conformist and inward-looking. Species remain healthy and thriving when they are able to ensure 'new blood', the input of new and diverse traits rather than more of the same, and thus ensure a diverse gene pool. Knowledge communities require the same diversity to sustain the 'epistemological rigour' essential to the thinking university. In the absence of such rigour, recessive traits of thinking can become dominant, causing problems and distortions. A plurality of ideas and perspectives is essential to the health of any academic discipline.

When Thought Gets Left Alone: The Case of Economics

To illustrate the social nature of thinking, when considered from a social justice perspective, I will focus on the discipline of economics. I do so for a number of reasons. One is personal, as my own first degree was in economics. I regard myself as lucky to have studied this discipline at a time (though change was imminent) when economics departments were staffed by a diverse range of economists, offering an equally diverse range of courses, considering the discipline from multiple, and not always compatible, perspectives. My undergraduate education featured instruction from Marxists, Keynesians, monetarists, labour economists and economic historians. I had extensive tuition in the history of economic thought, that gave me some literacy in the different thinkers whose names would be attached to so many different big ideas in the discipline – for example Smith, Friedman, Galbraith, Keynes and Marx. But as I have continued to take an interest in my first discipline over the intervening years I have witnessed a narrowing of the scope of the discipline, and a loss of variety and dissent. Neo-classical, monetarist forms of economics have become dominant, and alternatives rarely studied, and when done so often as mere footnotes in disciplinary history. The famous monetarist economist, and advisor to Margaret Thatcher, Milton Friedman, once declared that there are no different schools of economic thought, only good economics and bad economics. From such a perspective struggle, contestation and diversity are not needed; they are neither encouraged nor embraced in the disciplinary thinking.

The interesting case of economics is that we have a distortion of both the subject of thought and the approach to thinking. The disciplinary knowledge engaged with in economics has, since my student days, narrowed so that it almost exclusively focuses on the one tradition of neoclassical economics. Further, within this dominant tradition, the focus is not on social systems, but on the individual, assumed to be acting largely free of social context. Much of its analysis of human behaviour focuses on the autonomous individual. Thus in both its approach and its subject matter economics has eschewed the social, the cooperative and the inter-related. Assumptions are made about rational behaviour based on narrow, utilitarian notions of rationality. Recognition, or personal achievement, is seen as linked to market mechanisms, while other forms of society are regarded as naive and illusionary. The social justice implications are profound. Neoclassical economics, with its focus on the decontextualized individual, renders invisible much of the suffering within the social realm.

The contrast between the discipline economics has become and the work of its famous forefather, Adam Smith, could not be more marked. In Adam Smith we find a moral philosopher who has been sorely misread and misunderstood. Indeed, there is surprising resonance between Smith's work and the type of intersubjective social justice proposed by Honneth. In his work, *The Theory of Moral Sentiments*, Smith makes clear that co-operation rather than competition is key to satisfying social needs (Haldane 2014). This text reveals a thinker at odds with many of those who quote him today in the cause of economic individualism:

> Rather than a treatise on triumphant and uncontextualised individualism, Smith's Economics stresses intersubjectivity and cooperation. Economic actions are not the preserve of isolated individuals, but of social groups and deeply inter-related (Haldane 2014, p. 4).

There is, therefore, no reason to see the current state of this discipline as somehow natural or inevitable. There are strong epistemological as well as social justice reasons to argue against the narrowing of dominant economic thinking. The further problem in economics is that the disciplinary knowledge with which students and academics engage has become narrower over a period in which the social and economic worlds have arguably become more complex. This renders its graduates unprepared and unequipped with the necessary traits and abilities to usefully contribute to society. Indeed, the consequences of this neglect of disciplinary thought became dramatically apparent in the wake of the 2008 financial crisis. Economists were seen as not being up to the task of understanding and offering informed critique of the implications of the behaviour of the international markets. Unfettered pursuit of individual profit so lauded by neo-classicism, and devoid of grounding in any form of social understanding, led with tragic inevitability to financial doom.

Ironically, in this financial tragedy – which quickly manifested into many, many forms of human and social tragedy – we had a strong reinforcement of the fact that economics has relevance to society, and to justice: 'The power of economics is that it affects real lives in real ways; it matters' (Haldane 2014, p. 6). As a consequence students of economics should reasonably feel they are engaging with knowledge which will enable them to have the traits and abilities to contribute to society, and thus be deserving of esteem recognition. There is, however, an alignment between the lack of diversity within the economics discipline, over the past 30 years, and its capacity to usefully contribute to the wellbeing of the social world through its graduates. The consequence of this nicely demonstrates the close inter-relationship of the practical and the philosophical, for we see unfolding the consequences of *thought that gets left alone*. The social usefulness of economics as a discipline is diminished when it ceases to be a place of dissent, contestation and creativity: when it ceases to ground its work in the social realm in which it *intrinsically and unavoidably* exists.

Economics as a discipline was not up to the task of foreseeing the terrible human tragedy about to unfold because it had become weakened by its own conformity. This is not to suggest economics should be capable of clairvoyance, but it was found wanting when its expertise was so sorely needed. And, worse, there is a sense of economists having been complicit in the financial crisis – having given poor advice and been unaware of the mounting financial troubles: the markets could not be relied upon to self-regulate as neo-classical economic theory espoused.

The extent to which economics has drifted into 'self-imposed shackles' (Haldane 2014, p. 6) has given rise to student protests. The economic crash managed to gel student concerns about the narrowness of the approaches to economics into significant student movements. Across the UK, for example, 'Post-Crash Economics

Societies' have been formed offering a student perspective on the limitations of the accepted orthodoxy of the discipline within higher education. There are accounts in the UK and the US of student protests and even walkouts in the face of this narrow, socially disarticulated curriculum. In this chapter I want to draw particularly on a thoughtful critique published by students from Manchester University (see PCES 2014) in which they outline the problems associated with the narrowness of the knowledge engaged with in economics programmes, and its social isolation. The critique offered by the students at Manchester University is analytical, considered and comprehensive. It is testament to the standards of thought and debate our students are capable of. The students describe economists as potentially holders of 'enormous power and responsibility…. The quality of their advice and guidance is essential to our society's future prosperity and sustainability as evidenced so clearly by the Financial Crisis' (PCES 2014, p. 8).

Honneth is useful here to appreciate the nature of the injustice that such disciplinary conformity gives rise to. We have here an example of the sort of misrecognition that occurs if the opportunities for thinking in higher education become confined within canonical norms, while dynamic and critical engagement is discouraged. The problem is threefold. Firstly, only one school of economic thought is taught: economics departments and schools become monocultures (PCES 2014) with an ever-decreasing gene pool of new knowledge and perspectives. The contestation, disagreement and academic conflict required for new knowledge and new insights into old knowledge are silenced. Without complex and contested knowledge students never get to experience academic, cognitive struggle and thereby fully develop their own intellectual skills. To return to Bruner, the astonishing capacity to understand the minds of others becomes limited in a discipline which largely closes itself off to the minds of anyone but the accepted orthodoxy. Indeed, Honneth refers to struggle as 'an enormously productive force in our human life-world' (Honneth in Marcelo 2013, p. 217). And there are rich traditions of economic thought, potential critique and intellectual struggle which could add diversity to the economics' curriculum, including post-Keynesian, Marxist, feminist and ecological economics. As the students argue, the teaching of only one school of thought precludes:

> the development of meaningful critical thinking and evaluation. In the absence of fundamental disagreement over methodology, assumptions, objectives and definitions, the practice of being critical is reduced to technical and predictive disagreements. A discipline with a broader knowledge of alternative perspectives will be more internally self-critical and aware of the limits of its knowledge. Universities cannot justify this monopoly of one economic paradigm (PCES 2014, p. 9).

Secondly, neo-classical economics focuses on individual economic actors, and de-emphasises the importance of social groups and interactions. Further, such individuals are assumed to be rational actors whose behaviour can be predicted in allegedly value-free ways. Indeed, there is a close connection in neo-classical economics between the assumptions about rational individual actions and the claims to be a 'neutral' and 'value-free' discipline. As Honneth's work makes clear, the interactions between people are complex and messy, and they reflect and shape normative positions. The simplification of the human world is essential because neo-classical economics also aspires epistemologically to replicate the natural sciences. Indeed, Haldane (2014, p. 3) refers to economists having 'physics-envy', striving for the assumed robust certainties of other disciplines. The insistence on the value-free rigour of economics has affected its relationships with other disciplines it once exchanged ideas with:

> It is also the process that has allowed economics to cut itself off from communication with other social sciences such as political science or sociology while claiming superiority over them (PCES 2014, p. 25).

The esteem and mutual recognition, which is fundamental to leading socially just lives, is denied by the assumptions which underpin neo-classical economics.

Finally, this engagement with economic thought also disconnects the disciplinary knowledge from history, culture or wider society. Courses on the history of economic thought, economics and philosophy or comparative economic systems become minority, specialist interests, rather than standing at the centre of disciplinary engagement. Modules that explicitly link economics to social or philosophical concerns are relegated to optional at best, and often actively discouraged. As the Manchester students argue:

> This state of affairs violates the University's own guidelines for undergraduate education at Manchester. The Manchester Matrix sets out the knowledge and skills the University expects graduates to have. To take just one example, it states that university education should 'prepare graduates for citizenship and leadership in diverse, global environments'. In a discipline such as economics this seems particularly relevant, and yet social, political and philosophical issues are divorced from the discipline and are removed to optional modules in other departments. Pure economics students are encouraged not to take these modules as they are seen as less valuable (PCES 2014, p. 10).

A heart-breaking example of this is also provided by Richardson (2004), and the story of an economics first year student called Pauline. Pauline chooses to study economics because she is interested in the social and political world around her; she looks forward to gaining knowledge she can apply to this world. Indeed, in an early assignment on opportunity cost she is required to explain the concept and also give a *real world* example. Pauline comes up with some very topical and interesting examples, drawing on current social debates in the city of Melbourne where she lives. She considers how recent decisions about the venue for a Grand Prix and a new casino have economic consequences that in turn have important social implications. It is clear she is particularly concerned about the social repercussions of a large casino and the associated rise in gambling. However, Pauline has learned through the processes of assessment that this is not what is really meant by a *real world* example. She is self-deprecating and refers to herself as opinionated, implying this is not a trait required, or valued, in economics. Thus her chosen example is, in the end, the impact of a shortage of cotton on the cotton industry. This is a more straightforward example, and more in keeping, she believes, with what is expected. She tells the interviewer it is:

> Much more straightforward. No chance for me to get in there and say what I think (517).

So experience, and conscientious attention to the assessment task, teaches Pauline that it is not appropriate *to get in there and say what I think*. To be clear, what is so compelling about this case is that Pauline wasn't thinking just anything, she wasn't wanting to pepper her assignment with uninformed opinions. She *had* thought carefully about the *real world* examples of opportunity cost and related these to the society she lived in. But a distant example drawn from a textbook and cleansed of its social relevance was deemed more appropriate.

If we teach thinking out of our students in first year, then how do we expect it to magically reappear later? As the Manchester students illustrate so well, what is at stake here is what we should expect of undergraduate education within our universities. If we strive for the thinking university then it seems unacceptable to me to exclude the vast majority of our students from genuinely participating in it. It makes no sense to make debate and alternative theories the preserve of postgraduate education, moreover as the Manchester students say, this is 'completely unacceptable' (30).

Conclusion

The thinking university cannot truly exist without being grounded in our social world. As such we should be ambitious about the social justice role this university can play. Such a role is linked intimately to the nature of knowledge with which we engage in higher education. We fall short of our responsibilities if our students do not have opportunities to engage with knowledge in such ways that it affords the sense of purpose and achievement inherent in Honneth's notion of esteem recognition. The costs of such failure permeate through the social world in which these students go on to live and work. We do injustice to our students if we truncate or distort their engagement with knowledge. We perpetuate injustice in the world around us if we produce graduates ill-equipped to be active, thoughtful and transformative citizens.

Economics has been, and should be again, a fascinating, colourful and rich discipline, resplendent with insights into the social and economic world in which we live. The more economics has striven for some caricature of certain and uncontested knowledge, the more it has diminished its social usefulness. The example drawn from the great financial crash is a compelling one, but other disciplines would be unwise to consider themselves immune from similar mistakes. Driven by an audit agenda of simplified certainties we have become uncomfortable with the messy realities of thought and learning, particularly at the undergraduate level. Our students are capable of so much more than our sometimes rigid and unresponsive assessment systems allow them to show – as demonstrated by Pauline and by the Manchester economics students. There is, therefore, potential to be unleashed in realising the goal of the thinking university.

References

Brown, J. S., & Duguid, P. (2000). *The social life of information*. Boston: Harvard Business School Press.

Bruner, J. (1996). *The Culture of Education*. Cambridge, MA: Harvard University Press.

Haldane, A. (2014). The revolution in economics. In PCES (Ed.), *Economics, Education and Unlearning*. Manchester: Post-Crash Economics Society (PCES).

Honneth, A. (1996). *Struggle for recognition*. Cambridge: Polity Press.

Honneth, A. (1999). Pathologies of the social: The past and present of social philosophy. In D. M. Rasmussen (Ed.), *The Handbook of Critical Theory* (pp. 369–398). Oxford.

Honneth, A. (2003). Redistribution as recognition: A response to Nancy Fraser. In N. Fraser & A. Honneth (Eds.), *Redistribution or recognition? A political-philosophical exchange* (pp. 110–197). London: Verso.

Honneth, A. (2004). Recognition and justice: Outline of a plural theory of justice. *Acta sociologica [Norway], 47*(4), 351–364.

Honneth, A. (2010). The political identity of the green movement in Germany: Social-philosophical reflections. *Critical Horizons, 11*(1), 5–18.

Honneth, A. (2014). *The I in we: Studies in the theory of recognition*. Cambridge: Polity Press.

Løvlie, L., & Standish, P. (2003). Introduction: *Bildung* and the idea of a liberal education. In L. Løvlie, K. P. Mortensen, & S. E. Nordenbo (Eds.), *Educating humanity: Bildung in postmodernity* (pp. 1–24). Malden: Blackwell.

Marcelo, G. (2013). Recognition and critical theory today: An interview with Axel Honneth. *Philosophy and Social Criticism, 39*(2), 209–221. https://doi.org/10.1177/0191453712470361.

McArthur, J. (2013). *Rethinking knowledge in higher education: Adorno and social justice*. London: Bloomsbury.

PCES. (2014). *Economics, education and unlearning*. Manchester: Post-Crash Economics Society (PCES).

Richardson, P. W. (2004). Reading and writing from textbooks in higher education: A case study from economics. *Studies in Higher Education, 29*(4), 505–521.

Chapter 12
The Worldhood University: Design Signatures & Guild Thinking

Rikke Toft Nørgård and Søren S.E. Bengtsen

Introduction

Universities and higher education today are sites for entanglement of multiple forms of agency and lifeworlds. Enhanced focus is given to higher education strategies and frameworks that integrate more traditional forms of higher education curriculum with moral and political awareness, social agency, and economic consciousness.

An example of such initiatives within teaching and learning is the 'Connected Curriculum' at University College London (UCL) (Fung 2017). The Connected Curriculum strives to merge different disciplinary, professional, social, political and economic realities and contexts. Closer to our own national context, Aarhus University (AU) is in the middle of a process where it is trying to define and redesign the physical campus through a purchase of an old hospital ground for 800 mill. DKK creating a 110.00 square meters new campus area. One of the aims here is to create a future campus where living labs, sustainability, student-staff partnerships and engagements with the public are interconnected as can be seen when looking at the "Ten principles for the university campus of tomorrow" (http://newsroom.au.dk/en/news/show/artikel/ti-principper-for-fremtidens-universitetscampus/). Related trends are visible within research as well, where new centres emerge that are established and funded based on enhancing relations between policy making, societal engagement, intellectual leadership, business cooperation, and HE practice. Examples of such centres are the newly established centres Centre for Global Higher Education (UCL) and Centre for Higher Education Futures (AU).

Such initiatives and socio-political forms of institutional agency are highlighted in current research on the ecological university and higher education ecologies (Barnett 2017; Wright 2016), the global education industry and professionalisation

R.T. Nørgård (✉) · S.S.E. Bengtsen
Centre for Teaching Development and Digital Media,, Aarhus University, Aarhus, Denmark
e-mail: rtoft@tdm.au.dk; ssbe@tdm.au.dk

© Springer International Publishing AG, part of Springer Nature 2018
S.S.E. Bengtsen, R. Barnett (eds.), *The Thinking University*,
Debating Higher Education: Philosophical Perspectives 1,
https://doi.org/10.1007/978-3-319-77667-5_12

of higher education (Verger et al. 2016; Andres et al. 2015), and the social responsibility of higher education institutions (Marginson 2016; Macfarlane 2007).

As Ronald Barnett (2004), Finn T. Hansen (2010), and others have argued we have left the mode 1 university behind, where the institution steadfastly manages and imposes the right forms of knowledge, ideas and values on the world for it to follow. Also, we are now moving beyond the mode 2 university, where the university is 'for sale' (Shumar 1997) and where higher education curricula are being defined and shaped by the needs and current drivers of the job market and the shifting neoliberalist company strategies. As Ronald Barnett underlines "the contemporary vocabulary of the university [is] terribly thin - relying as it does on the terminology of performance indicators, worldclass-ness, knowledge transfer, 'third space professionals', 'the student experience', students-as-consumers, league tables, outcomes, impact, [and] internationalisation" (Barnett 2013, p.43–44).

Currently, we are now in the process of approaching the mode 3 university, which is a university for, in, and of the world. This notion has recently been described by Barnett (2017) as an 'eco-philosophy for the university', and Barnett argues for the need for "Earth philosophies, conveying a sense of the embeddedness, of humanity in the world in its fullest sense and its inter-connectedness, and urging an orientation towards the world." (Barnett 2017, forthcoming).

This chapter is one such example of trying to materialise such an 'earth philosophy' through the notion of the 'worldhood university' as a way for a university to be integrated *in* the world in distinctive ways and to be a distinctive world *for* the people living there. Whay we call 'designed signatures' and 'guild thinking.' Through the concept of 'worldhood' we intend, on the one hand, to focus on the ways the different designs of university structures and systems create specific signatures for being, doing and knowing at the university. Something universities can work with intentionally to shape thinking in certain ways and create unique worldhood signatures for themselves. On the other hand, we also wish to draw attention to how particular ways of thinking conjures different worlds. Here, thinking becomes a guild's craft embedded in and emanating from the sinews of the university.

However, new difficulties and challenges become visible, if universities as higher education institutions are to be for, in, and of the world. As we have argued elsewhere (Nørgård and Bengtsen 2016) making the university belong to the world, and vice-versa, is a challenge politically, socially, ethically, and philosophically. It requires new conceptions of academic citizenship, belonging in higher education, and what we have called 'placeful universities' where "academic citizenship emerges through dialogical integration and 'Mitsein' in the critically open bond between university and society as they are *in* and *for* each other [...] That entails designing universities that allows for openness, dialogue, mutual integration, joint responsibility and care" (Nørgård and Bengtsen 2016, p. 14).

Paul Temple (2014) has likewise argued for the university as a potential *place* as "[t]he creation of a community and its culture turns, I suggest, the university space into a place. As a result, locational capital becomes transformed, through the mediation of an institutional culture, into *social capital.*" (Temple 2014, p.11). If this transformation from locational to social and educational capital does not occur successfully, the university is at risk of becoming a monologic world design of exclusion and power (Waite 2014).

As Peter Scott (2015) has argued the dialogue between institution and society risks breaking down, when the purpose of the university world is no longer clear to the public. Nixon further this point by calling attention to how this might make the university a secluded disconnected world as "[t]he loss of all values other than the values of the marketplace further erodes public trust in the universities by restricting the notion of public concern to narrow self-interests of the commercial sector." (Nixon 2008, p.22). Following Nixon (2008) and Macfarlane (2007), the fusion of the university and the public into a shared world is mandatory to ensure the continued dialogue between university and society. As Barnett argues, the university itself needs to be imaginative and to promote imaginative thinking, being, and doing in the higher education curriculum. Only the imaginative university "can offer transport to a new world, freeing the university from its entrapment within dominant discourses and working towards social emancipation." (Barnett 2013, p.45). Such an imaginative university, we shall argue in the following, is dependent on being *an integrative worldhood university* by establishing dialogues between the 'thought crafters' of the university guilds and the broader range of social, cultural and political lifeworlds.

Conceptual Framework for the Worldhood University

In the following section we present a conceptual framework for the worldhood university resting on four core philosophical pillars, namely

1. the philosophy of things (Harman 2002, 2005; Lingis 1998, 2011),
2. the philosophy of place (Casey 1997; Tuan 1997/1977; Bachelard 1958, Malpas 1999),
3. the philosophy of design (Nelson and Stolerman 2012; Flusser 1999; Verbeek 2011), and
4. the philosophy of thinking (Heidegger 2000, 2001, 2011; Bhaskar 2008, 2011).

Below we present the framework and the core concepts derived from the pillars. The framework demonstrates how the worldhood university is concurrently emerging from the world through the things and places that constitute it and creating the world through the designs and thinking it constitutes (Fig. 12.1).

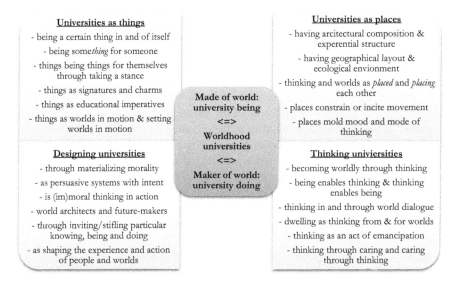

Universities as things
- being a certain thing in and of itself
- being some*thing* for someone
- things being things for themselves through taking a stance
- things as signatures and charms
- things as educational imperatives
- things as worlds in motion & setting worlds in motion

Designing universities
- through materializing morality
- as persuasive systems with intent
- is (im)moral thinking in action
- world architects and future-makers
- through inviting/stifling particular knowing, being and doing
- as shaping the experience and action of people and worlds

Made of world: university being

<=>

Worldhood universities

<=>

Maker of world: university doing

Universities as places
- having arcitectural composition & experential structure
- having geographical layout & ecological envionment
- thinking and worlds as *placed* and *placing* each other
- places constrain or incite movement
- places mold mood and mode of thinking

Thinking univiersities
- becoming worldly through thinking
- being enables thinking & thinking enables being
- thinking in and through world dialogue
- dwelling as thinking from & for worlds
- thinking as an act of emancipation
- thinking through caring and caring through thinking

Fig. 12.1 Conceptual framework for the worldhood university

The Universty as World-Made: Things & Places

Worldhood Things

If we apply the object-oriented philosophies of Graham Harman (2002, 2005) and Alphonso Lingis (1998, 2011), the university can be seen as a thing in its own right, with its own particular ontology and an internally coherent and consistent reality. Instead of seeing universities as a uniform globalized or mass university for anyone, object-oriented philosophy argues that universities are in principle open *to* everyone but *for* someone. As Harman describes, things are "not ultimate materials but autonomous *forms*, forms somehow coiled up or folded in the crevices of the world and exerting their power on all that approaches them." (Harman 2005, p.19). As Harman continues, with his "definition of substance (...): an object or substance is a real thing considered apart from any of its relations with other such things." (ibid.). Transferred to this context, worldhood universities, on an ontological level, become things that "take a stance within the world and command our attention, lure us into taking them seriously even if only to ridicule them." (Harman 2002, p.241). In line with Harman we argue that universities must be dealt with as worlds through an effort of "ontological alchemy" (Harman 2002, p.237), where they respond to not only socio-political imperatives, but indeed that they respond to an ontological imperative within themselves as well. They are their own worlds.

However, in our object-oriented approach to worldhood universities as things we shall need to underline that the specific university as a world "is not only hard at work in being what it is, but is equally effective at drawing [others] into its orbit as *an individual thing*." (Harman 2002, p.242). If the university as such a worldhood being succeeds in making itself manifest as a particular power in the world, the effect will be that it will, powerfully and through the signature of its being, try to draw us in or repell us. To describe this power Harman can "think of no better technical term than *charm*." However, this word "should be heard with overtones of witchcraft rather than those of social skills. (...) The charm of objects is their innocent absorption in being just what they are, which in each case is something that we ourselves can never be." (Harman 2005, p.137).

To recognise each university as a thing or a particular worldhood in and of itself is to recognise that it is not only us that infuses educational imperatives into universities through sculpting them as things, but that they also, as Lingis argues, exert *their* powers and "shape our bodies, [and] imprint their forms on [us]." Indeed, we "find ourselves caught up in their images, their shadows, their reflections, halos, the harmonics of their colors, the rhythms of their forms." (Lingis 1998, p.101), and through such an ontological imperative, "[w]e find ourselves among them and carried on by them into a time of fate." (ibid.). As such, the university, and, more importantly, *each individual* university is a thing in itself – a field of forces, and a specific autonomous power at work in the world.

Worldhood Places

Seeing universities not only as things in themselves, but also as places for someone opens them up to being inhabited. We can, following Lingis, comprehend how universities "make us move as patterns in the world (...) [and] take possession of us and choreograph our movements". (Lingis 2011, p.67). Here, an ontological dialogue creates place, between the university as a particular thing and its inhabitants entering that thing. Through thinking universities as places, things and people necessarily becomes *located* and as such the concept of place becomes a pathway for humanity into the university. It is through following this pathway that the thinking university emerges as 'a world for someone': "A world of other persons as well as a world in which we find ourselves, so it is *this* world, and the place in which it unfolds, that our philosophical explorations must always be addressed and to which they must always return" (Malpas 1999, p. 196). By becoming something for someone, universities become places of felt value, they have a certain atmosphere and impart certain moods and modes of being.

But they also have a more concrete spatial and geographical being - places are *architectural rooms* for thinking that can be spacious or crowded, and can constrain or incite movement in body as well as mind. As Tuan writes: "Spaciousness is closely associated with the sense of being free. Freedom implies space; it means having the power and enough room in which to act" (Tuan 1997, p. 52). But conversely, "Enclosed and humanized space is [also] place. Compared to space, place is a calm centre of established values. Human beings require both space and place. Human lives [and thinking] are a dialectical movement between shelter and venture, attachment and freedom" (Tuan 1997, p. 54). This dialectical movement between fredoom and control can be established in numerous ways and as thus invite and prohibit ways of being and thinking at the university.

This potential humanising quality of placefulness is also accentuated by Bachelard who in the chapter "Nests" argues that belonging and dwelling in places is intimately connected to feeling at home. (Bachelard 1958, p. 91). Following Bachelard, the university holds the possibility of being *a worldhood nest* for us to dwell and dare to think in. But for a university to become a nest for daring thinking in the world it needs to ensure that it instils enough confidence for anyone to lodge there (Bachelard 1958, p. 103). That is, universities are environments of affect and experience. They are lifeworld signatures, functioning as a particular *localisation and placing of thinking* (our term) that has the power to define, refine and thwart what thinking is and could be. Universities are thinking guilds that can sharpen and extend thinking, or dull and restrict it.

That is, thinking as a particular world signature is integrated and identifiable in the very sinews of a university. As such, the university environment serves an educational purpose through which it can communicate its guild thinking: "Architectural space reveals and instructs" (Tuan 1997, p. 114). The university place is the spatiality that shapes, mutates, and grows thinking into a certain kind of university being. As such, intimate connections exist between the places we inhabit and the thinking we do. Our thinking becomes architecture and architecture becomes thinking.

Being a certain place is, then, also an annexation of thinking - as thinking is an annexation of place. Thinking becomes an affectionate relation with the place in which one thinks – thinking emerges through *topophilia*, 'the love of place,' where thinking emerges through constant dialogue with its worldly surroundings: "Thus one does not first have a subject that apprehends certain features of the world in terms of the idea of place; instead the structure of subjectivity is given in and through the structure of place" (Malpas 1999, p. 35).

Consequently, the signature of the university place also becomes the signature of that university's thinking. The university, as a placeful being, "stands as an environment capable of affecting the people who live in it [...] architecture 'teaches.' A planned city, a monument, or even a simple dwelling can be as symbol of the cosmos" (Tuan 1997, p. 102). Accordingly, the worldhood university intentionally teaches people to be, think, and act in the world in a certain way.

The University as World-Maker: Design and Thinking

Worldhood Design and Designing

A university is not still life - it is a world brimming with lifeforms. But it is not a neutral or natural ecosystem. It is an world designed by humans and a world designing humans. As Nelson & Stolterman states in *the design way – intentional change in an unpredictable world*: "Genesis is ongoing. As human beings, we continuously create things that help reshape the reality and essence of the world as we know it.

When we create new things – technologies, organizations, processes, environments, ways of thinking, or systems – we engage in design" (Nelson & Stolterman, 2012, p.1). A university is not just a thing and a place, it is also a design actively fashioning the being, doing and knowing that goes on there.

As a design, universities invite for certain forms of interaction and experience while it stifles or prohibits other kinds. This can be seen in the ways university buildings and interiors are designing for or against informal gatherings, social events or weekend visits through offering places to hang, managing rooms, and locking doors. On a very fundamental level, the university is a world that through its design dynamically act upon its inhabitants by letting them know who and where they should be and how they should act and think.

A design is never a neutral existential terrain – it has particular intents. What philosophy of design unearths, is the morality and intentionality designed into the things and places of the university (Verbeek 2011). Following Peter-Paul Verbeek, a university is a moralizing design, and, hence, we need to think carefully and critically about how universities are designed, and subsequently are designing us. As Verbeek accentuates: "Even when designers do not explicitly reflect morally on their work, the artefacts they design will inevitably play mediating role in people's actions and experience, helping to shape moral actions and decisions and the quality of people's lives" (Verbeek 2011, p. 90).

Consequently, worldhood universities are enacters of certain ethics and call upon us as institution makers and working inhabitants to take part in the responsibility arising from the circumstance that "designing is *materializing morality*" (Verbeek 2011, p. 90). Wether we come to care about thinking or each other, wether we are truthful or feel authentic in our being is to large extent dependent upon what we hear when we listen to the world we inhabit. How it design us. Here, the term 'culture' is important, as higher education and critical thinking do not happen in a social and cultural vacuum, but very much are influenced by the education environment they emerge from.

However, we suggest an ontological approach to culture, which means that higher education culture is not merely related to the social norms and codes of conduct, but is being co-constitued by the brick and mortar of the buildings and the design of the campus experience. This entails, that the experience, ethics, engagements, and action of the university and its inhabitants fall back on the designers that, as a consequence hereof need to be in constant critical dialogue and thoughtful inquiry with their design and its entanglement with people and worlds. At the core, higher education culture is what Verbeek calls *persuasive design*, that is, design that through its constitution convinces people to think, act and be in certain ways (Verbeek 2011, p. 122). Seen through the lens of design, the moral responsibility of the university is inescapable.

To offer and sustain enduring thinking and habitable existential terrains, universities need to critically reflect on their worldhood and take on themselves to be moral leaders through embodying ethics in both thinking and design: "This is a task that calls for good judgment – not problem solving. It calls for compelling compositions and effective creations – not true solutions [...] leaders and designers are often one and the same, and that it is important for leaders to recognize that their challenge is that of a designer – to determine direction and destination via the design tradition" (Nelson & Stolterman, 2012, p. 5).

Through the lens of design, to become a world, universities need to take charge and be the intentional architects of their own worldhood, rather than followers and opportunists in the world. From this also follows a moral obligation to take action and be proactive through ethically imagining that-which-do-not-yet-exist. This entails that the worldhood university is not only a spatial and social arena, but connects to past, present, and future time also. An ability that demands strong moral and great human capacity as:

> Possessing the ability to engage so powerfully in the world is the essence of human potential. But it is also true that humans are fallible. Design activities can do, and have done, great service to humanity. But design has done great harm as well. [...] At the most basic level, we as human beings are compelled to design – it is our calling as agents of free will, who through design intelligence, can act with *design will*. As humans with design will, we are impelled to create new meaning, new forms, and new realities. (Nelson & Stolterman, 2012, p. 12-13)

This presuppose that universities know themselves as designed and designing world and act upon people with ethical design will that take responsibility, whenever it is clear that their worldhood has unethical consequences for the people living there (Verbeek 2011). And this is a moral obligation that override any utilitarian, statutory or pragmatic purpose or task that the university might have (Verbeek 2011; Flusser 1999). Otherwise the university is risking its own worldhood and are in danger of becoming an inhabitable place for thinking.

Worldhood Thinking

We find Heidegger's understanding of thinking central here, as it becomes a link of academic being and engagement to the very place of this thinking. The university as a world, argued by way of Heidegger, "designates the ontologico-existential concept of *worldhood*." (Heidegger 2000, p.93). Heidegger importantly points out that thinking and world are closely linked, and that students and teachers at the universities become 'worldly' through their thinking. Here, to become worldly means that higher education thinking and learning thinks *from* a certain social, cultural, and political context *towards* a critical openness in that context.

Therefore, worldhood thinking is not a certain form of closing down the horison meaning, but a certain way of opening it up. Thinking is here a response to the worldhood nature of the university, and the university as "'world' does not in any way imply earthly as opposed to heavenly being, nor the 'worldly' as opposed to the 'spiritual'. For us 'world' does not at all signify beings or any realm of beings but the openness of Being." (Heidegger 2011, p.172). This way we argue that thinking has roots, which means that it emerges from a specific institutional, regional, and national context, which are often overlooked when discussing critical thinking in higher education. As Heidegger writes, thinking belongs to being, and "[a]t the same time thinking is of Being insofar as thinking, belonging to Being, listens to Being. (...) Being enables thinking." (Heidegger 2011, p.149). By foregrounding this point from Heidegger, we again wish to stress the point that thinking is being opened up through its grounded nature. This 'placefulness' (Nørgård and Bengtsen 2016) of higher education learning and thinking creates abundance in the very act of thinking itself – a surplus that makes criticality possible.

A kindred perspective is found in Roy Bhaskar's scientific realism, where he argues that the world is not opened up through science, but, the other way around, that science is opened up because of the open nature of the world. As Bhaskar writes, "a closed world entails either a completed science or no science (...), so a closed world entails the impossibility of science." (Bhaskar 2008, p.116). Bhasker goes on to conclude that "as science occurs the world must be open." (ibid.) Science, here understood as thinking at universities in the broadest sense of the term, is not the reason *why* the world is open. Rather it is "because the world is open that science, whether or not (and for how long) it actually occurs, is possible." (ibid.). Thinking, in this perspective, is a thinking submerged in the world, a thinking *from* an open world.

Thinking *from* the world is possible because thinking is a way of taking place in the world, it is, as Heidegger writes, 'dwelling' in the world. With Heidegger we argue that students and teachers at the worldhood university must be invited as worldhood "*dwellers*." (Heidegger 2001, p.146) where we "think for the sake of dwelling [wohnen]" (Heidegger 2001, p.159). Here, to dwell contains the meaning of "to cherish and protect, to preserve and care for (...)." (Heidegger 2001, p.145), and as Heidegger underlines by the use of italics: "*The fundamental character of dwelling is the sparring and preserving*." (2001, p.147). In this way, Heidegger connects dwelling to giving thanks, to preserve, and to care for someone or something, and a certain kind of alien "[n]oble-mindedness would be the nature of thinking and thereby of thanking." (Heidegger, 2010, p. 97).

As Gloria Dall'Alba points out in her work on Heidegger's notion of care in higher education contexts, "ontology is integrated with epistemology through developing the capacity to care", and that the "capacity to care promotes an interweaving of what students know and can do with how they are learning to be." (Dall'Alba, 2011, p.115). Understood as care, thinking links dimensions of personal meaning, social and cultural importance and relevance, disciplinary depth and academic rigour in the worldhood university. Also here, we find important overlaps with Bhaskar's realist philosophy of science. Bhaskar argues that the object of thinking, here called depth-investigation, is to locate and access emancipatory powers that are embedded within the world. Bhaskar writes that "[t]he object of the depth-investigation is emancipation. (...) Now if the emancipation is to be of the human species, then the powers of the emancipated human being and community must already exist (...) in an unactualized state." (Bhaskar 2011, p.112).

Thus, we wish to underline that thinking in the worldhood university is an academic dwelling where a particular university as a thing, place and design in itself

Fig. 12.2 The four pillars
of the worldhood
university

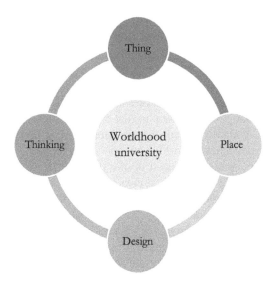

together with its capacity to be ethical, rooted and habitable constitutes an institutionally grounded *and* critically open higher education world.

In the above, we have invoked the idea of the worldhood university and established it as a certain engagement with the four pillars of philosophy of things, place, design, and thinking (Fig. 12.2).

In the last part of the chapter we will describe two central characteristics of the worldhood university, when these four domains intersect in productive ways. Firstly, this will be done be explicating how worldhood universities emerge as *guilds*, and secondly what forms of *signatures* such guilds leave on higher education practice.

Around the forge of a particular guild, craftsman come into being by way of 'Thinking through craft' (Adamson, 2007) and the guild perseveres and prosper though carrying its craftsmanship in its sinews. Powerful guilds are those that are able to perform their craftsmanship as and through being intentional thinking, design, place, and things (Sennett 2008). This comes forth as an embodiment and exhibition of a distinguishing signature that set it apart from other guilds. The craftsmen of the guild, living and thinking around the forge materialises that signature in their hands, heads, and hearts – what Lee Shulman and others have called a 'signature pedagogy' (Shulman 2005; Gurung et al. 2009). Following theories of craftsmanship and signature pedagogies, as well as thinking through the concepts of guilds and signatures – the remaining part of the article present a framework for thinking about the worlds of worldhood universities as constituting distinctive homes for thinking crafters to dwell.

Design Signatures and Guild Thinking

Worldhood Guilds

Like the workshop is the craftsman's home (Sennett 2008) the university contains in it the possibility to be a home for thinking. Through the lens of guilds and craftsmanship we argue that thinking at the university is also something generated by our hands, our being, our movements, and our ability to dwell and build in the world. Here, the university materialises by way of what Adamson calls *thinking through craft* (Adamson 2007).

Like craft, the university is not a fixed thing, but perpetually emerging from a particular guild's engaged craftsmanship practice. Through craftsmanship practice university thinking is simulatenously forged as way of thinking, acting and being (Adamson 2007, p. 3–4). Considering universities as craft and thinking as craftsmanship enables a break both with understandings of the university as an institution separate from the lifeworld of its inhabitants, and with academic work as abstract or immaterial. Firstly, we argue, by way of Sennett (2008), that the worldhood university is a guild where a certain thinking craft finds a 'home' in the sense that "[t]he workshop is the craftman's home." (Sennett 2008, p.53). The worldhood university as guild emphasises its collective endeavour and rooted dwelling of thought as a homefulness.

Secondly, academic work in the guild materialises as a *socio-material* practice - a "knowing how to make something" through integrating ways of thinking, doing and being (Adamson 2007, p. 69). In the guild, the craft of thinking emerges through critical-creative forging of materials wherein "the quality of the result is not predetermined, but depends on the judgment, care and dexterity which the maker exercises as he works" (Adamson 2007, p. 73). Following from this, the worldhood university as a guild is a geographically and socio-materially embodied and ethical university, a place where the "successful workshop will establish legitimate authority in the flesh, not in rights or duties set down on paper. "(Sennett 2008, p.54).

Looking at the worldhood university as a guild make thinking emerge, as Heidegger describes, "by taking to mind and heart", and "[t]he heart is the wardship guarding what lies before us" (Heidegger 2004, p.207). Here, the thinking university materialises as ethical wardship of the guild-members where having a university home means to participate in the craft practice of the worldhood university itself. Seen through the lens of Heidegger, the thinking within the guild becomes a "Homecoming" (ibid.), and the university as guild becomes the "homeland" (ibid.) of thinking.

As Barnett and Bengtsen (2017) write, "the ecological university is characterised by an ecological epistemology. Its work, its efforts to understand the world and to advance understandings in the world, are guided by a will to advance the ecosystems of the world." (Barnett and Bengtsen 2017, p.10). So, the 'homeland' or 'existential terrain' of the worldhood university is not expressed as a guarded and secret university that primarily nourishes its own 'family' of students and teachers. On the contrary, the university as guild "gives itself to the world, and has concerns for the world, and these concerns inflect its knowing efforts." (Barnett and Bengtsen 2017, p.10). However enriching the intersections between the different ecological domains may be, it is still important that the notion of embodied dwelling, and the ontological 'being-there', is anchored in a physical place. That thinking has things to work with and that the craftsmen has a forge to gather around. As Ossa-Richardson underlines, the university campus must congeal "as a place in its own right, with its own history and meanings, [for the students and teachers to] have the opportunity of finding their own part in a community and in a tradition - of participating in the idea of the university." (Ossa-Richardson 2014, p.154).

Craftsmanship thinking in the guild is the ability to take and manage risks as the process of thinking materialise in the guild in the form of a craftsmanship conversation between things for thinking at hand and crafting design will around the university forge. Craftsmanship practice is to not only know how to craft something (a thought/thing), but rather to know how to make something *just right* both in the ethical and critical-creative understanding of those words (Adamson 2007, p. 78).

Furthermore, every worldhood university has its own guilds with its particular craftsmen embodying certain ways of 'thinking through craft' and making things and thinking 'just right.' The worldhood university highlights the circumstance that thinking is always done in a place, surrounded by things and is carried out as a moral and intentional design practice. It is, as Adamson writes, a craft dialogue between process and material where the worldhood university is a 'tectonic' guild (Adamson 2007, p. 97) - a place bound to thinking through craft and a play of forces in the world calling forth a particular university which, as a guild, expresses and forges specific worlds through thinking. The guild is a place for the craftsman to think through building and dwelling - but also a place that through its design impact and shape our dealings with the world. Our thinking is crafted in the guild as we are crafting our thinking there, and so, we cannot walk away from the forge untouched.

The worldhood university as guild, therefore, is not a stagnant form of higher education that reproduces and reruns an overstretched and backward looking craft or curriculum. The university as guild sees into the many possible futures and creates thinking as craftsmanship practice *from* these futures, and "[a]s the future is dawning, our response through thinking dawns as well." (Barnett and Bengtsen 2017, p.7). Preparing craftsmen for the world ahead is an enduring ethical endeavour of the guild, and in this way the image of the guild suits the worldhood university well.

Designing Worldhood Signatures

The worldhood university as a practicing guild engraves its thinking into the world as a recognisable mark. A worldhood university that practices its craft intentionally gain a distinct signature that can be found in the way its inhabitants expresses their knowing, being and doing in the world. By creating a 'worldhood signature' – through excerting intentional design will on things, places and think-ing – the university becomes something that sets its thinking apart from other uni-versities. A guild that distinguishes itself from other guilds through the way thinking is forged and wielded in the world by its craftsmen. One such example could be the 'worldhood signature' of UCL's Connected Curriculum described in the beginning and put forward in *A connected curriculum for Higher Education* (Fung 2017).

Drawing on Shulman's (2005), Gurung et al. (2009), and Horn's (2013) works on signature pedagogies, we argue that a defining feature of the worldhood university is its signature. As Shulman writes, signature pedagogies "define how knowledge is analysed, criticised, accepted, or discarded. They define the functions of expertise in a field, the locus of authority, and the privileges of rank and standing. [...] these pedagogies even determine the architectural design of educational institutions, which in turn serves to perpetuate these approaches." (Shulman 2005: 54). As this quote underlines, the worldhood signature works as a higher education nexus, a point of gathering in the Heideggerian sense, where "habits of the head, heart, hand" (Shulman 2005, p. 59) are united in the things, place, design and inhabitants of the university and its environment.

We find attempts to gather university signatures in Barnett's comprehensive list of sightings of different universities in the literature (Barnett 2013, p.67–70), and in Staley's own inventions of university tyoes (Staley 2015). However, such sightings and inventions need to be further developed into real signatures with a clear "epis-temological footprint" (Barnett 2015, p.163). To develop a worldhood university with a distinctive signature that sets it apart entails an ability to make it manifest as thing, place, design, and thinking. And to make it come alive in the world through its inhabitants ability to unfold and express the signature and its qualities within the world. Here, "universities have to decide how they are to be in the world. This is an existential moment for universities." (Barnett 2011, p.16) as the particular institu-tion needs to critically reflect and choose how it shall carry on, oppose, or rethink its social, cultural, and political rootedness in the world. Just because the particular institution has been 'grown' out of a certain culture, it is not determined by that culture, and so it needs to find a proper and determinate voice and worldhood of its own.

Following from this, worldhood as a university signature is a way of conceiving individual universities as having authenticity and distinctiveness. The authentic uni-versity enacts its voice and worldhood from the four-fold described above, and it emerges *from* the world as a distinctive signature. Here, authenticity as a signature qualia, includes a continued ethical questioning of search for its place in the world and as part of that world. As Barnett underlines "[t]he authentic university is not withdrawn from the world but is immersed in the world. The issue [of worldhood] concerns the grounds of that immersion." (Barnett 2011, p.136). Inspired by Bhaksar's concept of the powers of things, Barnett describes the range of powers that constitute the being of the university in the world. The worldhood university can be said to be 'signatured' into the world:

Practical powers are those powers internal to universities as organisations. (...) Pedagogical powers are self-evidently those that derive from the teaching role of a university. (...) Epistemic powers are those powers that derive from a university's engagement with fields of knowledge. (...) Powers of engagement are those powers through which a university connects itself to the wider society. (...) Discursive powers refer to the registers, the languages, and the narratives that a university employs both in relation to itself and in its relationships with the wider world. (...) Imaginative powers are those that universities possess to see the world and themselves in ways that depart from conventional images. (Barnett 2015, p.163)

Seen through the lens of the worldhood university, higher education becomes visible as an ontological imperative, a powerful signature, laid down by the specific university. Not to say that universities across the world cannot be comparatively discussed and reflected, but they each hold within them the footprint of their own institutional forms of being and becoming. Such "imperatives that extend a space [for higher education] of our own are vitalizing forces that do not have the form of law but of portentous events." (Lingis 1998, p.167). The university signature extends into thinking as well. Thinking as worldhood. Thoughts as emergences *from* the university as a particular world with its own thing, places and designs. Seen this way thinking in higher education unfolds as a footprint within the world, visible to other worlds beyond the university, and other university-worlds. Again, the notion of embodiment can be helpful here. A university world has its own visage (emblem, coat of arms), its own voice (motto or saying, even its own songs), its corpus (the buildings and campus environment), and its heart and soul (its curriculum and academic values and visions).

A similar point is noted by Temple (2017 - forthcoming) in his description of the difficulty in separating a place from the habitus and modes of being of the people living there. Temple writes that it is notoriously difficult to "saying just what a place *is* - we have to rely on those in it, those creating it, to tell us" (Temple 2017 - forthcoming, p.8). With the words of Lingis the "[r]eality of [the worldhood university] weighs on us; we cannot be indifferent to it." (Lingis 1998, p.119). The signature of the worldhood university lies in its socio-material existential terrains and 'geographies of thinking'. Life in the worldhood university becomes real because we work amongst its *things*, inhabit its *place*, shape and get shapes by its *design*, and engage its *thinking* through thinking with it. Thinking in the worldhood university becomes the "geography of primary and secondary paths [that] open from it and return to it" (Lingis 1998, p.87). Signatures manifest themselves as indwelling powers of the university, as "practical fields that extend about [them]" (Lingis 1998, p.87), and as "sites that take form when we come upon the reality [of them]" (ibid.) as places for living in research, teaching, and learning.

Conclusion

Based on our exploration and conceptualisation of the idea of the worldhood university and its design signatures and guild thinking, we foreground three concluding points: Firstly, the worldhood university could be seen as a moving away from the discourse about the uniform or globalised university that is nowhere rather than now-here and for no-body rather than some-one. Contrary, the worldhood university is a re-guildification and re-grounding of the university into time and, here more importantly, place. This is not a nostalgic argument for a return to pre-modern times and the walled gardens of university knowledge. On the contrary, the worldhood university thinks and acts not only in the world, but *from* the world. It becomes an inhabited lifeworld and a place for thinking and things to dwell. This point brings back the meaning of 'home' to universities. Not home in the meaning of the private sphere or egoistic thinking, but home as a submersion into society and the greater good.

Secondly, the chapter has provided an analytical model for worldhood thinking by way of the philosophies of thing, place, design, and thinking. This model has been applied on understandings of the university and the life taking place there. This 'worldhood model' should not be seen as a normative ideal, but rather as both an analytical tool for further analysis and discussion of the role of universities within contemporary societies and cultures, and as a prospective framework for imagining and designing future universities. The worldhood model, we argue, has a wider potential than this chapter and may be used outside the university context even, when analysing or designing institutions for all levels of educations.

Thirdly, and finally, the concepts of guild and signature reaches beyond these concepts' own point of origin and contribute with more far-reaching understandings of the university and its societal environment. This has wider philosophical implications too. It opens up a pluralistic ontology of the university, captured in the concepts of worldhood, design signatures and guild thinking. This contribution to the philosophy of the university and higher education ontology asks for further research and thinking into the ways that worlds grow out of, and into, the university as world-maker and world-hood.

References

Adamson, G. (2007). *Thinking through craft*. Oxford: Berg Publishers.
Andres, L., Bengtsen, S., Crossouard, B., Gallego, L., Keefer, J., & Pyhältö, K. (2015). Drivers and interpretations of doctoral education today: National Comparisons. In *Frontline Learning Research* (Vol. 3, pp. 63–80).
Bachelard, G. (1958). *The poetics of space. The classic look at how we experience intimate places*. Boston: Beacon Press.
Barnett, R. (2017 – in print). *The Coming of the Ecological University*. London/New York: Routledge.

Barnett, R. (2015). *Understanding the University. Institution, Idea, Possibilities*. New York: Routledge.

Barnett, R. (2013). *Imagining the university*. London: Routledge.

Barnett, R. (2011). *Being a University*. New York/London: Routledge.

Barnett, R. (2004). Learning for an unknown future. *Higher Education Research & Development, 23*(3), 247–260.

Barnett, R., & Bengtsen, S. (2017). Universities and epistemology: From a dissolution of knowledge to the emergence of a new thinking. *Education Sciences., 7*(38), 1–12.

Bhaskar, R. (2011). *Reclaiming reality. A critical introduction to contemporary philosophy*. London /New York: Routledge.

Bhaskar, R. (2008). *A realist theory of science*. London: Verso.

Casey, E. (1997). *The fate of place. A philosophical history*. Berkeley: University of California Press.

Dall'Alba, G. (2011). Re-imagining the University: Developing a capacity to care. In R. Barnett (Ed.), *The future University*. London/New York: Routledge.

Flusser, V. (1999). *The shape of things. A philosophy of design*. London: Reaktion Books.

Fung, D. (2017). *A connected curriculum for higher education*. London: UCL Press.

Gurung, R. A. R., Chick, N. L., & Haynie, A. (2009). *Exploring signature pedagogies. Approaches to teaching disciplinary habits of mind*. Stylus Publishing.

Hansen, F. T. (2010). The phenomenology of wonder in higher education. In M. Brinkmann (Ed.), *Erziehung. Phänomenologische Perspektiven* (pp. 161–177). Würzburg: Königshausen & Neumann.

Harman, G. (2005). *Guerrilla metaphysics. Phenomenology and the carpentry of things*. Chicago: Open Court.

Harman, G. (2002). *Tool-being. Heidegger and the metaphysics of objects*. Chicago and La Salle, Illinois: Open Court.

Heidegger, M. (2000). *Being and Time*. (J. Macquarrie and E. Robinson, Trans. Oxford: Blackwell.

Heidegger, M. (2001). Poetry, language, thought (trans: A. Hofstaadter). New York: HarperCollins.

Heidegger, M. (2004). *What is called thinking?* (trans: J.G. Gray). New York: Harper Perennial.

Heidegger, M. (2010). *Country path conversations* (B.W. Davis, Trans.). Bloomington: Indiana University Press.

Heidegger, M. (2011). *Basic Writings*. London: Routledge.

Horn, J. (2013). Signature pedagogy/powerful pedagogy: The Oxford tutorial system in the humanities. *Arts & Humanities in Higher Education., 12*(4), 350–366.

Lingis, A. (2011). *Violence and Splendour*. Illinois: Northwestern University Press.

Lingis, A. (1998). *The imperative*. Bloomington: Indiana University Press.

Macfarlane, B. (2007). *The academic citizen: The virtue of service in university life*. London: Routledge.

Malpas, J. E. (1999). *Place and experience. A philosophical topography*. Cambridge: Cambridge University Press.

Marginson, S. (2016). Higher Eduction and the common good. MUP Academic.

Nelson, H. G., & Stolterman, E. (2012). *The design way. Intentional change in an unpredictable world*. Cambridge: The MIT Press.

Nixon, J. (2008). *Towards the virtuous university. The moral bases of academic practice*. New York: Routledge.

Nørgård, R., & Bengtsen, S. (2016). Academic citizenship beyond the campus: A call for the placeful university. *Higher Education Research & Development, 35*, 4–16.

Ossa-Richardson, A. (2014). The idea of a university and its concrete form. In P. Temple (Ed.), *The physical university. Contours of space and place in higher education* (pp. 131–158). London: Routledge.

Shulman, L. S. (2005). Signature pedagogies in the professions. *Daedalus, 134*(3), 52–59.

Schumar, W. (1997). *College for Sale. A critique of the commodification of higher education*. London/New York: Routledge.

Sennett, R. (2008). *The craftsman*. London: Penguin Books.

Scott, P. (2015). Higher education, the public good and the public interest. In O. Filippakou & G. Williams (Eds.), *Higher education as a public good. Critical perspectives on theory, policy and practice* (pp. 41–58). New York: Peter Lang.

Staley, D. (2015). The future of the university: Speculative design for innovation in *higher   education.   EDUCAUSEreview*,   http://er.educause.edu/articles/2015/11/ the-future-of-the-university-speculative-design-for-innovation-in-higher-education

Temple, P. (2017). Space, place and university society: Insights from common-pool resource theory. (forthcoming).

Temple, P. (2014). Space, place and university effectiveness. In P. Temple (Ed.), *The physical university. Contours of space and place in higher education* (pp. 3–13). London: Routledge.

Tuan, Y. (1997). *Space and place. The perspective of experience*. Minneapolis: University of Minnesota Press.

Verbeek, P. (2011). *Moralizing technology. Understanding and designing the morality of things*. Chicago: The University of Chicago Press.

Verger, A., Lubienski, C., & Steiner-Khamsi, G. (2016). The Emergence and Structuring of the Global Education Industry: Towards an Analytical Framework. In *World Yearbook of Education 2016: The global education industry* (p. 2016). New York: Routledge.

Waite, P. (2014). Reading campus landscapes. In P. Temple (Ed.), *The physical university. Contours of space and place in higher education* (pp. 72–83). London: Routledge.

Wright, S. (2016). Universities in a knowledge economy or ecology? Policy, contestation and abjection. *Critical Policy Studies, 10*(1), 59–78. https://doi.org/10.1080/19460171.2016.114 2457.

Chapter 13
The Thinking University: Two Versions, Rival *and* Complementary

Ronald Barnett

Introduction

Thought is difficult. Perhaps it is especially difficult in and for the university. But it is necessary, if a university is to be a 'university'.

Already, hares are running in different directions, and that is indicative of challenges ahead. The two pronouns – 'in' and 'for' - and their associated syntax in either case indicates two paths. On the one hand, with thought 'in' the university, there are matters concerning the ways in which, and the extent to which, the university is an institutional space that supports, prompts and nurtures thinking. Is it a space of thought? Could it be more so? Might thought take justifiably different forms *in* the university? Could students or academics think more *or* in other ways? On the other hand, there are matters concerning the university as an institution that thinks, that thinks about its purposes and projects and that reflects upon itself; that thinks about itself. This would be thought *for* the university, thought that might carry it forward, thought that helps it thrive as an institution, as a thoughtful institution.

And so the thinking university is a university that exhibits thought at two levels: thought *in* the university and thought *for* the university. These are profoundly different logics, as it were. The first is manifestly *epistemic thought*, concerned with understanding the world beyond the university. Here, questions arise as to the legitimacy of different and even widening forms of knowledge to which the university might be attracted.

The second, though, is more an *ontological thought*, concerned with the university itself as an institution in the world and in society. Here, questions arise as to how the university might orchestrate its thinking so that those thought processes

R. Barnett (✉)
University College London, Institute of Education, London, UK
e-mail: ron.barnett@ucl.ac.uk

© Springer International Publishing AG, part of Springer Nature 2018
S.S.E. Bengtsen, R. Barnett (eds.), *The Thinking University*,
Debating Higher Education: Philosophical Perspectives 1,
https://doi.org/10.1007/978-3-319-77667-5_13

help the university to flourish (and don't diminish it). With such thought, too, the university can develop itself as a learning institution, reflexively learning about itself and helping itself to develop and to move into new forms and new spaces. But, then, this is an ontological form of thought in a further sense, for such thought – if it is to be serious thought – has to concern itself with the world, with the way the world is. If it is to live and thrive as an institution in the world, the university has to take account of the world. In this sense, the thinking university will think not just about itself but also about the world, not least to assist it in acting in the world.

This chapter, accordingly, will amount to an examination of these two logics. *Prima facie*, it may seem that there is tension between them, between thought concerned to understand the world and thought concerned to help the university as an institutional actor in the world. Disinterestedness on the one hand and instrumentalism on the other hand. I shall accept that there are such tensions here but I shall argue further that the two kinds of university thinking are – surprisingly perhaps – reciprocals. Each has a level of dependency on the other. They even take in each other's washing. In the university of the twenty-first century, these two forms of thinking – epistemic and ontological – hold uneasily together. Indeed, the tensions between them have become part of what it is to be a university.

A Space of Thought

The university is a remarkable institution if for no other reason that it is an institution of thought. It might be said that it is not unique in this way, for a monastery is also an institution of thought. But the thought of the two institutions differ. The thought of the monastery is primarily contemplation on the works of God, and human being within that great panorama. It is thought intended to assist in realizing God's purposes on Earth. The thought of the university has Earthly and more worldly aspects. It does not help our purposes to say of this thought – in contradistinction to contemplative thought – that it is pure, or disinterested, or thought or for-itself or even, as Newman might have put it, 'its own end'. Thought in the university has its sources in multiple interests, many of them outwith the university. But what marks out the thought of the university is that the thinking that characterises the university is disciplined and inquisitive thought.

It is a form of thought that has *in-itself* qualities. That is to say, it is thought that subjects itself to rules and conditions that are concerned with what it is to think; rules and conditions of reasonableness, argumentation, openness to critique, attentiveness to the world, comprehensibility, intellectual freedom and so forth. Of course, all such terms are themselves open to dispute and elaboration; and just such conversations are pursued in the university. And, so far as I am aware, the university is the only institution the particularity of which is marked by its adherence to such rules and conditions. (Contemporary debates over intellectual property, plagiarism (not only among students but among academics who draw on their own work), copyright and open access are testimony to an inner interest in the tacit rules and conditions of academic thought processes). If we are presented – as we actually are around the world at this time – with an institution that did not follow such rules and conditions, we would not be able to say with any seriousness that we were in the presence of a university, whatever its title might be.

A university is, minimally, therefore, an institutional space *of* thought. It is an institution where such disciplined inquisitive thought is to be found. But if any such institution is to survive over centuries, and is to be found amid different cultures and political systems across the globe, as is the case with the university, then it also has to be a space *for* thought. That is to say, it has to take it upon itself to nurture thought, to provide the institutional conditions under which such thought will flourish – and not merely 'might' flourish. Maintaining such institutional conditions will not be easy. It may even be impossible. We see several examples in the world today where powerful states are imposing themselves upon universities such that the foundational rules and conditions cannot be maintained. Indeed, university leaders and academics may be incarcerated and their institutions closed or sacked purely on account of their attempting to maintain those universities as spaces for thought.

Apposite here is the observation of Deleuze and Guattari (2013:41) that 'thinking provokes general indifference. It is a dangerous exercise nevertheless'. Thinking is liable to be neglected both by the university and by the dominant powers that surround the university until and unless the interests of the powerful are in jeopardy. But that the university can be and is attacked even by or especially by the state suggests that thought is liable to be dangerous; or at least sensed as such by national powers.

How can this be, that thought might be dangerous? Is it that it is thought of a particular kind that is dangerous *or* is it that thought itself, thought as such, is dangerous? It is surely both of these. Thought that concerns itself with the social, ethical, cultural, human, and even economic foundations of society are liable to discomfort, or at least have the potential to discomfort, the order of things in society and maintained by the state. Thought may have dangerous *consequences*. It is partly on this account that an interest in academic freedom and institutional autonomy arose, so as to ensure that universities and their academics could enjoy – if that is a convenient term – a space to pursue their academic interests unmolested by external powers. And it is partly on this account, it might be felt, that we are seeing states around the world connive in the marginalisation of the humanities, and sometimes framing national policies towards that end, so limiting their effects in their capacities for critique and even disruption.

But surely it is also thought itself that causes a frisson in powerful states for the very presence of thought brings with it a sense of an openness, a freedom, that will be anathema to power. The presence of thought itself represents a limit on power, and a potential challenge to power. Thought is dangerous in itself.

There are a number of dimensions of this matter that we cannot go fully into here but should at least be flagged. Firstly, that space is granted to the university such that it could be said to constitute a space for thought does not entail that, in practice, it *is* a space of thought. Over the centuries, academic life has not always been characterised by a rigorous criticality or even an academic professionalism. Rather, the university historically has been content to play its part in sustaining cultural elites on the fringes of society. More recently, two other movements can be identified. On the one hand, higher education has multiplied in size, embracing professions that had hitherto been outside of the university and understandably do not possess an inquisitive culture. On the other hand, and at the same time, universities have been incorporated into the apparatuses of the state and have been subjected both to increased 'productivity' expectations and intrusive audit requirements. The upshot has been a quiescence within the academic community, brought about by heightened workloads and a cautiousness to play within the rules – explicit and tacit – now in place. In turn, thought diminishes, both in volume and in intensity.

Secondly, matters of space, time and communication are working together, again with implications for thought in the university. The academic world has witnessed a combination of a compression of time and space, and a proliferation of modes of communication and a speeding-up of flows of data. All of this cuts in two ways. The individual academic, now increasingly working in teams, finds herself bombarded with messages, terms, concepts, ideas, and information and from across the disciplines. This is a homelessness that both prompts thought and undermines thought. Thought patterns are disturbed, so prompting *more* thought. But there is both a busy-ness here and a shallowness; and these features are combined, such that there is *less* thought.

Thirdly, that thought has the capacity to disturb the powerful suggests that the university, contains powers of thought that it does not always realize that it possesses. And perhaps these powers are actually widening in some ways in the contemporary world.

What is Called 'Thought'?

And here Heidegger's (2004) question, 'What is called thinking?' comes to us and with some force. For it might appear, *prima facie*, that the modern university is characterised by more thought than ever. And, indeed, the productivity indices are all in that direction, as the number of academic papers, books and so forth grow exponentially. But an outpouring of words does not entail thought as such.

Thought is more than an ideational reflex, more than the coming into consciousness of a belief or an observation. Thought may be distinguished by such features as its depth, profundity, criticality, synoptic grasp, forensic interrogation, poetic nuance, scholarliness, insight, and originality. Thought is a kind of non-thought, for it does not take thought for granted. It questions, it critiques, it holds thought in suspension, it hardly dares to think in that it hesitates before any kind of assertion. This is a *deep thought*, but it is also a hesitant thought. In forming a thought, it seeks its support, its evidence, its reasoning, its foundations and its framing, and even its critiques.

This thought is ultimately thought about itself. Thus considered, thought is demanding, not only of time but of *being*. This thought has always an elusive quality to it. Thought can never catch up fully with itself. There is even an alien aspect to it, as awkward and even sinister murmurings are sensed, if not brought fully into the light.

It may be apochrophal but it is said that Bertrand Russell opined that 'the English would sooner die than think … and (he added) most of them do'. This thought, this thinking, is difficult. And, the difficulties are not merely material but are also ethical. Ultimately, if it is not to amount to casual wandering, thought has to yield to some kind of act, whether that be in the form of the taking up of a belief, or outlook and at least susceptible as being expressed in the world in a communicative act or in a physical action. This thinking is not merely about the way the world *is*, but also carries an *ought*ness. The thinker speaks – or writes – in such a way that he or she has a certain will to speak or write in a certain way. The thinker – or the writer – is committing to a particular connection with the world; even to a certain shaping of the world. To come to a thought, of the kind sketched here, has, therefore, to entail a *commitment*. Hence the naming of Habermas's (1989, 1990) grand project as one of an uncovering of 'communicative action': thinking has to yield to communication, which in turn is a form of action. To every thought there is the hidden affirmation that 'here I stand'.

Thought, therefore (again of the kind sketched here), is necessarily authentic, for it calls for a number of epistemic virtues such as courage, persistence, openness, resilience, inquisitiveness and carefulness (in the processes of thought and reasoning). And perhaps the need for such virtues is now heightened, not least in the wake of the emergence of the digital world. In this world, one both is bombarded with and has – literally – at one's fingertips an avalanche of counter-views and other frameworks. For every thought, there is a near-infinity of opposed thoughts or at least radical extensions and critical commentaries. *Thought is always relational.* Today's thinker, thereby, is perforce obliged to hear internally the voices of countless others: the inner conversation nowadays is a tempestuous affair.

Thinking in the Institution

These considerations impinge on the university as an institution in two ways. Firstly, there are matters concerning the ways in which and the extent to which the university provides the institutional conditions that are likely to sponsor the kind of deep thought we have just sketched out. Secondly, there is the matter of the university itself as a thinking institution. We may take these issues in turn.

Alistair MacIntyre (1985: 187-195) distinguished between practices and institutions. For him, practices were distinguished by their internal goods. Institutions, on the other hand, characteristically had their eyes on external ends or at least ends that entailed instrumental modes of thought; concerns such as income, reputation, making it in the world and so forth. This distinction goes to the heart of our reflections here. Thought, or at least processes of thought, are distinctive sets of practices of universities with their own internal goods. The university as an institution provides an institutional set of supports for such thinking. Indeed, it is not fanciful to say that thinking as a set of practices requires succour and support from its institutional host, the university. And MacIntyre seems to say just this. In other words, universities are not to be dismissed on account of their being institutions; as being marginal to the practices that constitute the university. To the contrary, the university as an institution is necessary for deep, critical thought to be sustained.

But this set of reflections, at once philosophical and social-theoretical, has these days to be bracketed. Over the last half century or so, universities have taken on corporate manifestations, orchestrating themselves so as collectively to promote their interests in the world and to the world. Partly, they have been protecting and advancing their interests vis-a-vis the state, as the state has itself sought to organize a system of higher education to its purposes. Phrases and terms such as 'the entrepreneurial university', 'the corporate university' and 'the world-class university' speak to such developments. In turn, phenomena such as a professionalised managerial cadre, 'academic capitalism' and 'cognitive capitalism', and a public playing up of the university's 'excellence' have emerged, not least against a background of world rankings, international competition and often reduced public finance.

This complex of developments has resulted in a diminution of space within the university. There has been much concern over the loss of academic freedom and institutional autonomy but much less observed is a diminution in intellectual space; in the space for thought. Beyond the formal and material conditions of academic life lie immaterial conditions. Of course, there is a fluidity here. The internet has had a massive explicit impact on the character of academic life, as academics are bombarded with unending messages and data, much of which demands a response of some kind. And so academic life expands, as it were, temporally. But this expansion brings with it a tendency towards diminution. The sheer cascade of communications, material, messages, data, and information, not least when added to the busyness and even freneticism of academic life, crowd out thought.

What is this crowding-out of thought? It has a number of components. Its originating source lies in a natural reluctance to contend against the dominant frameworks. Kuhn's (1970) 'normal science' has its counterpart in all disciplines: certain approaches, theories and large ideas take over. Thought neutralises itself and gives itself smallish safe harbours, reluctant to venture out into choppy waters. But the new governmentalities of academic life reinforce this natural risk adverseness. Audits of various kinds – internal to the university, national and international – come armed with their inner criteria by which academic performance is now judged. The criteria, whatever they are, are constraining and the auditing process has an added domesticating effect, for in an audited environment, academics are compelled to have an eye over their shoulder. They are induced always to be monitoring their utterances, in whatever form, for the possibly low evaluation that might ensue. In addition, there is the freneticism of academic life, itself the result of a combination of massification and limits on public spending, internal bureaucratic requirements wrought by a heightened managerial environment and the arrival of the internet, which has unleashed an onslaught of data to be managed.

An effect of all of these phenomena is that thought shrinks. It shrinks in volume in that effort is put in simply on getting through the day, of managing the flow of demands and data, from wheresoever it comes. (And such demands come increasingly too from students, encouraged to see themselves as customers with claims on their university and professors.) Priority is given to the immediate, the quick-paced and the short-term. Matters that are of longer duration or that require a more measured rhythm are put off until tomorrow. But thought shrinks too in its scope, in that in a risk-averse environment, the horizons of thought contract. Thought that might critique the dominant frameworks becomes too risky and such paths are not entered. After all, the risk-averseness spreads to the journals, for they are captured by the audit environment. The algorithms of the corporations that monitor the journals focuses in part on 'keywords', a process that is bound to have conservative rather than innovative functions.

Ultimately, any such shrinking of thought in and of the university will be bound to have wide repercussions. Thought in and across society is likely to draw in, its stock of concepts diminished, its horizons limited and the extent to which critique is permitted curtailed. With any such non-comprehension within the university, society itself will tend towards a non-thinking situation.

The first sentences of this chapter, it will be recalled, were 'Thought is difficult. Perhaps it is especially difficult in and for the university.' We now see why this is so. Academic life has become one of surveillance, of compliance with protocols, of risk averseness, and of coping with the onrush of data. In turn, thought is compressed, narrowed, avoided, and put off for another day. We may here recall, too, the earlier quotation from Deleuze and Guattari (2013), that 'thought is dangerous'. Now, it turns out not just that thought is dangerous to the dominant powers, including the state but that thought is dangerous *to the thinker*. Thought might lead to excommunication from one's disciplinary community, or from one's institution or even to incarceration; or it may just dislodge one from one's framing assumptions. Thought may be dangerous to oneself. Under these conditions, it is hardly surprising if thought withers.

Against the background of such considerations, a fair judgement could be made to the effect that the university is no longer a space for thought. Not only does it no longer offer the conditions for thought but rather many of the elements in the environment that the university now provides conspire to *diminish* thought. Thought, it might be felt, is being sucked out of the university.

The Thinking University

We should now turn to the matter of the university as a thinking institution; that is to say, not merely as an institution that sponsors and encourages thought but as an institution that thinks qua institution. This would be a university that has self-reflective capacities and is able to learn about itself and collectively to forge projects for itself and develop itself. It would be, in the terminology of List and Pettit (2011), a 'corporate agent'.

Such an idea raises both empirical and conceptual problems. Empirically, inquiries could be put in hand to ascertain the most effective forms of university organization for forging such a university. What connections might there be, both horizontally across its departments and vertically between its senior team and its academic cadre? But such empirical inquiries would make sense only when foundational conceptual matters had been addressed. For example, for a university to be accorded the title - in the sense envisaged here - 'a university that thinks', is it a necessary requirement either that all its members should be part of those thought processes or, to the contrary, that, in the limit, such a university could be heralded even though some of its members were not party to its 'thinking' processes? This is conceptual matter in that it turns on what might be meant here just by the term 'a university that thinks'.

Against the background of our reflections so far, it would be understandable if such a quest for the thinking university was to be abandoned. The contemporary manifestations of the university – caught in such neologisms as 'the entrepreneurial university', 'the corporate university', 'the digital university' or the university of 'excellence' – are deflecting away from such an institutional identity. Now, the university aims just to get by, swimming rather directionless and without boundaries in turbulent waters or at most to win the day through its innovative efforts amid 'cognitive capitalism' (Boutang 2011. In such a context, the idea of a thoughtful university, attempting to forge a path for itself, in which it works out collectively its values, projects and goals, may seem fanciful. But, yet, just this must be a necessary condition of the thinking university being realized.

It is important to be clear where we have reached in the argument. It is not being suggested that the thinking university is to be identified by a university that lays down specific goals for itself and neatly brings them off. In itself, such a depiction would conjure the instrumental university, liable to be devoid of institutional thought as it has been characterised here. There are two lines of consideration.

Firstly, we may bear in mind Alistair MacIntyre's recent (2009:174) observation that it is becoming increasingly difficult for certain questions and issues even to be raised in universities. For a university intent on rising in the world rankings, and on maintaining good relationships with the dominant powers, it is better to maintain a degree of discursive quietness while pursuing the university's instrumental goals. Even talk of values becomes otiose in this climate. The thinking university, in contrast, and as earlier implied, is a resolute institution, and establishes an environment that is conducive to open debate. But open debate, as indeed MacIntyre recognized, is liable to lead to fractiousness, both within the university and between the university and the wider society and polity. It is understandable, if undesirable, that a university will wish to keep its corporate head down, and restrict hostilities to a minimum.

Secondly, open debate cannot yield a sure way forward. The world is changing, and the evidential and reasoning basis for any institutional stance has always to be deficient. The idea of the university as a space of reason, accordingly, always exceeds its logical and empirical instantiation. The idea of the university can never be fully redeemed. Adorno (2008:75, 79) made this point as an observation about concepts in general: they always contain a remainder in relation to their manifestations in the world. And so it is for the university, a situation exacerbated therein because ideas of the university will – or should – always be subject to critical scrutiny within the university. The university qua institution will always be wanting compared to the university as an idea.

It follows, therefore, that – for example – a university may well legitimately choose to produce a 'corporate strategy' for itself but such a strategy should be understood as constituting a set of hopeful fictions. For the thinking university, thought does not and in fact will seldom lead to definite outcomes. The thinking university understands that goals are seldom realized. What matters, though, if the thinking university is to be its own agent, is that there be collective processes of institutional reflection and consideration. And for that, three conditions have to be respected, of (i) discursive tolerance and spaciousness, (ii) institutional capacities to entertain novel frameworks so as to provide a university's members with a critical distance from immediate constructs, and (iii) an institutional criticality, to inject a sense that a university could – at least over the medium term – come to be quite other than it is.

Recapitulation and Development

The thinking university thinks at two levels, at (i) the level of its inner practices (in inquiry and in teaching) and at (ii) the level of itself as an institution. It is thoughtful in the ways in which its central activities are undertaken and it is thoughtful in the ways in which its conducts its affairs as an institution. It is not, therefore, that thinking, *thoughtful* thinking as we may term it, is confined to the university's characteristic activities in research and learning. To the contrary: the thinking university is especially characterised in its exhibiting capacities for collective self-reflexivity.

But then issues arise as to the relationship between the two levels of thought in the university. The university is a strange place. It may be thoughtful at the level of (i) its research and teaching activities even while thoughtfulness is lacking at (ii) the level of the institution itself. Thoughtfulness at the level of (ii) the institution is *not* a necessary condition of thought in (i) its central practices. However, thoughtlessness at (ii) the level of the institution can *impair* thoughtfulness in (i) its research and teaching activities.

Secondly, thoughtfulness at (ii) the level of the institution is more problematic and more difficult than in (i) its inner practices (and it is difficult enough at the latter level). It is more *problematic* at the level of the university qua institution since identifying its manifestations is far from straightforward. Just how might this thinking university be recognized? Is it that it allows controversial academic visitors on campus? Is it that permits its own academics to speak out publicly on issues? Is it that it mounts a university-wide debate in formulating its key strategies? Is it that it confronts its students with challenging situations and declines to afford them safe spaces? Is it that it tolerates open dissent with management decisions? Is it that it sponsors 'blue-skies' thinking about itself and invites critical and imaginative thought processes, even from constituencies beyond itself?

But then, is the thinking university to be recognized more in its discursive environment or in its governance environment? More, that is, in its culture of thought *or* in its total politics of thought? Admittedly, there is overlap here, for both environments ultimately concern matters of hierarchy, and the right of university members to speak freely on issues affecting the university as a whole. But all these reflections are tantamount to making the point that specifying the thinking university is problematic.

What then of the difficulties facing the thinking university? Sufficient intimations have perhaps been made. The thinking university is faced with near-intractable forces that would press it in other directions, and which tend to diminish the university as a space for open thought, not least about itself. And these forces pull the university in different directions. Worldwide, the university is being encouraged to be more instrumentally-minded, looking for opportunities to be innovative in the wider economy and competitively demonstrate its capacities amid 'cognitive capitalism'; it is having to heed national and international audit regimes, which subject it to public scrutiny through performance indicators over which the university sector has little influence; and it is now held in a global internet environment that heaps upon it an instantaneity of data and information that it feels the need to digest, for some of it may disturb the university as an institution.

But in addition to these matters of the societal and global environment, there are major practical matters. The thinking university is a reflexive institution. It is able to reflect upon itself such that it might heed its own thoughts about itself. Such reflexivity builds not only into the university's thought processes but in its processes for collective decision-making and action. Issues emerge here of feedback loops and of interconnections between institutional thought processes and action. These matters of organizational systems within the university are literally complex, involving a myriad of practical aspects with unpredictable inter-connections. Constructing the thinking university in the twenty-first century is far from easy.

Thinking, then, is difficult and it is perhaps especially difficult for the would-be thinking university.

Thought about What?

But what is it that the thinking university has characteristically to think about? Several responses are called for; and cumulative responses at that.

Firstly, there is no one topic or subject about which the university should *especially* think. On the contrary. The university is a *universal* space of reasoning. Nothing should *a priori* be excluded from its purview, including – as stated – the university thinking about itself. This, of course, should not need to be said. However, the university has come to censure itself and, as we have seen, for understandable reasons. The university is now caught in a turmoil of currents, massive and largely unyielding, that bend the university to their interests. The university has to operate in an interest structure that is not of its making. But perhaps the university succumbs without too much of a struggle.

Secondly, it follows that the university should concern itself with the conditions of thought, and the conditions of thought at each level of thought. Conditions of thought attach to the pedagogical situation: which pedagogical conditions need to be satisfied so as not just to release but to prompt and to cajole students into thinking? They attach to groups of researchers and scholars: which conditions of inquiry are likely to dislodge understandings from their taken-for-granted frameworks into more daring and even subversive ways of thinking? And conditions of thought attach to the university as an organization: which conditions have to be heeded in order that a university might come to think and to act differently and in ways in which its members feel that they are playing a part?

Thirdly, all such conditions of the thinking university have to play out, as stated, within a larger context of global currents. A convenient shorthand – deployed here - for such currents is that of 'cognitive capitalism' but within it lie multiple forces, of global re-arrangements of commerce and knowledge, of universities and their host states, of students and changing labour markets, and of the internet of people and of things.

The tea-leaves here can be read in different ways. Most evince gloom and despondency but more nuanced positions are surely more fitting. Michael Peters sees in the digital economy prospects for a 'knowledge socialism' (Peters et al. 2012). Perhaps the most powerful commentary today is that of Bernard Stiegler (2015) who, against the backdrop of an analysis of the world in the twenty-first century, both sees a massive global 'stupidity' reflected in the realignment of universities and the world which arises from the 'toxicity' of contemporary forces, and also sees 'therapeutic' possibilities for the role that the university might play in relation to the multiple publics now emerging on the internet.

It turns out, then, that a proper answer to the question 'What is it that the thinking university should think about?' must include the consideration that the thinking university should think about the conditions of its own thinking and the possibilities that those conditions, both old and *new*, are making possible. It just may be that while the conditions in which the university finds itself are doing much to constrain thought – and at all levels in the university – still *spaces may be opening anew in which new kinds of thinking for and in the university are possible.*

Valuing Thinking

However, such a position cannot be the end-point of our reflections here. For the question has at least to be put on the table: thinking to what end? Let us come directly to the matter. Are there values that the university should heed that might at least set boundaries to its thinking processes? It may be – a la Weber (1991) - that values cannot point in any particular direction, but they might set up a stance, an orientation to the world. A start could be made by recalling that serious processes of inquiry install or presuppose certain kinds of value, of openness, criticality, truthfulness, sincerity, respect for participants in the inquiry and so forth. Any list of such 'epistemic virtues' would be both open to debate – would they include courage and even fearlessness? Is sincerity crucial, for what of the 'devil's advocate'? – and would be liable to extend into a list so long and so nuanced as to render it useless as a set of principles for the thinking university.

There is, though, a more serious problem with the 'epistemic virtues' approach as a way of supplying an orientation for the thinking university. It is that it is too inward, too self-serving. It is a way of the academic world falling back on its own particularities when the matter before us is much more serious and more demanding. If the world is in difficulty, and if the university has become party to many of the difficulties of the world, generally complying with the tasks that have come its way, a values stance has to be found that will enable the university not just to think about its survival in the world but that also both enables the university, first, to think about *the world* and, second, to think about its possibilities *in* the world.

This is close to the position that Nicholas Maxwell has been advocating for the past 40 years. For Maxwell (1984), the university's thought processes have been unduly closed since the Enlightenment, when inquiry was put onto a basis in which fundamental rules of reasoning were disregarded. Problems were to be broken down and isolated. As a result, synoptic understandings of the world were repudiated and 'wisdom' as a way of inquiring into what is of value in the world was outlawed. Maxwell's analysis is powerful but his analysis needs surely to be taken further: to his story of the epistemological deficiencies of the university we should add an ontological account - and I have tried here to intimate what such an account might look like. The university is now caught in a maelstrom of forces acting on it, visible and invisible. The thinking university, accordingly, has to become knowledgeable about and *think about the conditions of its place in the world* (and thereby the conditions of its own thinking) and seek out – and engage with - the spaces that might be spotted such that the university just might lend its considerable resources to improving life on this planet.

The thinking university, then, thinks about all manner of things, including itself. And it thinks at all manner of levels, again including itself but going well beyond itself. Ultimately, the thinking university thinks about the world and its possibilities in the world. But it thinks also about the conditions of its thinking and of ways of living with those conditions – and even ameliorating them or circumventing them – such that it might be better placed to help the world.

Conclusions

Three sets of conclusions may be drawn from these reflections.

Firstly, inherently, there are tensions between, on the one hand, thought within the characteristic activities of the university – its disciplines, its teaching and learning, its research and scholarship – and, on the other hand, thought at the level of the university as an institution. This is not because thought within the disciplines is free-flowing, fearless and imaginative while thought at the level of the institution is closed, narrow and instrumental. No such dichotomy should be entertained. Thought within the disciplines and in teaching and learning may well, in practice, be narrow and unduly limited. But, with it being hedged in as it is by massive global and national forces in favour of cognitive capitalism, the university qua institution may unwittingly act to constrain thought in the disciplines still further. The boundaries of academic life shrink, as it falls in with the university's corporate aspirations.

We have, then, as it were, two versions of the thinking university: one in which its activities – such as research and teaching – are characterised by deep thought about the world and one in which the university itself is characterised by deep thought about *itself*, its evolving place and possibilities in the world, its values and its major projects. And there will be rivalry between these two modes of the thinking university. Thought in the disciplines has, to a large extent, take its bearing from lines of thought and their conditioning within the disciplines; it is to that degree thought-in-itself. Thought about the university, on the other hand, is bound to have a large element of instrumentality to it, as the university considers the impact both on the world and on itself of its possible ventures. Disinterestedness on the one hand and instrumentalism on the other hand. These two orientations of the thinking university are bound to be rivalrous, to some extent.

However, and secondly, new spaces are opening for universities that have a propensity to encourage new thinking in the university. As it was remarked in a slightly different context: 'We find ourselves in a kind of historical breathing space', not least because 'it is once again possible to give serious attention to thought, thanks to current material conditions' (Adorno 2008:57–58). The university is being encouraged to engage with the wider society and new media are opening paths. Now, the university has to think as to what might be meant by the public sphere and how it can help to advance that sphere, not least when there are multiple publics in cultural, scientific, human, and environmental communities, as well as private persons concerned with matters of societal and individual wellbeing. So, in positioning itself afresh in the world, the university can act to encourage thought in *and across* the disciplines.

This would be a style of thought concerned with making connections with the wider world. In this way, the university may actually grow as a space of thought. Complementarily, work in the disciplines – and not only in the humanities and social sciences but even in the so-called STEM disciplines – can prompt fresh thinking in the university about its possibilities in the world.

And so the two versions of the thinking university – in the disciplines and about the university itself – even while they stand characteristically in a rivalrous relationship, are yet complementary to each other. There are grounds for optimism.

Thirdly, and precisely in this more optimistic vein, responsibilities are emerging here: being a university in the twenty-first century is fundamentally a matter of the university thinking through the ways in which it can help to advance the wellbeing of the world in all its manifestations. Such thinking-through requires that a university, collectively, goes on thinking about itself, and especially its value-stance in and towards the world. This thought is not concluded by a single consultation within a university on the occasion of its new corporate strategy. Rather, this reflexivity has to become a way of the university being and continuously becoming itself. As observed in our opening statements, this kind of thought is difficult. Perhaps it is especially difficult in and for the university. But it is necessary, if a university is to be a 'university'; and it may even be possible.

References

Adorno, T. (2008). *Lectures on negative dialectics*. Cambridge: Polity.

Boutang, Y. M. (2011). *Cognitive capitalism*. Cambridge, UK and Malden: Polity.

Deleuze, G., & Guattari, F. (2013/1994). *What is philosophy?* London and New York: Verso.

Habermas, J. (1989). *The theory of communicative action: The critique of functionalist reason (Vol Two)*. Cambridge: Polity.

Habermas, J. (1990). *The theory of communicative action: Reason and the rationalization of society (Vol One)*. Cambridge: Polity.

Heiddeger, M. (2004). *What is called thinking?* New York and London: Harper Perennial.

Kuhn, T. (1970). *The structure of scientific revolutions*. Chicago: University of Chicago.

List, C., & Pettit, P. (2011). *Group Agency: the possibility, design and status of corporate agents*. Oxford and New York: Oxford University Press.

MacIntyre, A. (1985). *After virtue: A study in moral theory*. London: Duckworth.

MacIntyre, A. (2009). *God, Philosophy, Universities: A Selective History of the Catholic Philosophical Tradition*. Lanham: Rowman and Littlefield.

Maxwell, N. (1984). *From knowledge to wisdom: A revolution in the aims & methods of science*. Oxford and New York: Blackwell.

Peters, M., Gietzen, G., & Ondercin, D. J. (2012). Knowledge socialism: Intellectual commons and openness in the university. In R. Barnett (Ed.), *The future university: Ideas and possibilities*. New York and London: Routledge.

Stiegler, B. (2015). *States of shock: Stupidity and knowledge in the 21st century*. Cambridge, UK and Malden: Polity.

Weber, M. (1991). Science as a vocation. In H. H. Gerth & C. Wright Mills (Eds.), *From max weber: Essays in sociology*. London: Routledge.

Coda: There is Much to Play for

In relation to thought, thinking and thoughtfulness, universities are on a cusp. Malign forces work quite explicitly in some countries to subjugate thinking in universities and, in many other countries, to corral it or diminish it. Authoritarian states on the one hand; market forces, managerial over-tightness and audit processes on the other hand: both have the effect of limiting thought and turning it in the direction of interests that lack a care for thought. However, thought in universities has not disappeared; far from it. Indeed, thinking in universities can still be seen to alive and even vibrant.

In the contributions here, we see that universities are not merely passive agents that conduct their activities in an unreflective manner. On the contrary, universities remain places of hope and vision. The university as an institution is not at all in ruins, but can be seen to be venturing into new fields of agency in contemporary societies and political landscapes. This is far from easy and, continuously, institutions of higher education bear witness to falling in with the ideological currents of the age, albeit it with uncertainty, institutional strain, academic anxiety, and even social unrest. However, thoughtfulness on campus remains necessary, and the university knows this. That the university remains a centre for deep, reflective and critical and, yes, antagonistic thought remains its most important task today.

In this volume, we have heard of universities reaching out and engaging with the wider societal context. In this societal engagement, academic *thinking* can become the epitome of thinking in and by the university today. The contributions speak of university thinking as not only a preservation of culture, but of even creating culture. Thinking in universities is culture coming to life intellectually and socially too. In this sense, the idea of the university is not tied to a particular institutional context, but is a *living idea*. As a living idea, the thinking university does not always play according to rules of contemporary political agendas and social norms. It might be exhibited as dissident thought, even taking – in some nations at least – the form of radical revolt. Elsewhere, more subversive and subtle forms of resistance may be detected.

S.S.E. Bengtsen, R. Barnett (eds.), *The Thinking University*,
Debating Higher Education: Philosophical Perspectives 1,
https://doi.org/10.1007/978-3-319-77667-5

In whichever form, the vibrancy of the thinking university is characterised by care and responsibility. Indeed, it may be ideas of responsibility and social justice that sometimes challenge and provokes actual political discourses, and not only in the social sciences and the humanities. Global warming, the use of technologies, the ethical uses of science, and environmental degradation are only indicative of the wide array of ways in which the university's thoughtfulness can help the world in the twenty-first century. To take up this task in a responsible way, as evident in the contributions here, new questions are posed of citizenship, in relation both to academic citizenship and the citizen scholar.

The contributions here have also unearthed forces underlying the university's societal agency and engagement. The thinking of universities moves in a horizontal dimension across societal institutions, social and political domains, and individuals and personal life-worlds. Many of the chapters here bear witness, too, to its deeper structures and powers, making visible acts in which universities speak with their own voices to power or display institutional courage in the ways in which they comport themselves. Such powers do not seem to arise from contemporary educational programmes, but from a deeper purpose and aim. Contributions speak of universities as institutions of truth with concerns for social justice that may prompt a pause for thought in any political power that might suppress and undermine free speech, democracy, and critical thinking. Also, we hear the whisperings of a worldhood university, which exceeds the task of promoting higher education. Here, the university turns out to be a shelter and safe haven for advanced scholarly and critical thoughts and thinking that are not welcomed elsewhere.

Universities have a will to think that is not easily quelled, even though it may often be dimmed. And we do not really know to what end, and in what manner, they might think. Students, teachers, researchers, and academic leaders become caught up in that thinking to which then they add in turn. Contrary to some contemporary views, the universities are not in a crisis, and neither is the thinking that goes on in and with universities; but it is fragile and instances of that fragility can be witnessed daily, undermined both from outside and also from inside the university.

The thinking university needs continual vigilance if it is to flourish as it might and to be places of thought and *for* thought. The thinking university continues to think across the generations with those the ones who are no longer present and to think for the generations and times to come. The university as an institution that exemplifies thought is surely a condition of a flourishing wider world.

Lightning Source UK Ltd.
Milton Keynes UK
UKHW02n1354020518
322005UK00003B/190/P